The Fantastic in France and Russia in the Nineteenth Century
In Pursuit of Hesitation

LEGENDA

LEGENDA, founded in 1995 by the European Humanities Research Centre of the University of Oxford, is now a joint imprint of the Modern Humanities Research Association and Maney Publishing. Titles range from medieval texts to contemporary cinema and form a widely comparative view of the modern humanities, including works on Arabic, Catalan, English, French, German, Greek, Italian, Portuguese, Russian, Spanish, and Yiddish literature. An Editorial Board of distinguished academic specialists works in collaboration with leading scholarly bodies such as the Society for French Studies and the British Comparative Literature Association.

MHRA

The Modern Humanities Research Association (MHRA) encourages and promotes advanced study and research in the field of the modern humanities, especially modern European languages and literature, including English, and also cinema. It also aims to break down the barriers between scholars working in different disciplines and to maintain the unity of humanistic scholarship in the face of increasing specialization. The Association fulfils this purpose primarily through the publication of journals, bibliographies, monographs and other aids to research.

Maney Publishing is one of the few remaining independent British academic publishers. Founded in 1900 the company has offices both in the UK, in Leeds and London, and in North America, in Boston. Since 1945 Maney Publishing has worked closely with learned societies, their editors, authors, and members, in publishing academic books and journals to the highest traditional standards of materials and production.

Studies in Comparative Literature

Editorial Committee
Professor Peter France, University of Edinburgh (Chairman)
Professor Stephen Bann, University of Kent
Dr Elinor Shaffer, School of Advanced Study, London

ALSO PUBLISHED IN THIS SERIES

The Fantastic in France and Russia in the Nineteenth Century

In Pursuit of Hesitation

CLAIRE WHITEHEAD

Studies in Comparative Literature 10
Modern Humanities Research Association and Maney Publishing
2006

Published by the
Modern Humanities Research Association and Maney Publishing
1 Carlton House Terrace
London SW1Y 5DB
United Kingdom

LEGENDA is an imprint of the
Modern Humanities Research Association and Maney Publishing

Maney Publishing is the trading name of W. S. Maney & Son Ltd,
whose registered office is at Hudson Road, Leeds LS9 7DL, UK

ISBN 1 904350 56 9 / 978-1-904350-56-9

First published 2006

Printed in Great Britain

Cover: 875 Design

Copy-Editor: Nigel Hope

CONTENTS

FOR MY PARENTS
JOHN AND SARAH
AND MY SISTER
EMMA

ACKNOWLEDGEMENTS

I would like to thank the University of Bristol, whose award of a PhD scholarship allowed me to undertake much of the research for this book. I am also indebted to the Carnegie Trust for the Universities of Scotland and the University of St Andrews for generous financial aid.

Part of Chapter 1 appeared in a different form in my 'The Fantastic in Russian Romantic Prose: Pushkin's *Queen of Spades*', in *The Gothic-Fantastic in Nineteenth-Century Russian Literature*, ed. by Neil Cornwell (Amsterdam: Rodopi, 1999).

Part of Chapter 2 appeared in a different form in my 'The Impact of Multiple Voice on Reader Hesitation: The Case of Vladimir Odoevskii's *The Sylph*', *Modern Language Review*, vol. 98, issue 2 (2003), pp. 397-415.

I am enormously grateful to my PhD supervisors Neil Cornwell and Richard Hobbs, without whose encouragement and guidance this book could not have been written. Thanks are also due to those who have offered comments and advice at various stages of the preparation of this manuscript: Katy Testemale, Teresa Bridgeman, Ruth Coates, Peter France, Graham Nelson, and, in particular, Bettina Bildhauer. I would also like to express my thanks to Irina and Vladimir Rapoport, who kindly gave their permission for the use of Alek Rapoport's images on the front and back covers of this book.

My greatest debt, however, is to my parents for their encouragement and support over the years. This book is for them.

Claire Whitehead

St Andrews, December 2005

ABBREVIATIONS

To avoid cumbersome repetition, reference to the corpus of primary texts appears in abbreviated form. This practice is also extended to the principal text of Todorov, *Introduction à la littérature fantastique*. The abbreviations employed are as follows:

F. M. Dostoevskii, *The Double*	D
T. Gautier, *Onuphrius*	O
T. Gautier, *Spirite*	S
N. V. Gogol, *The Nose*	N
G. de Maupassant, *Le Horla*	H
P. Mérimée, *La Vénus d'Ille*	V
V. F. Odoevskii, *The Sylph*	Sy
A. S. Pushkin, *The Queen of Spades*	Q
T. Todorov, *Introduction à la littérature fantastique*	F

Translations in the text are my own, unless otherwise stated. In transliterating Cyrillic I have used the Library of Congress System (without diacritics). The only exception to this practice is the decision to use the widely accepted form, Gogol, and not Gogol´.

INTRODUCTION

This study investigates the genre of the fantastic as it was practised in France and Russia during the nineteenth century. With the rise of the novel, this was the century of the grand narrative which held out to readers the promise of a greater understanding of the world around them. As Peter Brooks (1984, xi) explains, during this period:

> authors and their public apparently shared the conviction that plots were a viable and a necessary way of organising and interpreting the world, and that in working out and working through plots, as writers and readers, they were engaged in a prime, irreducible act of understanding how human life acquires meaning.

Although postmodernism may have challenged the notion that the signifying structures of life are somehow recoverable through literature, the belief that writing and reading are two salient ways of making the world comprehensible remains popular today. However, there have always been literary works and genres whose aim is somewhat different. According to Roland Barthes's formulation (1973, 25–26), complementing the 'texte de plaisir' which confirms cultural values and allows a 'comfortable' reading, we find a 'texte de jouissance' which:

> met en état de perte, [...] déconforte (peut-être jusqu'à un certain ennui), fait vaciller les assises historiques, culturelles, psychologiques, du lecteur, la consistence de ses goûts, de ses valeurs et de ses souvenirs.
>
> [places in a state of loss, [...] discomforts (possibly even to the extent of causing some anxiety), shakes the historical, cultural, and psychological foundations of the reader, the consistency of his tastes, his values, and his memories.]

The fantastic is just one example of such a genre. Whilst not radically illogical or abstract, it is predicated on uncertainty, on an undermining of accepted knowledge about the world and on a destabilization of the values which both reader and fictional characters hold dear. Such frustration of the pursuit of knowledge and such deconstruction of accepted norms need not, however, as Barthes's label makes clear, be an unpleasant experience. With reference to the related genre of the uncanny, Nicholas Royle (2003, 52) argues:

> intellectual uncertainty is not necessarily or simply a *negative* experience, a dead-end sense of not knowing or of indeterminacy. It is just as well an experience of something open, generative, exhilarating (the trembling of what remains undecidable). (original italics)

The reader who enjoys the fantastic would concur: she embraces uncertainty as a positive and appreciates the ways in which the genre perverts the traditional knowledge-accumulating structure of fictional narratives.[1]

The fantastic not only challenges the reader's convictions about the way in which the world is organized. It also calls into question received ideas regarding the manner in which we read and process literary narratives. Perhaps ironically for a genre which was dismissed by some as a lightweight substratum of more worthy literature, one of the particular appeals of the fantastic is its subversion of conventional notions of storytelling. By contravening the laws which govern the world we recognize, the fantastic makes us more aware of their existence and of the belief-systems we construct around them. By appropriating and then undermining familiar models of storytelling, the fantastic makes us more sensitive to the ways in which we read and process narratives. It is this aspect of the genre which perhaps helps to explain the presence of so many 'big names' in any list of canonical fantastic stories. If an author is to subvert storytelling models successfully, (s)he must first master the non-subverted, traditional techniques. Writers such as Alexander Pushkin, Théophile Gautier, Fedor Dostoevskii, and Guy de Maupassant managed to produce successful fantastic narratives which skilfully undermine readers' conventional cognitive practices precisely because they understood these conventions so clearly. It is these two aspects in particular, the championing of uncertainty and the subversion of storytelling conventions, which make the fantastic such a rich genre for critical study.

This book attempts to reveal how the fantastic operates and how it produces its effects. More specifically, it analyses the devices and techniques used by the fantastic in order to produce hesitation in the mind of the reader. In the process, it reveals how the mechanics of the genre frustrate this reader's search for unambiguous knowledge and definitive interpretation. With a dual focus on both technique and reception, this study offers a more detailed and sustained examination of hesitation in the fantastic than has appeared to date. In placing an analysis of the production and potential resolution of hesitation at its heart, it also argues for the inclusion into the genre of works which have previously been considered liminal.

Critical investigation of the fantastic was revolutionized in 1970 by Tzvetan Todorov. Although interest had been steadily growing in the post-war years, discussion was still largely restricted to the history of the genre, the biographies of its practitioners and the cataloguing of its principal themes.[2] Todorov moved away from such approaches and in *Introduction à la littérature fantastique* he adopts a quasi-scientific attitude in an effort to examine the genre with greater critical rigour. Most notably, he employs a structuralist methodology in order to discover rules which operate across the genre rather than to note features which occur in individual texts. A second particular advantage of Todorov's approach is the structuralist belief he places in the text as a self-sufficient aesthetic entity. This results in almost exclusive focus being directed towards elements observable within the literary text. The poetics of the fantastic thus move to centre-stage as previously popular concerns such as author biography or social history are sidelined.

One of the most enduring contributions made by *Introduction à la littérature fantastique* is its proposal of a clear and persuasive definition for the fantastic which remains broadly shared by critics today.[3] This definition is inspired by a consideration of a principal precursor to the fantastic, Jacques Cazotte's *Le Diable amoureux* (1772), in which the hero, Alvaro, is pursued by a demonic figure. In what Todorov argues is a centrally important passage of the novel, Alvaro reflects upon the events he has experienced and asks himself:

Mais qu'y avait-il de concevable dans mon aventure? Tout ceci me paraît un songe, me disais-je; mais la vie humaine est-elle autre chose? Je rêve plus extraordinairement qu'un autre, et voilà tout. [...] Où est le possible? Où est l'impossible? (*F 28*)

[But what was there that was conceivable in my adventure? All of this seems like a dream, I said to myself; but is human life anything else? I dream more extraordinarily than another, and that's all there is to it. [...] Where is the possible? Where is the impossible?]

For Todorov, Alvaro's uncertainty about whether his experiences are real or illusory is a manifestation of the central tenet of the fantastic. Accordingly, Todorov makes this the cornerstone of the definition he proposes for the genre:

Dans un monde qui est bien le nôtre, celui que nous connaissons, sans diables, sylphides, ni vampires, se produit un événement qui ne peut s'expliquer par les lois de ce même monde familier. Celui qui perçoit l'événement doit opter pour l'une des deux solutions possibles: ou bien il s'agit d'une illusion des sens, d'un produit de l'imagination et les lois du monde restent alors ce qu'elles sont; ou bien l'événement a véritablement eu lieu, il est partie intégrante de la réalité, mais alors cette réalité est régie par des lois inconnues de nous [...].

Le fantastique occupe le temps de cette incertitude; dès qu'on choisit l'une ou l'autre réponse, on quitte le fantastique pour entrer dans un genre voisin, l'étrange ou le merveilleux. *Le fantastique, c'est l'hésitation éprouvée par un être qui ne connaît que les lois naturelles, face à un événement en apparence surnaturel.* (*F 29*; my italics)

[In a world which is indeed our world, the world which we know, without devils or sylphs or vampires, there occurs an event which cannot be explained by the laws of this same familiar world. The person who witnesses the event must opt for one of two possible solutions: either it is a case of an illusion of the senses, of a product of the imagination and hence the laws of the world remain as they are; or the event actually did take place, it is an integral part of reality, but this reality is now governed by laws which are unknown to us [...].

The fantastic occupies the duration of this uncertainty; as soon one or other response is chosen, we leave the fantastic for a neighbouring genre: the uncanny or the marvellous. *The fantastic is the hesitation experienced by a being who knows only natural laws when confronted by an event which is seemingly supernatural.*]

The fantastic is therefore defined by the presence of hesitation experienced as a consequence of an ambiguity between natural and supernatural interpretations of events. For as long as this uncertainty cannot be dispelled, we are in the realm of what Todorov calls the 'pure fantastic'. Even when this hesitation is resolved by the acceptance of one particular interpretation, we are still in modes related to the fantastic: the 'fantastic-uncanny' if a natural interpretation is decided upon or the 'fantastic-marvellous' if a supernatural interpretation imposes itself. The recognition of hesitation both in herself and in fictional characters portrayed in a literary text is a relatively straightforward task for the reader. It is this which informs my belief that Todorov's definition of the fantastic remains the most workable, and also the most laden with potential, of those which have been proposed to date.

However, this potential has not yet been fully realized. This is because no one has yet satisfactorily addressed the question which is its most logical consequence: *how* is this hesitation between interpretations provoked? Providing answers to this question is the principal aim of this book. Accounting for why Todorov and his various successors have left such a fundamental issue largely unresolved will allow me to begin to trace the intentions of the present work. In the case of Todorov, the decision not to interrogate the issue of hesitation in greater detail can be explained by two particular tendencies in his work. The first is a refusal to recognize the figure of the 'addresser' behind the literary text which is a hallmark of structuralist criticism.[4] This creative persona can be conceived of variously as the actual author, the implied author, or simply a narrative voice. The failure to acknowledge this presence means that the impact of decisions it takes concerning the nature of the text is neglected. Yet it is precisely these decisions which generate uncertainty. In Todorov's work, therefore, hesitation appears simply to be taken as a given and, as a consequence, the structures which provoke it are not adequately investigated. The second explanation for this neglect grows out of the first. Although both in *Introduction à la littérature fantastique* and elsewhere Todorov recognizes the distinction between events and narration of events, his discussion of hesitation in the fantastic does not display this awareness sufficiently rigorously. For example, in the second half of his first condition for the existence of the fantastic (of which more below), Todorov states that the reader must hesitate between a natural and supernatural interpretation of 'événements évoqués' ['events evoked'] (F 37). Throughout his analysis, the impression given is that greater significance is attributed to events than to their evocation. His explanation of the characteristics of the 'marvellous' is also typical: 'ce n'est pas une attitude envers les événements rapportés qui caractérise le merveilleux, mais la nature même de ces événements' ['it is not an attitude towards reported events which characterizes the marvellous, but the very nature of these events'] (F 59).[5] And yet, it is precisely the way in which the events are evoked or reported which is all-important to an appreciation of hesitation. The means by which a fantastic story prompts a reader to hesitate are difficult to understand if it is not acknowledged that this reader enjoys a different, less direct type of access to events than do fictional characters. Fictional characters confront fictional events directly; the reader's experience of fictional events can only ever be indirect because a narrative text does not comprise a series of events but, rather, '*the representation* of a series of events' (Onega & Landa 1996, 5, original italics). Because these events are represented verbally, the reader's access to these events is mediated through the prism of the various syntactic and narrative techniques employed to present them. Todorov's investigation of the triggers for hesitation in the fantastic is incomplete because he shows greater interest in the events than in the devices used to present them.

The failure of post-1970 critics of the fantastic to engage with the question of how hesitation is provoked can be explained by their preoccupation with other of the many issues raised by Todorov.[6] Rejecting his contention (F 169) that the birth of psychoanalysis at the end of the nineteenth century sounded the death knell of the fantastic, many of Todorov's successors have felt the need to broaden the historical parameters of *Introduction à la littérature fantastique*. Irène Bessière (1974), Christine Brooke-Rose (1981), Rosemary Jackson (1981), and Neil Cornwell (1990) are just some of those who argue that examples of the fantastic are still to be found in the modern and postmodern eras. The work of authors such as Franz Kafka, Alain Robbe-

Grillet, Kurt Vonnegut, Salman Rushdie, and Toni Morrison is cited as evidence of this. This concentration on a historical amplification of Todorov's work is accompanied by the perceived need for an extension of his generic scope. In *A Rhetoric of the Unreal*, Brooke-Rose argues that the twin elements of hesitation and the supernatural do not enjoy equal importance in the fantastic. Because 'the mere fact of the supernatural is not sufficient' (Brooke-Rose 1981, 63), the real basis of the fantastic is ambiguity. If the distinguishing feature of the fantastic is ambiguity, she argues, this is a trait it shares with non-fantastic texts. It is this which permits her broadening of the discussion of ambiguity to include genres such as science fiction and the French nouveau roman. In *Le Récit fantastique: la poétique de l'incertain*, Irène Bessière acknowledges the role of ambiguity but argues that it stems from the contradiction between different orders of 'le vraisemblable' (1974, 12). In her eyes, therefore, the fantastic is determined by the presence not of uncertainty but of antinomy, most frequently embodied in the oxymoron.

The spotlight Bessière casts upon verisimilitude as an essential element in the fantastic reveals a relatively widespread dissatisfaction with the work of Todorov amongst his successors. Numerous critics feel the need to counteract the structuralist belief that the literary text is devoid of reference outside itself by giving consideration to the context of the fantastic. For instance, Rosemary Jackson in *Fantasy: Literature of Subversion* and José Monleón in *A Specter is Haunting Europe* (1990) both undertake socio-historical investigations of the genre, assessing the fantastic in terms of the 'politics of its form' (Jackson, 1981, 6). Brooke-Rose (1981, 7) chooses to open her study with a discussion of twentieth-century concepts of the real and underlines three significant changes which distinguish that century from its predecessor in terms of man's relationship to this idea. As the real came to seem more and more unreal in the last century, it is not surprising, she argues, that fantastic art forms should have become increasingly pervasive. In *Fantasy and Mimesis: Representations of Reality in Western Literature* (1984), Kathryn Hume compensates for Todorov's 'work-in-itself' approach (1984, xi) by considering the 'artistic motives' for fantasy's departures from reality.[7] Consideration of both artistic motive and societal influence also informs the decision taken by Jackson and T. E. Apter in her *Fantasy Literature: An Approach to Reality* (1982) to discuss the genre in the light of psychoanalysis. Jackson (1981, 6) justifies this aspect of her approach by contending: 'Fantasy in literature deals so blatantly and repeatedly with unconscious material that it seems rather absurd to try to understand its significance without some reference to psychoanalysis and psychoanalytic readings of texts'. The desire amongst Todorov's successors to compensate for his context-free approach by referring to material reality is supplemented by the impulse to analyse the fantastic in terms of its relation to purely literary notions of reality. As hinted above, with her focus on the concepts of verisimilitude and literary realism, Irène Bessière is at the vanguard of this response. Echoing this approach, T. E. Apter (1982, 1) begins her work with the claim that 'the aim and purpose of fantasy in literature are not necessarily different from those of the most exacting realism'. Rosemary Jackson marries her socio-historical method with an analysis of the manner in which the fantastic operates by combining elements of the marvellous and the mimetic (1981, 33–37). Choosing to address the question of the interaction between the fantastic and literary notions of the real from an innovative angle, Neil Cornwell (1990, 24–25) makes reference to concepts associated with the theory of possible worlds. Marie-Laure Ryan (1992, 537) develops this potential much further when she uses the terminology of this theory to reformulate Todorov's definition of the fantastic.[8] This is very far from being an exhaustive account of all the responses elicited by *Introduction à la littérature fantastique*. What it does indicate, however, is how, in the plethora of critical endeavours inspired by Todorov's work, the specific issue of the provocation of hesitation might have been overlooked.

As references throughout this book will make clear, there is a great deal which is of value in the contributions of the critics who have investigated the fantastic since Todorov. However, because it takes the pursuit of hesitation as its central focus, this study engages most closely with his work in *Introduction à la littérature fantastique*. It tests out, and often challenges, a number of the claims that Todorov makes regarding the optimum conditions and techniques for generating ambiguity. For this reason, it is pertinent to outline the characteristics he identifies in the fantastic in the form of his triads of rules, properties, and functions. Todorov offers a refinement of his definition of the fantastic by proposing, in the first instance, three rules which govern its existence (*F* 37–38):

> D'abord, il faut que le texte oblige le lecteur à considérer le monde des personnages comme un monde de personnes vivantes et à hésiter entre une explication naturelle et une explication surnaturelle des événements évoqués. Ensuite, cette hésitation peut être ressentie également par un personnage; ainsi [...] elle devient un des thèmes de l'œuvre [...]. Enfin il importe que le lecteur adopte une certaine attitude à l'égard du texte: il refusera aussi bien l'interprétation allégorique que l'interprétation 'poétique'.

> [Firstly, the text must oblige the reader to consider the character world as a world of living people and to hesitate between a natural explanation and a supernatural explanation for events evoked. Next, this hesitation can be felt equally by a character; in this case [...] it becomes one of the themes of the work [...]. Finally, it is important that the reader adopts a certain attitude towards the text: he will refuse equally an allegorical interpretation as a 'poetic' interpretation.]

He argues that these three rules can be organized in a hierarchy of importance whereby the first and third are essential whilst the second is simply optional. Whilst this hierarchy exists in theory, Todorov maintains that, in practice, the majority of fantastic texts fulfil all three conditions equally. Complementing these rules is a series of three properties (*F* 82–94) which, he contends, a fantastic literary narrative should conventionally possess. These properties, which are determined by the three rules and serve to create the structural unity of the work, are: (1) 'un certain emploi du discours figuré, le surnaturel naît souvent de ce qu'on prend le sens figuré à la lettre' ['a certain use of figurative discourse, the supernatural is often engendered by taking the figural sense literally']; (2) 'le narrateur dit habituellement "je"' ['the narrator habitually says "I"']; and (3) 'le fantastique est un genre qui accuse [la convention qu'implique la lecture de gauche à droite] plus nettement que les autres' ['the fantastic is a genre which emphasizes [the convention of reading from left to right] more clearly than others']. Finally, in a show of typical structuralist symmetry, Todorov discusses three semantic features which can also be used to define the genre. These features (*F* 98) take the form of three functions which the fantastic serves in the literary text:

> Premièrement, le fantastique produit un effet particulier sur le lecteur — peur, ou horreur, ou simplement curiosité —, que les autres genres ou formes littéraires ne peuvent provoquer. Deuxièmement, le fantastique sert la narration, entretient le suspense: la présence d'éléments fantastiques permet une organisation particulièrement serrée de l'intrigue. Enfin, le fantastique a une fonction à première vue tautologique: il permet de décrire un univers fantastique, et cet univers n'a pas pour autant une réalité en dehors du langage; la description et le décrit ne sont pas de nature différente.

> [Firstly, the fantastic produces a particular effect upon the reader — fear, or horror, or simple curiosity —, that other genres or literary forms cannot provoke. Secondly, the fantastic serves the narration, maintains suspense: the presence of fantastic elements permits a particularly tight organization of the plot. Finally, the fantastic has a function which appears tautological at first sight: it allows the description of a fantastic universe and this universe for all that has no existence outside language; the description and the described are not different in nature.]

By reproducing at some length the nine propositions made by Todorov for the fantastic, I do not seek to suggest that they are all correct. Nor, for my purposes, are they all equally interesting. It is the rules and properties, rather than the semantic features, which prove to be of the most use to the investigation undertaken in this book. But it is largely through a process of interrogating and trying out these various claims that a fuller understanding of the mechanics of hesitation and the functioning of the fantastic can be gained.

As my critique of Todorov's structuralist failings above has suggested, the central idea that the current work interrogates is that hesitation in the fantastic is the consequence of the stylistic, narrative, and syntactic devices employed to present the fictional world to the reader. A reading of eight primary texts will reveal the variety of these devices, the manner in which they are deployed and combined in order to create the genre's defining interpretative ambiguity. Certain techniques will be shown to recur with great regularity across different texts; this will permit the identification of a series of stock generic tools. This analysis also reinserts the other figure marginalized by Todorov's structuralist focus on the text above all else: the reader. My discussion of narrative and syntactic techniques will be constantly accompanied by an assessment of their likely impact upon the reader's experience of the text. Of particular interest will be the question of how the reader's responses change as the narrative develops and how the degree or focus of hesitation alters. One critical issue which will constantly be kept in view is the likelihood that the reader will continue to sense uncertainty or that, for some reason, she will be persuaded to accept one definitive interpretation of events. This interest in whether hesitation endures or is resolved is what informs the clear extension of the scope of *Introduction à la littérature fantastique* that I propose in Chapters 3 and 4 below. Here, I will argue that the hesitation typical of the fantastic exists in texts which would ordinarily be dismissed by Todorov's criteria, notably those depicting madness or an ironic narrative attitude.

The belief that hesitation in the fantastic results from the techniques used to represent fictional events in the text leads me to adopt a methodological approach which allows the clearest interrogation of these factors: narratology. Developing out of 1970s structuralism, this critical framework proposes a systematic model of the structures that participate in story construction and narration. It is helpful to consider this model as a series of questions which the reader may ask of any narrative text. The answers to these can then be used to compare the structures which function both within a single work and between different works. Issues which are fundamental to narratology, such as the characteristics of the narrative voice, point of view, narrative levels, and temporal stance, prove to be invaluable to an understanding of how fantastic texts construct and maintain ambiguity. The models proposed by Gérard Genette in *Figures III* (1972) and by Susan Lanser in *The Narrative Act* (1981) are the most useful.[9] The work of Lanser serves as a valuable complement to that of her French predecessor in terms of the move she advocates away from his somewhat restrictive binary approach according to which a narrative feature must be either one thing or another. She initiates a system of sliding scales, allowing degrees of adherence to particular conventions, which facilitates an account of the subtle variations of representation within and between works. Where Genette's model has a tendency to lose itself in a confusing maze of technical terms, Lanser's framework comprises thirty-four axes, which can be tabulated on a single page. These axes are subdivisions of the three relationships which operate in the structure of point of view: status (which deals with the speaker's relationship to the speech act); contact (which refers to the speaker's relationship to the audience); and stance (which concerns the speaker's relationship to the message). Whilst Helmut Bonheim is correct when he argues (1990, 300) that 'it is hardly possible to apply [Lanser's model] as a whole', it nevertheless offers significant potential for the study of narrative in both its range and clarity. It is not my intention in what follows to feed my chosen texts wholesale into either of the models proposed by Genette or Lanser. Rather, the discussion of how a text triggers interpretative hesitation will select those axes, or questions, which appear to be the most pertinent and fruitful. Nor is narratology the only critical framework invoked in this book. At an early stage, the discussion of how a narrative text creates a mimetic fictional world has recourse to theories of realism. And in the final two chapters, where the spotlight falls upon the role of madness and irony in the fantastic, elements of reader-response theory prove to be especially valuable.

The answers to how the fantastic provokes hesitation are sought in eight works of prose fiction written in France and Russia between 1833 and 1887. The eight, in the order they are analysed below, are: Alexander Pushkin's *The Queen of Spades* (1834), Théophile Gautier's *Spirite* (1865), Vladimir Odoevskii's *The Sylph* (1837), Prosper Mérimée's *La Vénus d'Ille* (1837), Fedor Dostoevskii's *The Double* (1866), Guy de Maupassant's *Le Horla* (1887), Théophile Gautier's *Onuphrius, ou les vexations d'un admirateur d'Hoffmann* (1833), and Nikolai Gogol's *The Nose* (1836). This comparative approach offers a number of advantages and presents significant opportunities for a deeper insight into the functioning of the genre. It is generally agreed that the modern fantastic, as works written during this period are commonly categorized, grew out of the popularity of the Gothic novel in the late eighteenth and early nineteenth centuries. More specifically, development in the practice of the fantastic in both France and Russia can be traced to a common catalyst: the work of the German author E. T. A. Hoffmann. Owing to the widespread use of French in Russia during the nineteenth century, Hoffmann's works were often translated into Russian not directly from the original German but via the French. This meant that, in many cases, the literary tastes of the French audience came to influence what was presented to the Russian readership. Furthermore, it is well documented that writers in France and Russia enjoyed especially close contact, either directly or through correspondence. The present work does not engage with either of these issues specifically. However, although surveys of the European fantastic have highlighted the popularity of the genre in both countries, by aligning these two literatures directly, I hope to allow a new appreciation of their points of correlation. Moreover, the revelation of similarities between the devices used to create uncertainty in the two languages proves that fundamental generic features exist at a deeper, more trans-linguistic level than has previously been acknowledged.

The method of close textual analysis adopted here explains the restriction of the number of primary texts to be discussed to eight. The decision as to which works would make the final cut was arrived at only after long and painful consideration. The selection favours works which present the most fruitful and most interesting illustrations of how the wider canon of the fantastic functions. One important factor in this decision was the need for texts which offered the most extensive scope for discussion; the chosen works are eight in which hesitation is sustained for an extended period in the narrative. Therefore, while Gérard de Nerval's *Aurélia ou le Rêve et la vie* (1855), for example, presents the motifs of madness and the supernatural discussed in Chapter 3, its past-tense orientation means that the potential for ambiguity is restricted and the interest it holds as a primary text is reduced. However, the claims that the present work can make to be an account of hesitation in the *genre* of the fantastic stem from its extensive use of cross-reference to secondary texts. The combination and organization of devices used to provoke hesitation in an individual work may be unique, but the device itself is shown to have a trans-generic application.

This investigation of the fantastic falls broadly into two parts. The first, comprising Chapters 1 and 2, examines the mechanics of hesitation. The analysis of the first four primary texts reveals a series of techniques which the genre favours in the provocation of uncertainty. Establishing the model which will be maintained throughout this book, each chapter proceeds through an analysis of one French and one Russian work. The first two chapters engage closely with the proposals contained in Todorov's first rule of the fantastic:

> il faut que le texte oblige le lecteur à considérer le monde des personnages comme un monde de personnes vivantes et à hésiter entre une explication naturelle et une explication surnaturelle des événements évoqués.

> [the text must oblige the reader to consider the character world as a world of living people and to hesitate between a natural explanation and a supernatural explanation for events evoked.]

They pose two different, but interrelated questions: (1) How does the literary text persuade the reader to believe in the story world it presents? (2) How does the narrative text prompt the reader to hesitate about the interpretation of events? The answers to these questions are sought in Chapter 1 in two texts displaying a third-person or heterodiegetic narrative voice. In Chapter 2, they are investigated in two works narrated by a first-person or homodiegetic voice. This approach allows claims that third-person narrators are not compatible with the fantastic to be disputed. Both of these chapters address the first question from two angles. Part 1 of Chapter 1 examines how a mimetic fictional world is constructed through the appropriation of techniques associated with realist fiction. Part 2 of both Chapter 1 and Chapter 2 scrutinizes the creation of a fictional world which is not just verisimilar but stable and in which the narrative voice is authoritative and reliable. In the case of the heterodiegetic text in Chapter 1, these features are shown to depend upon the skill of the narrative voice. In the homodiegetic context examined in Chapter 2, they are more closely associated with the issue of narrator personality. In Chapter 1, answers to the second question, regarding reader hesitation, are provided in Part 3 where contributory syntactic and narrative factors are discussed side by side. Particular attention is devoted here to the impact of switches in point of view which, as a means of circumventing reliability, facilitate ambiguity. In Chapter 2, the appreciation of the role of syntax gained in the first chapter is extended by the discussion in Part 1. This illustrates how narratives of different diegetic modes exploit similar syntactic devices to similar effect. Part 3 of this chapter is devoted to an analysis of the impact of narrative techniques and reveals the crucial role played by the technique of multiple voice.

The second part of this study, comprising Chapters 3 and 4, moves on from a discussion of the basic tools of the genre to an analysis of a typology of hesitation in texts where this element is more profound and disruptive. Pursuing the all-important question of reliability, these chapters analyse the nature and degrees of hesitation in works where the narrative voices show a tendency towards mental instability or self-conscious playfulness. Whilst the focus remains trained upon the contribution of syntactic and narrative techniques, greater attention is devoted than in Chapters 1 and 2 to the effect of these devices upon the reader. Indeed, in Chapter 4, the profile and abilities of this reader come very much to the fore. The discussion of the four chosen works asks that the dismissal or marginalization of certain texts from the genre of the fantastic be reconsidered. In its analysis of the influence upon hesitation of voices displaying signs of insanity, Chapter 3 challenges the contention that the parallel portrayal of madness and the supernatural invariably leads to a resolution of ambiguity. Part 1 of this chapter discusses the contradictory indications given in the opening passages of both primary texts regarding the stability of the fictional world and the competence of the narrative voice. Part 2 provides a detailed analysis of how, in a homodiegetic text, an impression of discursive disintegration is achieved by means of syntax and narrative techniques deployed by a voice standing in virtual isolation. Part 3 of Chapter 3 examines how effectively this sense of incoherence can be achieved in a heterodiegetic text, where the figure of the narrator is conventionally expected to act as a barrier between the reader and the alienated experiences of the protagonist. The irony revealed by the second and third parts of this chapter is that it is the heterodiegetic, filtered account of madness which proves to be the most unsettling for the reader.

Chapter 4 interrogates how the reader's experience of hesitation is influenced by narrative personae which play with the conventions of the fantastic. The two texts examined in this final chapter ask the reader to use the generic competence either already possessed or acquired through reading the preceding three chapters to recognize ludic departures and ironic deformations of these conventional models. The central issue here is whether the combination of narrative playfulness and apparently supernatural events provokes a type of hesitation which can still be considered to conform to generic requirements. Part 1 of Chapter 4 uncovers elements of narrator performance which, in terms of their effect on the creation of a verisimilar fictional world, are even more unsettling than the contradictions revealed in Chapter 3. Part 2 examines how the expectations that the initiated reader has of the fantastic are made the subject of irony by a trivialized depiction of the supernatural. Furthermore, this part illustrates how even the reader capable of recognizing this ironic exploitation of generic norms does not escape becoming the target of narrative play. Part 3 of Chapter 4 engages most explicitly with the issue of how the fantastic makes the reader aware of her reliance on storytelling conventions. It demonstrates how, at its peak, a playful, self-reflexive narrative attitude interrogates not only the depiction of the supernatural but the status of the entire discourse. The final question addressed by this study becomes, therefore, whether, as Todorov claims, hesitation concerning the status of the discourse rather than the nature of fictional events should be considered to be inimical to the fantastic.

Notes to the Introduction

1. The reader is referred to throughout this study as 'she'. This decision is informed by two main factors: firstly, it allows an easy distinction between references to the reader and the narrator, whom I uniformly call 'he'; and secondly, it indicates that, although I believe the reactions ascribed to the reader in this book to be largely universal, this figure bears the closest resemblance to myself.

2. The work of Pierre-Georges Castex is typical of the scholarship of this era. The first part of his *Le Conte fantastique en France de Nodier à Maupassant* provides an historical overview of the fantastic from the end of the seventeenth century until the close of the nineteenth; the second part is dedicated to an account of the particular contribution made by eight French authors. The thematic and affective perspective which dominates this second part is clearly evident in the type of chapter titles employed: 'Nodier et ses rêves', 'Gautier et son angoisse', and 'Maupassant et son mal'. There is much which is of value in Castex's study. However, it is his tendency to equate literary detail with biographical fact which seems out of date in the present day. A similar approach is adopted by both Louis Vax (1960) and Marcel Schneider (1964).

3. Pre-1970 critics of the fantastic had offered their own definitions of the genre, but these have been largely superseded by that proposed by Todorov. For instance, Castex (1951, 8) defines the fantastic in terms of its relation to the real and its similarity to various affective states:

   [Le fantastique] se caractérise [...] par une intrusion brutale du mystère dans le cadre de la vie réelle, il est lié généralement aux états morbides de la conscience qui, dans les phénomènes de cauchemar ou de délire, projette devant elle des images de ses angoisses ou de ses terreurs.

   [The fantastic] is characterized [...] by a brutal intrusion of mystery into the framework of real life, it is generally linked to morbid states of consciousness which, in the phenomena of nightmare or delirium, project images of anxiety and terror.]

   Both Schneider and Vax echo this idea of the fantastic as being an intrusion into the real. Schneider (1964, 8) argues that the fantastic is 'un produit de rupture, une déchirure soudaine dans l'expérience vécue du quotidien' ['a product of rupture, a sudden tear in the lived experience of the everyday'], while Vax (1965, 169) believes that it appears 'comme une rupture des constances du monde réel' ['like a rupture in the constancies of the real world']. Whilst these definitions cannot be said to be incorrect, they remain abstract and fail to pay sufficient attention to specifically textual criteria.

4. The term 'addresser' is borrowed from Roman Jakobson's model for verbal communication (1960,

353) in which 'the addresser sends a message to the addressee. To be operative the message requires a context referred to [...], seizable by the addressee, and either verbal or capable of being verbalised'. Todorov's definition of the fantastic admits only two of the four basic elements of Jakobson's communicative model: message and addressee. Such selectivity was typical of structuralists who endeavoured to switch the focus away from issues of author and context.

5. The misplaced emphasis in Todorov's 1970 study could have been rectified if he had reiterated sufficiently strongly his prior statement (1966, 141):

En lisant une œuvre de fiction, nous n'avons pas une perception directe des événements qu'elle décrit. En même temps que ces événements, nous percevons bien que d'une manière différente, la perception qu'en a celui qui les raconte.

[In reading a work of fiction, we do not have a direct perception of the events which it describes. At the same time as these events, we perceive, albeit in a different manner, the perception of the figure who recounts them.]

6. This failure can also be explained by the fact that no theoretical frameworks exist for an analysis of hesitation.

7. The use by Hume and Jackson of the term 'fantasy' reveals an area of some confusion in discussion of the genre. Unlike Todorov and Brooke-Rose, these two authors fail to distinguish sufficiently clearly between the associated terms 'fantasy' and 'the fantastic'. Jackson talks throughout, seemingly interchangeably, of 'literary fantasies' or the 'literary fantastic', while Hume criticizes Todorov for his claims regarding fantasy without acknowledging that this is not, in fact, the specific subject of his work. This terminological confusion is largely dispelled by Cornwell (1990, 31) when he defines fantasy as a wider concept than its narrower counterpart, the fantastic. He argues that fantasy has an equivalent value to the term 'mimesis' and can be considered to be a trans-generic literary quality. In contrast, the fantastic is essentially a generic form which can stand alongside other examples such as the realist, Gothic or modernist novel.

8. Ryan claims that Todorov's work can be easily translated into possible world theory terminology and offers the following discussion of the fantastic and its related genres (Ryan 1992, 536):

From the point of view of the reader this problem translates into a hesitation concerning the relation of the AW (actual world) to FW (fictional world). The protagonist approaches the FW with the same expectations we bring to our experience of AW. If the extraordinary event can be explained away as dream or hallucination — this is to say, expelled from the center of the fictional universe — these expectations prevail. Todorov calls this situation the fantastic-uncanny. If the extraordinary events turn out to be verified in TAW (textual actual world), this universe as a whole breaks the natural laws in effect in AW. The resulting subgenre is the fantastic-marvellous.

9. Although the work of Genette and Lanser is most commonly used, this book also makes reference to proposals offered by other narratologists, such as Mieke Bal, Shlomith Rimmon-Kenan, Seymour Chatman, and Monika Fludernik.

CHAPTER 1

Reliability and Shifting Perspectives: Hesitation in Heterodiegesis

Introduction

Before a reader can be prompted to hesitate, she must be encouraged to believe. If a reader is to respond with uncertainty to an apparently supernatural event, she needs to have been persuaded previously that the world she is observing is essentially natural. This opening chapter takes these two fundamental strands of the fantastic, believability and hesitation, as its basis. In the early stages of *Introduction à la littérature fantastique*, Todorov identifies the essential precursor to ambiguity in the fantastic as 'un monde familier' (*F* 29). In the progression of his study, the idea of familiarity is superseded by the twin concepts of 'la réalité' and 'le réel' and he explains:

> Le lecteur et le héros [...] doivent décider si tel événement, tel phénomène appartient à la réalité ou à l'imaginaire, s'il est ou non réel. C'est donc la catégorie du réel qui a fourni sa base à notre définition du fantastique. (*F* 175)

> [The reader and the hero [...] must decide if a certain event, a certain phenomenon belongs to reality or to the imaginary, if it is real or not. It is therefore the category of the real that has provided the basis for our definition of the fantastic.]

However, having invoked these concepts as centrally important, Todorov defines them with disappointing vagueness: reality is simply 'telle qu'elle existe pour l'opinion commune' (*F* 47), for instance. Rather than relying on such unquantifiable factors as public opinion, it would be more helpful to consider the notion of reality within a fictional text in purely literary terms. The likelihood that a text will be considered to represent reality depends upon its creation of a fictional world which stands in a mimetic relationship with the real world; it needs to portray a fictional world which resembles the extrafictional actual world. The first two parts of this chapter investigate the dual methods used in fantastic narratives to convince the reader of this resemblance. In Part 1, methods employed to create a sense of 'vraisemblance' in the fictional world are analysed. In Part 2, the spotlight falls upon the specific elements of the reliability and authority of the narrative voice and how these factors contribute to the construction of a stable fictional world. Part 3 of this chapter then turns its attention more specifically to the provocation of hesitation once the natural status of the fictional world has been established. It specifically challenges Todorov's contention that third-person narrators are ill-suited to the fantastic by examining uncertainty in the heterodiegetic context. It reveals the ways in which elements of syntax and techniques of narrative can be combined to problematize the status of fictional events and the reader's interpretation of them.

My analysis of these questions of believability and hesitation takes as its twin testing grounds Alexander Pushkin's *Пиковая дама* (*The Queen of Spades*) and Théophile Gautier's *Spirite*. Pushkin (1799–1837) is widely known as Russia's greatest poet, but he also made a remarkable contribution to the country's literary development in almost every other available genre. With the popularity of poetry in decline during the late 1820s and early 1830s, Pushkin turned increasingly towards prose fiction. Following on from the success of his first prose effort, *Повести Белкина* (*The Tales of Belkin*) in 1830, *The Queen of Spades* was first published in 1834 in the journal *Библиотека для чтения* (*Library for Reading*). The story is generally considered to be Pushkin's prose masterpiece and has, accordingly, received an enormous amount of critical attention. The hero of the story is a Russified German, transparently named Germann, who becomes obsessed with the tale of a gambling formula which could secure his fortune. In order to gain access to the holder of this formula, countess ★★★, Germann decides to court her ward, Lizaveta. An invitation to a late-night tryst with Lizaveta provides the perfect opportunity for Germann to confront the old woman. Fatefully, in a scene replete with erotic overtones, when he threatens her with a pistol, the countess dies of fright without revealing her secret. An overwrought and inebriated Germann is subsequently visited by the dead countess who reveals the sequence of three cards he needs to win at faro: three, seven, ace. Germann's first two nights of gambling prove successful as he wins 47,000 and then 94,000 roubles. However, disaster strikes on the third night when, having laid what he believes to be the winning ace, he realizes he has actually staked on the queen of spades — and lost. Bearing more than a passing resemblance to the dead countess, the queen of spades then appears to wink at Germann from the losing card. The story concludes with a description of the hero confined to a mental asylum, maniacally repeating: 'three, seven, ace', 'three, seven, queen'.

The story's status as an exemplary text in the genre of the fantastic was signalled by Fedor Dostoevskii in a letter of 1880. During correspondence with a young writer, Iu. F. Abaza, the novelist offered advice on how a fantastic story ought to be written by praising the example of Pushkin in *The Queen of Spades*. He recommended:

> Фантастическое должно до того соприкасаться с реальным, что вы должны почти верить ему. Пушкин давший нам почти все формы искусства, написал *Пиковую Даму* — верх искусства фантастического. И вы верите, что Германн действительно имел видение, и именно собразное с его мировоззрением, а между тем, в конце повести, то есть прочтя ее, вы не знаете, как решить: вышло ли это видение из природы Германна, или действительно он один из тех, которые соприкоснулись с другим миром, злых и враждебных человечеству духов... Вот это искусство.[1]

> [The fantastic must be so closely aligned with the real that you have almost to believe in it. Pushkin, who has provided us with all forms of art, wrote *The Queen of Spades* which is the very pinnacle of the art of the fantastic. And you believe that Germann really did have a vision which complies precisely with his world-view; but, meanwhile, at the close of the story, when you have read it through, you do

not know how to resolve matters: was this vision a product of Germann's mind or
is he, in actual fact, one of those persons who is linked to another world and who
is one of those evil spirits, destructive to mankind... Now that is art!]

Despite an historical distance of almost one hundred years, there are clear echoes
between the opinions expressed here and the definitions of the fantastic proposed
by Todorov. Dostoevskii explains how the description of the dead countess's visit
to Germann causes him to hesitate between a natural explanation (the vision is
a product of the protagonist's imagination) and a supernatural one (the visit did,
actually, occur and the protagonist enjoys links with the 'other' world). Transposing
Todorov's definitions and categories onto Dostoevskii's comment that, at the end of
the story, you still 'do not know how to resolve matters' would lead to a classification
of Pushkin's story as an example of the 'fantastique-pur'. This can be confirmed by
an analysis of the linguistic and narrative devices which are employed in *The Queen
of Spades* to ensure that Germann's uncertainty is shared by the reader and is denied
any definitive resolution.

Like Pushkin, Théophile Gautier (1811–72) was a remarkable contributor in both a
range of literary genres and a variety of artistic spheres. While he is best known as the
author of poetry and prose fiction, he also wrote plays, ballet librettos, travelogues, and
was a noteworthy critic of art and literature for the Parisian press. His novella, *Spirite*,
was first published in feuilleton form in *Le Moniteur universel* during 1865. It marked
Gautier's return to the fantastic some thirty years after the appearance of his first
efforts in this field. He had revealed his taste and talent for the genre with a series of
stories published in the 1830s which included *La Cafetière* (1831), *Omphale* (1834), and
La Morte amoureuse (1836). *Spirite* recounts the story of a young man's encounters with
the spirit of a dead girl. This girl, referred to throughout simply as 'Spirite', reveals
that, in life, she was in love with the hero, Guy de Malivert, but that he remained
oblivious to her presence. Nevertheless, Spirite believes that fate has destined them to
be together and so returns from the ideal world she inhabits in death to convince him
of this. There is nothing frightening or foreboding in these supernatural interventions,
which is not the case in *The Queen of Spades*. Instead, the supernatural offers the
possibility of initiation into an ideal other world which will bring happiness and
fulfilment and not tormented insanity. Structurally, the novella can be considered to
fall into two sections. Broadly speaking, the opening six chapters describe Spirite's
unexpected visits to the hero while the remaining ten chapters present the story of
her life and the denouement of the plot, involving the hero's death and accession to
the ideal realm. By the point at which Spirite begins to dictate her story in chapter 7,
hesitation concerning the nature of events has been resolved. Like Guy de Malivert,
the reader now accepts that he is being visited by a spirit from beyond the rational
world, thereby placing the novella in Todorov's category of the 'merveilleux'. In
view of the present chapter's interest in techniques establishing verisimilitude and
provoking hesitation, my discussion will be restricted to the opening six chapters of
Gautier's work.

Part 1: Realist Borrowings in the Fantastic

The key to any text's ability to persuade the reader to believe in the reality of its fictional world is 'vraisemblance'. This notion is a central element in the practice of mimesis which is, in turn, the defining feature of literary realism. I have shown in the Introduction to this book that it is not unusual for critics to relate a discussion of the fantastic to mimesis or realism. As Louisa Jones (1972, 237) claims: 'the *fantastique* [...] complements rather than opposes realism in fiction, since *vraisemblance*, paradoxically, is a major organizing principle of both'. This sentiment is reiterated by Joyce Lowrie (1979–80, 14), who explains that 'because the hero in a fantastic tale confronts that which threatens the very basis of his perceptions of reality, the question of mimesis is a crucial one'. Despite the pertinence of these observations, there remains work to be done in order to understand more clearly the relationship between the fantastic and realism. The most obvious approach is to look at how fantastic narratives appropriate certain realist devices as a means of creating a 'vraisemblable' fictional world. This methodology is chosen by Christine Brooke-Rose (1981, 85–102) in her analysis of the similarities between science fiction and realism and she makes use of the typology of realist fiction's fifteen 'structures obligées' which is proposed by Philippe Hamon (1973, 411–45). My decision to re-employ Hamon's realist inventory is informed not simply by its applicability but also by the symmetry between his approach and that found in *Introduction à la littérature fantastique*. Hamon himself likens his work to that of Todorov, saying: 'il faudrait [...] faire pour le discours réaliste ce qu'a commencé de faire T. Todorov a propos du discours fantastique' ['it is necessary [...] to do for realist discourse what T. Todorov has begun to do with regards to fantastic discourse'] (1973, 417). By considering which of the procedures identified by Hamon can be seen at work in fantastic narratives, I hope to show how the genre establishes the necessary verisimilitude by borrowing realist techniques.

Both *Spirite* and *The Queen of Spades* succeed in creating a fictional world which stands in a mimetic relationship with the real world. Their methods of doing so, however, do not always coincide. Just as in many of Gautier's fantastic stories, the setting of *Spirite* is recognizably contemporary, perhaps even reminiscent of scenes from the author's own youth. The novella's opening pages provide an extended passage of orientation comprising detailed descriptions of Guy de Malivert and the layout and furnishing of his rooms. This description does not simply restrict itself to the physically observable facts. In a manner typical of realist discourse, the narrator also reveals that he has a certain knowledge of the protagonist's personality, financial position, and behaviour in society:

> il avait 40 000 francs de rente en terres et un oncle cacochyme plusieurs fois millionnaire dont il devait hériter. [...] Lorsqu'il se voyait trop bien accueilli dans une maison, il cessait d'y aller, ou il partait pour un grand voyage, et à son retour il avait la satisfaction de se voir parfaitement oublié. (S 204–05)[2]

> [he had an income of 40,000 francs from land and an ancient, multi-millionaire uncle from whom he was due to inherit. [...] Whenever he found himself too well received in a house he would stop visiting or would leave on a long trip, and on his return he was pleased to see that he had been completely forgotten.]

The narrator's revelation of knowledge in the form of references to heredity and the psychological motivation of the character corresponds respectively to the first and second realist procedures identified by Hamon. A similar display of narrator knowledge is also manifest in *The Queen of Spades*, albeit at a later stage. For example, the reader is told towards the end of the second chapter:

> Германн был сын обрусевшего немца, оставившего ему маленький капитал. Будучи твердо убежден в необходимости упрочить свою независимость, Германн не касался и процентов, жил одним жалованьем, не позволял себе малейшей прихоти. (*Q* 330–31)[3]

> [Germann was the son of a Russified German who had left him a small inheritance. Firmly convinced of the need to consolidate his independence, Germann did not even spend the interest, he lived on his income alone, allowing himself not the slightest extravagance.]

These summaries establish a sense of mimesis in each story by making the hero appear rooted in the real world. More tellingly, though, they also reveal the desire of fantastic narrators to persuade their reader that they possess the degree of knowledge and insight which is typical of their realist counterparts.

The resemblance between the fictional world of the text and the real world is further promoted in *Spirite* by the information that, 'Guy habitait une des rues les moins fréquentées du faubourg Saint-Germain' ['Guy lived on one of the quietest streets in the Saint-Germain district']. We are also told that he purchased his horse from 'le célèbre marchand de chevaux des Champs Elysées' ['the famous horse dealer on the Champs Elysées']. For Hamon (1973, 426), such references to actual geographical places constitute an important third feature of realist discourse because they:

> renvoient à des entités sémantiques stables, qu'il ne s'agit d'ailleurs pas tant de comprendre, que de reconnaître comme noms propres (et la Majuscule en est la marque typographique différentielle), fonctionnent donc un peu comme les *citations* du discourse pédagogique: ils assurent des points d'ancrage [...] en embrayant le texte sur un extra-texte valorisé, permettent l'économie d'un énoncé descriptif, et assurent un effet de réel global qui transcende même tout décodage de détail. (original italics)

> [refer to stable semantic entities which do not so much need to be understood as recognized as proper names (and the capital letter is the differentiating typographical mark), function therefore a little like *quotations* in pedagogic discourse: they ensure points of anchorage [...] by switching the text to a valorized extra-text, they enable a description to be efficient and they ensure a global effect of reality which goes beyond any deciphering of detail.]

References to actual geographical places are less frequently encountered in *The Queen of Spades*. Nevertheless, mention is made of St Petersburg while, in his anecdote revealing the existence of the gambling formula, Tomskii states that his grandmother, the countess, was fêted in Paris as 'the Muscovite Venus' (*Q* 320). The extent to which fantastic stories employ such geographical references is striking. For example, in the opening lines of Hoffmann's *Der goldne Topf* (*The Golden Pot*) (1814) a young man runs through 'the Black Gate in Dresden', in Charles Rabou's *Le Ministère public*

(1832), reference is made to Beaugency, Orléans and its place du Martroi, as well as to Paris, while Dostoevskii's *The Double* repeatedly cites street names in St Petersburg. The lesser frequency of geographical reference in *The Queen of Spades* is counterbalanced by the depiction of various actual historical figures such as the duc d'Orléans, Richelieu, and the Count Saint-Germain with the same aim. While the first two of these are mentioned only in passing, the third occupies a central and intriguingly ambiguous role. It is Saint-Germain who is said to have helped the countess by revealing to her the gambling formula some sixty years previously. This creates the ironic situation in which an actual historical figure, who would conventionally be expected to act as a guarantor of the realness of the fictional world, is made complicit in action which undermines its very rationality.

The effect of mimesis created by these references to place and person is reinforced by the repeated inclusion of precise temporal references. Hamon (1973, 442) contends in his seventh procedure that there exists '[une] prédilection du discours réaliste pour les temps et les espaces "articulés" ' ['a predilection on the part of realist discourse for "articulated" times and spaces']. In both *Spirite* and *The Queen of Spades*, particular care is taken to situate the scene or action of the opening pages in the universally recognized framework of time. It is appropriate here to consider the system of time as an embodiment of the rational nature of the real world: man makes sense of his world by dividing time up according to the rules of this system. And if a reader is shown that she shares this same temporal framework with characters, she will be persuaded of the verisimilitude of the fictional world. This explains why time references are so prevalent and important in fantastic stories. For instance, the opening scene of Guy de Malivert relaxing in his room is said to take place 'en hiver' (*S* 203) whilst the gathering at Narumov's, which opens *The Queen of Spades*, also happens one 'зимняя ночь' ['winter's night'] (*Q* 319). Subsequent temporal references become increasingly specific. In Pushkin, the card players sit down to eat 'в пятом часу утра' ['at five o'clock in the morning'] and they retire to bed 'без четверти шесть' ['at a quarter to six'] (*Q* 323). As Gautier's protagonist congratulates himself on not being out in society, 'dix heures venaient de sonner' ['it had just struck ten'] (*S* 203). Like their geographical counterparts, temporal references are also almost ubiquitous in the fantastic. To give just two further examples: in *The Golden Pot*, the hero runs through Dresden 'on Ascension Day at three in the afternoon' whilst in Charles Nodier's *Une Heure ou La Vision* (1806), the narrator's nocturnal walks do not begin, 'qu'après que onze heures du soir étaient sonnées' ['until after 11 o'clock at night had struck'] (1961, 15). The effect of combining specific time references with the introduction of the apparently supernatural will be discussed later in this chapter.

Spirite is also notable for its exploitation of Hamon's fifth realist procedure: semiotic complementarity. This is the technique whereby a realist text 'overcodes' itself in an effort to provide information to as wide an audience as possible. Reference is made to other signs and codes in order to provide the reader with maximum information: if she does not have access to code (a), she might have access to code (b). This complementarity of signs can take various forms but, in *Spirite*, it is the references to works of art announcing the protagonist's destiny that are of especial interest. Overcoding can be seen primarily through the intertextual reference implied by Guy de Malivert's choice of reading matter in the opening scene: 'la lueur en tombait sur un volume que Guy tenait d'une main distraite et qui n'était autre que l'*Evangeline* de Longfellow' ['the light fell on a volume which Guy held in a distracted hand and which was none other than Longfellow's *Evangeline*'] (*S* 202). In *Evangeline*, the lovers are separated on the eve of their marriage and condemned to search eternally for each other in vain in a manner that prefigures the fate of Guy de Malivert in *Spirite*. Precisely because of the parallel between the stories of Longfellow's lovers and the protagonist of Gautier's novella, the reference to *Evangeline* must also be recognized as a discreet *mise en abyme*. This, along with further such references, covertly signals the fictionality of *Spirite* and, in particular, its literarity.[4] However, highlighting the fictional status of the text need not undermine its claims for 'vraisemblance'. Fictionality and 'vraisemblance' are entirely compatible concepts; simply because something is signalled as not being fact does not mean that it cannot be made to resemble the real world. Semiotic complementarity is also present in the description of the contents of Guy de Malivert's library which characterize him as an artist and 'un savant'. The presence of works such as 'la *Symbolique* de Creuzet, la *Mécanique céleste* de Laplace, l'*Astronomie* d'Arago' ['Creuzet's *Symbolic*, Laplace's *Celestial Mechanics*, Arago's *Astronomy*'] (*S* 204) again obliquely announces the protagonist's predestination to accede to an ideal world beyond material reality.

In part, perhaps, because of its much shorter length, Pushkin's story provides far less orienting information than *Spirite*. This does not mean, however, that its fictional world is lacking in verisimilitude. In place of the extended passages of informative description which open Gautier's novella, *The Queen of Spades* presents an extended section of dialogue after only seven lines of orienting narration. This dialogue takes advantage of the widely held belief that 'showing' a reader the verisimilitude of a fictional world can be just as effective as 'telling' her about it. Because in direct dialogue 'le narrateur fait semblant de céder littéralement la parole à son personnage' ['the narrator pretends to cede speech literally to his character'] (Genette 1972, 192), it is a discourse which can appear to be more life-like. This opening section of dialogue in *The Queen of Spades* clearly demonstrates the extent to which the voice of the narrator can be withdrawn from the forefront of the discourse. During the relatively extended passage of exchanges between the card players, Pushkin's narrator intervenes a mere seven times to utter a total of only twenty words. On six of these seven occasions, he does no more than attribute speech to identified characters whilst on the other he provides a bare minimum of additional information: 'сказал один из гостей, указывая на молодого инженера' ['said one of the guests, pointing to a young engineer'] (*Q* 320). Other parts of this dialogue stand entirely unattributed by the narrator in a move which renders the speech even more 'free' and so gives an even greater impression of mimesis. Although it is not specifically identified by Hamon, the use of direct dialogue can be associated with his eighth realist procedure which concerns the narrative concretization of the performance of the discourse.[5] The narrator takes a back seat during the exchanges between the card players and subsequently allows Tomskii to tell his all-important story about the gambling secret for himself. This guarantees a degree of authenticity for the anecdote because it is narrated by a quasi-witness, the countess's grandson, who can make claims for its veracity. This is a small-scale version of the practice recognized by Hamon in realist fiction whereby the whole of a narrative is delegated to a narrator-character.

Hamon makes no suggestion that even the most conventional realist text exhibits every one of the fifteen generic procedures he identifies. His inventory is intended to function more as a checklist against which the realist pretensions of a given text can be assessed. What both *Spirite* and *The Queen of Spades* show is an appropriation of a sufficient number of the procedures to establish realism as an important informing genre for the fantastic. Even if not entirely consciously, these procedures are recognized by the reader as building blocks of the mimetic in realism and so can be efficiently deployed to create the all-important sense of the real necessary to the fantastic. Both of these works also reveal another typically realist trait, but one which poses potentially significant problems to Todorov's conception of the fantastic.

Part 2: Narrative Authority and the Fantastic

In every literary text, the potential for creating a sense of the real also depends to a significant extent upon the characteristics of the narrative voice. In order to encourage the reader to invest belief, fantastic stories must endeavour not only to create a fictional world which is mimetic, but one which is stable and reliable. The narrative voice is the primary constructor of any such stability. Quoting Roland Barthes in *S/Z*, Hamon (1973, 427) acknowledges this state of affairs in realist fiction when he says that there exists '[un] évitement au maximum par le discours réaliste du pronom "je" [...], car "l'absence de nom [...] provoque une déflation capitale de l'illusion réaliste"' ['[an] avoidance as far as possible by realist discourse of the pronoun "I" [...], because "the absence of a name [...] provokes a significant deflation of the realist illusion"']. This claim is reinforced by Rosemary Jackson (1981, 34) when she argues that 'classic narrative fiction, which is exemplified by so many "realistic" nineteenth-century novels, represents as "real" the events it tells, using as mouthpiece a knowing third-person voice'. Both *Spirite* and *The Queen of Spades* employ this type of narrative voice which, following Genette's model, I choose to call 'heterodiegetic'.[6] The narrator simply records the action he describes and gives no indication that he will actually be a participant in the story.

While the heterodiegetic status of the narrative voice is made immediately evident in *Spirite* with the opening words 'Guy de Malivert était étendu' ['Guy de Malivert was lying'], Pushkin's story initially proves to be less explicit. It opens with the following lines:

> Однажды играли в карты у конногвардейца Нарумова. Долгая зимняя ночь прошла незаметно; сели ужинать в пятом часу утра. (Q 319)

> [One day (they/we) were playing cards in cavalry officer Narumov's quarters. The long winter night passed imperceptibly; (they/we) sat down to eat at five in the morning.]

In the original Russian, the verbs 'играли' ['were playing'] and 'сели' ['sat down'] appear in the plural past tense but without an accompanying subject. Whilst this omission is perfectly acceptable in colloquial Russian, it does serve to provoke a degree of ambiguity as to whether the missing pronoun should be 'they' or 'we'. At this very early stage, this non-specificity means that the narrator could potentially be either heterodiegetic or homodiegetic. Any confusion is swiftly resolved in the third sentence of the story as the demonstrative pronouns 'те' ['those'] and 'прочие' ['others'] clearly indicate that the narrator is not one of those present and therefore possesses heterodiegetic authority. In the light of the comments made by Hamon and Jackson, it is clear that the use of a heterodiegetic voice in *Spirite* and *The Queen of Spades* represents a further instance of cross-pollination between realist and fantastic fiction.

However, when viewed in the light of Todorov's theory of the genre, it constitutes a fundamental problem. In his second property, Todorov claims that, in diametric opposition to realist fiction, the fantastic usually employs homodiegetic narrators (or what he calls 'represented narrators'). His explanation of this perceived preference is based upon the status of the literary text, which means that the narrative assertions made therein cannot be subjected to a 'truth test'. The distinction Todorov draws can be more clearly understood by referring to what Lubomir Doležel calls the relative 'authentication authority' of each mode: that is, the likelihood that statements made by a homodiegetic or heterodiegetic voice will be taken to be narrative fact. Doležel argues that the 'Er-form' (heterodiegetic) narrator carries a greater level of authority because 'motifs introduced in the speech act of the anonymous Er-form narrator are *eo ipso* authentic' (1980, 12). By contrast, the 'Ich-form' (homodiegetic) enjoys a lesser degree of such authority: 'the world constructed by the Ich-form narrator is relatively authentic. It is not the world of absolute narrative facts' (ibid.). Doležel summarizes this distinction (1980, 18) by saying that 'the Ich-form narrator has to earn his authentication authority, while to the anonymous Er-form narrator this authority is given by convention'. In justifying his claim that the fantastic prefers homodiegetic narrators, Todorov explains:

> Le narrateur représenté convient donc parfaitement au fantastique. Il est préférable au simple personnage, lequel peut facilement mentir [...]. Mais il est également préférable au narrateur non représenté, et cela pour deux raisons. D'abord, si l'événement surnaturel nous était rapporté par un tel narrateur nous serions aussitôt dans le merveilleux [...]. En deuxième lieu et ceci se lie à la définition même du fantastique, la première personne 'racontante' est celle qui permet le plus aisément l'identification du lecteur au personnage, puisque, comme on sait, le pronom 'je' appartient à tous. (*F* 88–89)

> [The represented narrator thus suits the fantastic perfectly. He is preferable to the simple character, who could easily lie [...]. But he is equally preferable to the non-represented narrator, and for two reasons. First, if the supernatural event had been reported to us by such a narrator, we would immediately be in the marvellous [...]. Second, and this is linked to the definition of the fantastic itself, the 'narrating' first person is the one which most easily facilitates the identification between reader and character because, as we know, the pronoun 'I' belongs to us all.]

So, by presenting a heterodiegetic narrative voice, both *Spirite* and *The Queen of Spades* challenge Todorov's theory for the successful functioning of the fantastic. However, whilst the hesitation in *Spirite* is resolved into the 'marvellous' at the close of the sixth chapter, this is not as a direct result of its narrative voice. Equally, Pushkin's story in no way 'distances itself' from the fantastic, as Todorov claims its heterodiegetic narrator should oblige it to do.

My intention here is to challenge the claim that heterodiegesis is not compatible with the fantastic. In so doing, I align myself with Theodore Ziolkowski's argument (1977, 251) that: 'it is an oversimplification to say the first-person is *per se* the mode of the fantastic'. This discussion will begin, however, with an illustration of how certain characteristics of heterodiegesis might explain realist fiction's propensity towards it. Its alleged unsuitability to the fantastic will, concomitantly, be revealed. Once this has been shown, it will be possible in Part 3 of this chapter to highlight how the particular heterodiegetic performance in the two works under discussion suggests ways in which this unsuitability might be bypassed.

When it comes to establishing the authority and reliability enjoyed by a given narrative voice, its access to knowledge is of paramount importance. The heterodiegetic voice obviously benefits from the convention which states that it has the authority to be omniscient (Lanser 1981, 161). Omniscience 'is the kind of privilege that one most wishes a narrator to have, since it affords the reader the comforting illusion of reliability, objectivity and absolute knowledge' (Fludernik 1996, 167). And so omniscience is a key guarantor of a narrator's authentication authority in the eyes of the reader. In the opening pages of *Spirite*, the narrative voice repeatedly displays its omniscient privilege when, for example, it observes of Guy de Malivert: 'il était heureux sans qu'il lui fût arrivé aucun bonheur' ['he was happy without having been visited by any particular good fortune'] and 'il jouissait délicieusement de ce temps d'arrêt de son cerveau' ['he savoured this period of rest for his mind'] (*S* 202–03). Consistent with the distinctions between the opening passages of the two works noted above, the heterodiegetic voice in *The Queen of Spades* initially displays fewer indications of omniscience. In part, this is explained by the early presence of dialogue during which the narrator is restricted to an external perspective. In the second chapter, however, as the voice of the narrator comes more consistently to the fore, its unlimited access to information is displayed. For instance, upon Tomskii's mention of the death of one of his grandmother's friends, the narrator notes that 'он вспомнил, что от старой графини таили смерть ее ровесниц' ['he remembered that they kept the deaths of her contemporaries from the old countess'] (*Q* 325). Revealing a more internal perspective, he also records the old woman's reaction to Tomskii's slip: 'но графиня услышала весть, для нее новую, с большим равнодушием' ['but the countess heard the information, which was new to her, with the utmost indifference'] (ibid.). The apparent obstacle to the provocation of hesitation in a text featuring an omniscient heterodiegetic narrative voice is the implication that this voice possesses 'absolute knowledge'. One obvious means of sowing doubt in the reader's mind about the interpretation of events is to supply her with incomplete information. However, in texts where the voice is heterodiegetic and omniscient, and where the ability to read characters' thoughts and emotions has been established at an early stage, providing insufficient information is problematic. Generating ambiguity has the potential, therefore, to become a more transgressive process precisely because it cannot be naturalized to the limited knowledge of the narrator.

Omniscient privilege is only one factor in establishing the reliability of the narrative voice. Expectations of 'absolute knowledge' are also conditioned by the temporal relationship between event and narration of event. In both *Spirite* and *The*

Queen of Spades, the heterodiegetic narrator adopts what Lanser (1981, 198) calls a 'posterior' temporal stance.[7] Such a temporal attitude is signalled, very simply, by the use of the past tense: 'Guy de Malivert [...] éprouvait cette sorte de béatitude physique, résultat de l'accord parfait de ses organes' ['Guy de Malivert [...] felt that sort of physical bliss which comes from the perfect harmony of one's organs'] (*S* 202); 'однажды играли в карты' ['one day they were playing cards'] (*Q* 319). Posteriority is the most common temporal attitude encountered in literature and implies that all the events which constitute the 'fabula' have been completed by the point in time at which the narrator begins to relate the 'siuzhet'.[8] Consequently, the reader expects the narrator to enjoy a relatively high degree of knowledge because, by the time he starts to recount his tale, nothing should remain (temporally) to be found out. This is quite different from the case pertaining in simultaneous or interspersed narratives where the narrator acquires information as the tale progresses. Any piecemeal supply of information in posterior narration can reasonably be considered to be the result only of retardatory devices employed by the narrator: he possesses all of the relevant knowledge but chooses to withhold some of it in the interests of suspense. Like omniscience, therefore, posterior temporality might theoretically appear to be ill-suited to the provocation of hesitation.

A narrator can convince the reader of the stability of the fictional world not simply by revealing his access to knowledge but also by persuading her of his competence and skill as a storyteller. Lanser (1981, 170–71) subdivides her discussion of such skill (or what she calls 'mimetic authority') into three sections: honesty, reliability, and competence. The narrator's honesty concerns, self-evidently, the degree to which he gives the impression of speaking the truth. A narrator is deemed reliable if he displays to the reader that he is 'intellectually and morally trustworthy'. And he is skilled if he possesses 'sufficient competence as a storyteller to present the story in a manner that is coherent, complete, and skilful enough for it to remain "tellable"' (Lanser 1981, 171). Crucially, it is the convention in the literary transaction for the reader to 'infer felicity' as regards the narrator's mimetic authority. That is, the reader assumes the narrator to be competent and skilful unless there are aspects of, or markings in, the narrative to persuade her otherwise.

On the whole, the voice of the narrator in *Spirite* displays a high degree of mimetic authority and the reader trusts this voice. The examples given above where the narrator describes Guy de Malivert's past, his habits, and his motivations are clear evidence of this. Indeed, the only notable exception occurs when the narrator gives the age of the protagonist as 'vingt-huit ou vingt-neuf ans' ['twenty-eight or twenty-nine'] (*S* 204). In view of his omniscient privilege and the confidence he has shown in providing a myriad of other details up to this point, such a straightforward question as Guy de Malivert's age ought to cause the narrator no problems whatsoever. The reader is therefore briefly perturbed by this momentary vagueness as it constitutes an unexpected crack in the narrator's image of competence. However, it does not persist. In the subsequent paragraph, the narrator recovers himself and is far more confident: 'arrivé à cet âge solonnel de vingt-neuf ans, où le jeune homme va devenir homme jeune, il ignorait l'amour' ['having reached the solemn age of twenty-nine, when the youth is to become a young man, he knew nothing of love'] (*S* 205). Peter

Whyte (1984, 13) considers this temporary breach in reliability to be an example of the 'selective omniscience' occasionally employed by Gautier's narrators. He insists that it would be a mistake to consider it an unintentional oversight on the part of the narrator; he does not accidentally forget his omniscience and with it his access to this information. It is, on the contrary, a deliberate move whose purpose is to prepare the reader for the situation that will arise when supernatural events are subsequently introduced. And it plants a seed of doubt in the mind of the reader, which constitutes a weak point in the barrier omniscience constructs against uncertainty.

In the first two chapters of *The Queen of Spades*, Pushkin's narrator displays far less skill and competence than his counterpart in Gautier. Exaggerating the type of momentary weakness found in *Spirite*, the narrator raises doubts about his reliability by being inconsistent in his attitude towards omniscient privilege. For example, having established his omniscience by means of Tomskii's recollection about shielding his grandmother from unpleasant news, the narrator undermines it only a few lines later. During the conversation between Lizaveta and Tomskii, the reader is intrigued by the ward's persistent enquiries as to the identity of his friend: 'кого это вы хотите представить? [...] Он военный или статский? [...] Инженер?' ['Who do you want to introduce? [...] Is he in the military or civil service? [...] Is he an Engineer?'] (Q 325). The reader fully expects the narrator to reveal why Lizaveta is so interested in these details; his privilege says he possesses the information. However, on this occasion the narrator does not do so, simply reporting: 'барышня засмеялась и не отвечала ни слова' ['the young girl laughed and did not reply'] (ibid.). The decision not to supply this information might be considered, as in *Spirite*, a moment of selective omniscience intended to pique the reader's interest. However, when taken alongside other examples of apparently limited reliability, this seems less likely. For instance, in the opening pages of the story, the narrator fails to provide sufficient orienting information regarding the location of the action and, as we have seen, the identity of those speaking during the first dialogue. Indeed, this failure to provide full information extends to the names of one of the principal characters in the story: Tomskii's grandmother is simply referred to as 'графиня ★★★' ['countess ★★★'] for the duration of the story. Admittedly here a tension arises between realist fiction's impulse towards full information and the game it plays with the propriety of not naming characters who might actually exist. Nevertheless, more conventional confusion over identity exists temporarily at the opening of the second chapter when it is not immediately revealed that the characters Paul and countess ★★★ are, in fact, Tomskii and his grandmother from the previous chapter.

One of Pushkin's most subtle methods of casting doubt upon the competence of the narrator in the first chapter is to compare his skills as a storyteller unfavourably with those of Tomskii. For the time that he relates his anecdote of the gambling formula, Tomskii is an example of what Lanser calls a 'private narrator'. This type of narrator is 'usually a character in the text, bound to the fictional world, and dependent upon the existence of that world for his or her authorisation to speak' (Lanser 1981, 138). They are frequently delineated by the public narrator or by other characters and the purposes of their narration are subordinate to the design of the story as a whole. Because a private narrator occupies a narrative level immediately inferior to that of the public narrator, it is considered by the reader to enjoy a lesser degree of authority. Convention would therefore lead us to expect that Tomskii would display less skill in the telling of his tale than the heterodiegetic narrator. In fact, the opposite proves to be the case. Unlike the narrator, Tomskii clearly identifies the geographical location of his story (Paris), its temporal location (sixty years ago), and he names the participants in the action. He appears to provide his audience with all the information he possesses. Such a competent performance undermines, by implication, the heterodiegetic narrator's claims to possess skill and reliability.

In spite of these examples, and precisely because of the convention of inferring felicity, however, the heterodiegetic narrator in *The Queen of Spades* is not ultimately considered to be unreliable or incompetent. This is also explained by the fact that the majority of these oversights exist either only temporarily or concern details of more peripheral importance. For instance, the mystery surrounding Lizaveta's interest in Tomskii's friend is resolved as the narrator describes the repeated appearance of Germann outside her window. The confusion regarding the temporal link between the first and second chapters is cleared up in the middle of the second when the narrator explains that Germann's first appearance under Lizaveta's window occurs 'два дня после вечера, описанного в начале этой повести, и за неделю перед той сценой, на которой мы остановились' ['two days after the evening described at the opening of this story and a week before the scene on which we have stopped'] (Q 329). In fact, by overtly indicating his awareness of the storytelling act in this manner, the narrator goes a long way to reassuring the reader of his reliability. Overall, therefore, the performance of the heterodiegetic narrative voices in both *Spirite* and *The Queen of Spades* lends a stability to the fictional world which complements the sense of reality created by the appropriation of realist procedures. These same factors, however, also make the provocation of hesitation upon which the fantastic relies seem a less acceptable and less likely possibility.

Part 3: Hesitation and the Heterodiegetic Voice

Spirite and *The Queen of Spades* get around such apparent difficulties by exploiting two particular methods. These are switches in the point of view of the narrative (particularly spatial and psychological) and the use of elements of syntax which introduce ambiguity. Whilst the first technique is more conventionally associated with heterodiegetic narrative situations, the latter enjoys a more universal potential, as will be discussed in Chapters 2 and 3 below. In heterodiegetic texts, it is very often the case that the two techniques operate in tandem. Switches away from the heterodiegetic perspective are employed to bypass the obligations imposed by the access to information and reliability associated with this voice. A consideration of three pivotal incidents from each work will provide a clear illustration of this.

The scene in *The Queen of Spades* which describes Germann's attendance at the countess's funeral offers a fruitful starting point. The opening lines of the fifth chapter reveal a trio of techniques intended to reinforce both the 'vraisemblance' of the fictional world and the reliability of the narrative voice. The reader is told: 'три дня после роковой ночи, в девять часов утра, Германн отправился в ★★★ монастырь' ['three days after the fateful night, at nine o'clock in the morning, Germann set off to the ★★★ monastery'] (Q 347). Not only does the narrator provide a specific time reference, he also locates the action clearly in the time-line of the fabula. In the next lines, he reminds the reader of his omniscience by reporting Germann's feelings as he approaches his destination: 'не чувствуя раскаяния, он не мог однако совершенно заглушить голос совести, твердившей ему: ты убийца старухи!' ['whilst not experiencing any remorse, he could not quite silence his conscience which kept telling him: you are the old woman's killer!'] (ibid.). This is all quite straightforward, unambiguous, and revelatory of realist techniques.

The first, very brief description of the church is given from a detached, bird's eye perspective: 'церковь была полна' ['the church was full'] (ibid.). However, the focalizing perspective then immediately shifts to a position alongside the protagonist:

> Германн насилу мог пробраться сквозь толпу народа. Гроб стоял на богатом катафалке под бархатным балдахином. Усопшая лежала в нем с руками, сложенными на груди, в кружевном чепце и в белом атласном платье. (ibid.)

> [Germann had difficulty pushing through the crowd. The coffin was standing on a rich catafalque under a velvet canopy. The dead woman lay in it with her arms crossed on her breast, wearing a lace cap and a white satin dress.]

This switch in perspective is indicated by the fact that a description of the countess in her coffin is only given once Germann has forced his way through the crowd. Its effect is to produce a greater sense of mimesis in the scene. The reader is encouraged to believe that she experiences events alongside the protagonist: she only sees the countess when Germann does. Such reader–protagonist sympathy is a crucial preparatory step on the path towards hesitation. It is when Germann approaches the coffin to pay his respects that the apparently supernatural event takes place:

> Он поклонился в землю и несколько минут лежал на холодном полу, усыпанном ельником. Наконец приподнялся, бледен как сама покойница, взошел на ступени катафалка и наклонился... В эту минуту показалось ему, что мертвая насмешливо взглянула на него, прищуривая одним глазом. (Q 348)

> [He bent down to the ground and, for several minutes, lay on the cold floor, which was strewn with pine branches. He eventually got up, looking as pale as the dead woman, walked up the steps of the catafalque, and bent over... At that moment it seemed to him that the dead woman looked at him mockingly and winked.]

The impact of this first direct appearance of the irrational in *The Queen of Spades* is heightened precisely because of the brevity of its description. The report that the countess winks at Germann provokes hesitation because it contradicts the rules operating in the rational world. Dead women do not wink. The reader now has two interpretative avenues open to her. Either she can decide that the wink did occur, in which case, despite previous indications to the contrary, the rules pertaining in the fictional world are not the same as in the real world. Or she can decide that the dead woman did not actually wink (it was an illusion or a figment of Germann's imagination) and so the rational rules of the fictional world remain intact.

Key to the ambiguity provoked by this event is the syntax used in its description. The reader is not told that the countess winked at Germann; she is told that 'показалось ему' ['it seemed to him'] that she did. Todorov recognizes that such modal verbal phrases make a significant contribution to the experience of hesitation in the fantastic. Taking Gérard de Nerval's story *Aurélia ou le rêve et la vie* (1855) as his example, he notes the impact of certain introductory locutions which, without changing the meaning of the phrase as such, modify the relationship between the speaker and the speech act. De Nerval, he says, uses such 'modalization' phrases throughout his story, his favoured examples being: 'il me semblait que', 'je crus', and 'j'eus le sentiment' (*F* 43). The key point of modalization for the fantastic is that it 'indique [...] l'incertitude où se trouve le sujet qui parle, quant à la vérité de la phrase qu'il énonce' ['indicates [...] the uncertainty of the speaker with regards to the phrase he utters'] (ibid.). The Russian 'показалось ему' is just such a modalization phrase and it achieves the same effect.[9] Clearly, modalization is commonly found in all literary genres because uncertainty is endemic. But, as Todorov explains, its impact upon interpretation is fundamental to the fantastic:

> Si ces locutions étaient absentes, nous serions plongés dans le monde du merveilleux, sans aucune référence à la réalité quotidienne, habituelle; par elles, nous sommes maintenus dans les deux mondes à la fois. (*F* 43)

> [If these phrases were absent, we would be plunged into the world of the marvellous with no reference whatsoever to everyday reality; but thanks to them we are held in both worlds at the same time.]

And so it is clear that, during this passage from *The Queen of Spades*, the reader does not hesitate simply because of the nature of the event. The uncertainty is the consequence of the ambiguity contained in the description of this event.

Bearing in mind the proven omniscience of the heterodiegetic narrator in this story, if the uncertainty were to stem from this voice, a significant threat to the decorum of the text would be encountered. Textual decorum simply expects a narrative voice to observe, more or less, the rules of status and performance which it has created for itself. In *The Queen of Spades*, this decorum dictates that, thanks to its absolute knowledge, events should not have to 'seem' to the heterodiegetic narrator. However, no breach of decorum occurs here because of a second switch in point of view. During the description of Germann lying on the floor and then approaching the coffin, the point of focalization is alongside the hero but, importantly, still external to him. Crucially, however, the points of ellipsis which separate the second and third sentences in the extract quoted above signal a further shift in focalization. The experiencing perspective now moves from an external position alongside the protagonist to an internal point. Therefore, for the limited duration of the single line which describes the countess's apparent wink, the reader is being presented with Germann's perception of events. By implication, this coincides with the temporary removal of the privileged perspective of the narrator. Omniscience is now replaced by the limited human knowledge appropriate for a character anchored in the story world. The modalizing 'показалось ему' ['it seemed to him'] then becomes a justified result of this shift to lesser authority. Hesitation is, thus, the quite acceptable consequence of the suppression of the more reliable and knowledgeable voice and not a more transgressive breach of decorum.

In the fantastic, though, it is not simply a question of hesitation being provoked. It needs also to be sustained. Following the description of the countess's wink from Germann's perspective, the external 'bird's-eye' focalization of the heterodiegetic narrator is reinstated as two events occurring in different places are observed almost simultaneously:

> Германн, поспешно подавшись назад, оступился и навзничь грянулся об земь. Его подняли. В то же самое время Лизавету Ивановну вынесли в обмороке на паперть. Этот эпизод возмутил на несколько минут торжественность мрачного обряда. (Q 348)

> [Drawing back hurriedly, Germann stumbled and fell sharply backwards to the floor. He was picked up. At the same time, Lizaveta Ivanovna was carried out to the porch in a faint. This episode disturbed the solemnity of the sombre ceremony for several minutes.]

The return of this omniscient voice could theoretically permit the resolution of reader hesitation. The narrator could now provide information to confirm or deny the intervention of the supernatural. However, as the lines above show, what this voice actually does is ignore the event entirely. It contents itself with a simple description of physical events rather than offering any interpretation. This shortcoming is compounded a few lines later when the narrator reports the absurdly irrelevant conversation between two guests about whether or not Germann is the countess's illegitimate son. Although this may be linked to the network of erotic motifs operating in the story, for the reader desiring information about the status of the wink, it is frustratingly inappropriate.

This passage from *The Queen of Spades* highlights the role played in the creation of hesitation in the fantastic by three specific techniques. Firstly, the use of modalizing syntax which indicates the speaker's lack of conviction in his utterance. Secondly, the switch in narrative point of view which accounts for the presence of such indefinite description. And finally, the failure of the heterodiegetic voice, subsequent to the apparently supernatural event, to provide any additional, interpretative commentary. An examination of the passage in *Spirite* which describes the second incursion of the supernatural will reveal the exploitation of the same combination of three techniques. This permits their identification as central structural tenets of the genre of the fantastic. Following his first apparent encounter with the supernatural, which will be discussed below, Guy de Malivert decides to visit his sometime companion, Mme d'Ymbercourt:

> Il s'habilla rageusement, et, comme il allait sortir de sa chambre, il crut entendre un soupir, mais si faible, si léger, si aérien, qu'il fallait le profond silence de la nuit pour que l'oreille pût le saisir.
>
> Ce soupir arrêta Malivert sur le seuil de son cabinet, et lui causa cette impression que le surnaturel fait éprouver aux plus braves. Il n'y avait rien de bien effrayant dans cette note vague, inarticulée et plaintive, et cependant Guy en fut plus troublé qu'il n'osait se l'avouer à lui-même. (S 209)

> [He got dressed in a rage and, as he was about to leave his room, he thought he heard a sigh, but one so weak, so faint, so ethereal, that it required the profound silence of the night to be heard.

This sigh stopped Malivert in the doorway of his study and caused the same impression in him as the supernatural provokes in the bravest of men. There was nothing particularly frightening in this vague, inarticulated, plaintive note; nevertheless, Guy was more troubled by it than he even dared to admit to himself.]

With its betrayal of omniscient privilege, the adverb 'rageusement' suggests that the first clause of the opening sentence is given from the narrator's point of view. Earlier information has told the reader that Malivert is alone in his room apart from his dog. This absence of human company should rule out the possibility of hearing such a sigh. In fact, just as in *The Queen of Spades*, the use of the modalizing 'il crut entendre' ['he thought he heard'] means that the reader cannot even be sure that Malivert does hear a sigh. And as with Pushkin's 'показалось ему', this modalization phrase can be attributed to a shift in the point of narrative focalization. The all-knowing perspective of the heterodiegetic narrator is temporarily withdrawn and it is replaced by the point of view of the protagonist. Hesitation is introduced in the heterodiegetic situation when the rules regarding the knowledge possessed by this voice are suspended.

In a manner which extends the understanding of how the fantastic operates, the uncertainty provoked in this passage can also be traced to the syntax employed in the description of the sigh. On two occasions here a sense of uncertain perception is created by the use of multiple adjectives to qualify a single noun. The sigh is 'si faible, si léger, si aérien' and '[une] note vague, inarticulée et plaintive'. This multiplicity of adjectives suggests that the perceiver struggles to arrive at a single, definitive description of what might have been heard. And so reader uncertainty at this point is double-edged: did Malivert actually hear a sigh and, if he did, what was it like? The third technique identified from *The Queen of Spades* (the lack of corroborative interpretation from the narrator) is encountered in a slightly different form at this stage in *Spirite*. In the Pushkin passage, the voice of the narrator seemingly refuses to co-operate and provides trivial information instead. In Gautier, reaction is supplied by Guy de Malivert himself rather than by the heterodiegetic narrator. His response indicates his essentially rational character at this stage, as he says: 'Bah! c'est mon angora qui aura poussé une plainte en dormant' ['Ah, my angora must have let out a moan as he slept'] (*S* 209). This attempt to explain away the sigh is unsatisfactory, however, on two counts. Firstly, by implying its hypothetical status, the future perfect tense 'aura poussé' ['must have let out'] undermines the validity of the claim from within. Unlike the use of the simple perfect tense, 'a poussé', the future perfect indicates that the protagonist himself is not convinced by his own explanation.[10] The second weakness in this explanation concerns its provider. As a character bound to the fictional world, the protagonist exists at an inferior narrative level to the heterodiegetic narrator. Consequently, in an extension of the conventions regarding omniscience, his voice is granted lesser authority. The explanation for the sigh proposed by Malivert is therefore less convincing than if it had come from the narrator. The end result in the case of both *The Queen of Spades* and *Spirite* is that the reader's hesitation is sustained because of a lack of definitive interpretation from the narrator.

These first two passages have involved only short-lived switches in the narrative point of view. A consideration of two further passages where this shift is maintained for longer will reveal the use of a wider variety of techniques to provoke uncertainty.

The first is a description taken from the fifth chapter of *Spirite* in which Guy de Malivert apparently begins to see a female figure taking shape in a mirror. The voice of the heterodiegetic narrator is very much to the fore at the beginning of this chapter, describing the protagonist's thoughts and surroundings. In the last four lines of the third paragraph, however, a clear switch in focalization to the perspective of the protagonist is signalled: 'insensiblement les yeux de Malivert, comme sollicités par un avertissement intérieur, se dirigèrent vers un miroir de Venise' ['imperceptibly Malivert's eyes, as if attracted by an internal warning, moved towards a Venetian mirror'] (*S* 234). This shift in point of view is then sustained over the course of the next three pages of the novella.

The mirror is initially described as being nothing out of the ordinary; it is a mirror 'comme on en voit souvent' ['the like of which is often seen'] (ibid.). However, its apparently extraordinary nature soon begins to become apparent:

> Au milieu de ce scintillement, la glace, de petite dimension comme tous les miroirs de Venise, paraissait d'un noir bleuâtre, indéfiniment profond, et ressemblait à une ouverture pratiquée sur un vide rempli d'idéales ténèbres.
>
> Chose bizarre, aucun des objets opposés ne s'y réfléchissait: on eût dit une de ces glaces de théâtre que le décorateur couvre de teintes vagues et neutres pour empêcher la salle de s'y refléter. (ibid.)
>
> [In the middle of this shimmering, the mirror, small like all Venetian mirrors, appeared to be blueish black in colour, indefinitely deep, and it resembled an opening out towards a void filled with ideal darkness.
>
> A strange thing, none of the objects in front of it were reflected in it: one would have said it was one of those prop mirrors which stage-dressers cover in vague and neutral colours to prevent the auditorium being reflected.]

Rosemary Jackson argues that the fantastic is preoccupied with problems of vision and visibility and that this explains why one frequently encounters mirrors, eyes, reflections, and portraits in such narratives. She believes (Jackson 1981, 43) this preoccupation is due to the fact that this spectral imagery 'affect[s] a transformation of the familiar world into the unfamiliar'. Gautier's Venetian mirror is therefore generically conventional in its resemblance to a portal opening onto another world. At least in part as a consequence of this, the narrative voice struggles to provide a confident and definitive description of the mirror as betrayed by the approximative adjective 'bleuâtre' and the uncategorical 'indéfiniment profond'. Because of their ability to inject ambiguity into descriptions, approximative adjectives constitute an important syntactic device in the fantastic. They are employed repeatedly by Gautier in *Spirite*, particularly in reference to Malivert's initiator into the ideal realm, the baron de Féroë. He is described as having eyes 'd'un gris bleuâtre' ['of a blueish grey'] with 'une expression indéfinissable' ['an indefinable expression'] and which are veiled by 'de longs cils blanchâtres' ['long whitish eyelashes'] (*S* 214). Such indefinite terminology appears to imply the baron's existence on the threshold between two worlds. His appearance somehow defies, or goes beyond, the standard descriptive terms that are employed in relation to the rational world.[11] The effect of the future perfect tense in the earlier account of the sigh is reproduced in the description of the mirror by the pluperfect subjunctive, 'on eût dit' ['one would have said']. This is just one of a number of expressions Todorov identifies as preparing the ground for the incursion of the supernatural by introducing a figurative comparison (*F* 85). The use of figurative language, it will be recalled, is Todorov's first property of the fantastic and expressions such as 'on dirait' ['one might say'], 'ils m'appelleraient' ['they would call me'], and 'comme si' ['as if'] are just some examples. Discussing the use of the specific phrase 'on eût dit' in Gautier's work, Lowrie (1979–80, 16) indicates why it proves to be such an effective technique for the fantastic. It establishes, she argues, 'a condition that is contrary to fact. [...]. The simile maintains the duality even while assimilating the units, verbally, into one'. Therefore, in the example quoted above, the mirror's lack of reflective capacity is compared to the effect achieved in a theatrical prop, and yet in the very same phrase this rational explanation is implicitly dismissed.

This combination of linguistic devices announces the potential involvement of the supernatural by introducing a significant degree of ambiguity into the description of the mirror. This potential is then realized as the reader is told how Malivert senses apparent movement in it:

> Enfin il crut démêler dans cette ombre comme une vague blancheur laiteuse, comme une sorte de lueur lointaine et tremblotante qui semblait se rapprocher. Il se retourna pour voir quel objet dans la chambre pouvait projeter ce reflet; il ne vit rien. [...] La tache lumineuse du miroir commençait à se dessiner d'une façon plus distincte et à se teindre de couleurs légères, immatérielles pour ainsi dire, et qui auraient fait paraître terreux les tons de la plus fraîche palette. C'était plutôt l'idée d'une couleur que la couleur elle-même, une vapeur traversée de lumière que tous les mots humains ne sauraient la rendre. (*S* 234–35)

> [Finally he thought he could make out in this shadow something like a vague milky whiteness, like a sort of distant, trembling light which seemed to be getting nearer. He turned around to see which object in the room could be the source of this reflection; he saw nothing. [...] The luminous patch in the mirror began to sketch itself more distinctly and to take on light, one might almost say immaterial, colours, and colours which would have made the tones on the freshest palette seem earthly. It was more the impression of a colour than a colour itself, a vapour shot through with light which no human words would be capable of expressing.]

This description reveals the use of a modal lexical verb, 'il crut démêler' ['he thought he could make out'], and a modal verb of perception, 'semblait se rapprocher' ['seemed to be getting nearer'] which both indicate the difficulty in arriving at a single, definitive description. This difficulty, betrayed earlier by the use of multiple adjectives, is also shown here in the repeated attempts to approximate this image to another phenomenon through the use of the comparator 'comme une'. And modalization through tense is employed to good effect once again. As above, the conditional perfect ensures that the reality of the colours of the image is undermined by the internal syntax of the sentence. The colours 'auraient fait paraître' ['would have made'] other tones seem dull if they had existed; but the question as to whether they really did exist or not is left open-ended.

The continuation of this description is worthy of brief discussion for its revelation of two further techniques which render interpretation ambiguous:

> ce qu'il voyait, quoique *semblable*, ne *ressemblait* en rien à ce qui passe, en cette vie, pour une tête de belle femme. C'était bien les mêmes traits, mais épurés,

transfigurés, idéalisés et rendus perceptibles par une substance en quelque sorte immatérielle [...]. Il se rapprocha de la glace, croyant saisir plus distinctement encore les traits de l'image: elle resta comme elle lui était apparue d'abord, très près, et cependant très loin [...]. La réalité de ce qu'il voyait si l'on peut se server d'un tel mot en pareille circonstance, était évidemment ailleurs, dans des régions profondes, lointaines, énigmatiques [...] Guy essaya vainement de rattacher cette figure à quelque souvenir terrestre; elle était pour lui entièrement nouvelle, et cependant il lui semblait la reconnaître [...]. (*S* 236; original italics)

[what he saw, whilst *similar*, did not *resemble* in any way that which passes, in this life, for the head of a beautiful woman. It had, granted, the same traits, but purified, transfigured, idealized, and made perceptible by a substance which was somehow immaterial [...]. He approached the mirror, thinking that he would be able to perceive the traits of the image even more distinctly: it remained as it had seemed to him initially: very near and, nevertheless, very distant [...]. The reality of what he saw, if one can use such a word in similar circumstances, was clearly somewhere else, in deep, distant, enigmatic regions [...]. Guy tried in vain to link this face to some earthly memory: it was entirely new to him and, nevertheless, it seemed to him that he recognized it [...].]

Firstly, as in the description of the sigh, multiple adjectives qualifying a single noun are repeatedly employed to suggest the difficulty of likening this image to anything in the natural world. The first instance of this device incarnates on a verbal level the initial claim that the woman's head is unlike any known 'in this life'. The second use, qualifying the noun 'régions', expresses the impossibility of finding a conformity between the reality of the actual world and the 'reality' of what Malivert witnesses in the mirror. The difference in the nature of these two realities is further illustrated by the second device of epistemological paradox. The reality governing appearances in the mirror distinguishes itself from that operating in the 'familiar' world because the image of the woman can appear, at one and the same time, to be 'very near and, nevertheless, very distant'. Such seeming contradiction in linguistic terms, which is used to represent the conceptual problems thrown up by the vision in the mirror, is echoed in the report that the female image is entirely new to Guy de Malivert, and yet he somehow still recognizes it. By maintaining a balance between adjectives which conventionally are mutually exclusive, epistemological paradox is perfectly suited to the genre of the fantastic.

I would like to turn my attention now to an example of an extended shift in narrative perspective from *The Queen of Spades*. The description of the nocturnal visit of the dead countess reveals the exploitation of a number of different devices dependent upon this shift. As noted above, at the close of the description of the funeral, the voice of the narrator returns to the forefront of the discourse. It remains there as the reader is told how Germann embarks upon a bout of heavy drinking, returns home, and finally falls asleep. Of fundamental importance to the interpretation of subsequent events is the narrator's description of how the hero wakes up:

Он проснулся уже ночью: луна озаряла его комнату. Он взглянул на часы: было без четверти три. Сон у него прошел; он сел на кровать и думал о похоронах старой графини. (*Q* 349)

[It was already night when he woke up: the moon illuminated his room. He looked at the clock: it was a quarter to three. Sleep had left him; he sat on the bed and thought about the old countess's funeral.]

The reader should not doubt that what happens next is experienced by a protagonist who is awake; the events are not part of a dream. The waking state of Germann is reinforced by the reference to concrete time; indeed, the fantastic favours the use of such references immediately prior to the incursion of the supernatural.[12] The measured construction of the lines in the quoted passage also reflects the rational atmosphere which pervades. This short paragraph contains three sentences, two of which are divided in half by a colon. This choice of punctuation creates a very particular impact. As Heidi Faletti remarks (1977, 115) during a discussion of parataxis: 'the use of a colon is especially forceful and points to the immediate consequence of an incident or the effect of an event or perception on a character'. The causal link between the two halves of the sentences is invoked by means of this strong punctuation in order to insist upon the predominance of rational logicality at this point in the scene. The second half of each sentence describes the natural consequence of what is stated in the first half: the moon shines into Germann's room because he awakes in the middle of the night, for instance. It is precisely the lack of causal links between events that characterizes the world of the irrational. Despite the hesitation provoked by the description of events at the funeral, therefore, the narrator is now acting to persuade the reader to believe in the reality of this nocturnal scene.

N. K. Gei (1983, 189) contends that, in the paragraph following the description of Germann waking up, there occurs a twofold shift in focalization. The first shift is in visual perspective and is effected in the sentence: 'в это время кто-то с улицы взглянул к нему в окошко — и тотчас отошел' ['at that moment someone in the street looked in at him through the window and immediately walked off'] (Q 349). The markers of spatial deixis employed here clearly locate the focalizing perspective inside the room and alongside Germann. This shift in visual perspective is reinforced by a change in the audible perspective: 'чрез минуту услышал он, что отпирали дверь в передней комнате' ['a minute later he heard the door in the hall unlock'] (ibid.). The reader is now in the position of experiencing events at the same time and from a similar location as the protagonist. These shifts in perspective are maintained throughout the account of the apparently supernatural nocturnal visit. Perspective is shifted back to the narrator in the description of the same events as have signalled the initial shift, but in reverse: 'Германн слышал, как хлопнула дверь в сенях, и увидел, что кто-то опять поглядел к нему в окошко' ['Germann heard the door in the passage slam shut and saw someone again look in at him through the window'] (Q 350). Although the visual and audible perspectives move towards the protagonist in the passage between these two lines, the voice in the discourse still belongs to the narrator. Consequently, as in the description of the countess's wink, the reader confronts a narrative in which both narrator and protagonist are present as informing personae. Gei (1983, 189) comments:

Смешение авторского и персонажного планов повествования, способствуя амбивалентности очевидного и невероятного, порождает из себя глубинные изобразительно-выразительные повествовательные пласты.

[The interference of the perspectives of narrator and protagonist, which creates the ambivalence of the obvious and the improbable, gives rise to deepened and graphically expressive narrative levels.]

The crucial point here is that this perspectival interference is constructed during the highly important description of how the dead countess apparently visits Germann to reveal the gambling formula. The event alone is not sufficient to account for the reader's interpretative difficulties. What also needs to be taken into account is the effect of the quality of information provided as a consequence of the shift in narrative perspective.

One of the most obvious contributors to ambiguity in this passage is the indefinite personal pronoun. In the course of the final four paragraphs of the fifth chapter, 'кто-то' ['someone'] is used on three occasions. Two of these appear in the lines quoted above. The third example occurs in the description of the footsteps Germann hears: 'но он услышал незнакомую походку: кто-то ходил, тихо шаркая туфлями' ['but he heard unfamiliar footsteps: someone was coming, quietly shuffling in slippers'] (Q 349). These indefinite pronouns stand in marked contrast to the more informative time references and controlled punctuation employed earlier. They are accounted for, however, by the shift towards Germann's perspective. Sitting in his room, with his human perspective dictating that his view is limited to this room, he cannot be aware of who is performing these actions. This cognitive gap would not need to exist if the perspective still belonged to the narrator; he has previously shown himself able to report actions occurring in two places simultaneously. But it is entirely appropriate for Germann. This omission of identity is reinforced by the use of two verbs with passive force. The first occurs in the sentence which shifts the audible perspective: 'услышал он, что отпирали дверь' ['he heard the door [...] unlock'] (Q 349). The second comes four lines later as the unidentified figure enters Germann's bedroom: 'дверь отворилась, вошла женщина в белом платье' ['the door opened and a woman in a white dress came in'] (ibid.).

Verbs in their passive form, particularly in Russian, represent a significant syntactic construct in the provocation of hesitation. This is because they describe actions without revealing the identity of the performer; as such, they complement the use of indefinite pronouns. And the reflexive form in the second example is particularly suggestive. 'Дверь отворилась' gives the impression that the door opens of its own accord, that the action is somehow performed by the object itself. This form represents what Paul Simpson (1993, 88) calls a 'material process of supervention', where the event just happens and where human agency is supervented.[13] Such supervention processes will be seen to figure repeatedly in fantastic narratives. The combined effect of indefinite pronouns and passive or reflexive verbs is to provide the reader with no more than an uncertain and imprecise description of events. This is in contrast to the assured information supplied immediately prior to this scene and, therefore, emphasizes the different capabilities of protagonist and narrator. The shift in narrative perspective which engenders these two syntactic devices leads to a gap in cognition which generates ambiguity. The reader is prevented from being able to make a definitive assessment: is Germann actually visited during the night? And if so, is his visitor really the dead countess? The fifth chapter, and indeed the entire story as Dostoevskii noted, close without the reader being able to answer these questions.

In none of the four passages from *Spirite* and *The Queen of Spades* discussed thus far has the presence of ambiguous syntax transgressed the authority of the omniscient narrator. In each, the various devices which prompt uncertainty have been perfectly acceptable in terms of the text's decorum because they result from the presence of the protagonist's point of view and not the narrator's. However, at certain points in both works, interference between these two perspectives makes attributing ambiguous descriptions to either protagonist or narrator with any confidence more problematic. It is in such cases where textual decorum comes under threat and where hesitation becomes more profound. I would like to discuss two such episodes briefly in order to show how skilfully each work undermines the storytelling norms it has constructed for itself.

In the closing pages of the first chapter of *Spirite*, Guy de Malivert sits down to write a note to his companion, Mme d'Ymbercourt, giving his apologies for not attending her soirée. It is here that the supernatural makes its first appearance in the novella as he manages to write the word 'Madame', but:

> Là, il fit une pause et appuya sa joue sur la paume de sa main, sa faconde ne lui fournissant rien de plus. Pendant quelques minutes il resta ainsi le poignet en position, les doigts allongés sur la plume et la cervelle involontairement occupée d'idées contraires au sujet de sa lettre. Comme si, en attendant la phrase qui ne venait pas, le corps de Malivert se fût ennuyé, sa main, prise de fourmillements et d'impatiences, semblait vouloir se passer d'ordre pour accomplir sa tâche. Les phalanges se détendaient et se repliaient comme pour tracer des caractères, et enfin Guy fut très étonné d'avoir écrit absolument sans conscience neuf ou dix lignes qu'il lut et dont le sens était à peu près de celui-ci:
> 'Vous êtes assez belle et entourée d'assez d'adorateurs pour qu'on puisse vous dire sans vous offenser qu'on ne vous aime pas.' (*S* 208)

> [There, he paused and rested his cheek in the palm of his hand, his loquacity offering him nothing more. For several minutes he remained in the same position, his hand poised, his fingers stretched along the quill and his mind involuntarily taken up with ideas unrelated to the subject of the letter. As if waiting for the words that would not come, Malivert's body was agitated, his hand, seized by pins and needles and fidgeting, seemed to want to act unbidden in order to accomplish its task. His fingers relaxed and contracted as if to trace letters, and finally, Guy was quite astonished to have written, entirely unconsciously, nine or ten lines which he read and the sense of which was roughly the following:
> 'You are beautiful enough and surrounded by sufficient admirers for one to be able to say without causing offence that one does not love you.']

In light of the extracts discussed previously, it might be tempting to consider this passage as an account of the protagonist's perceptions of what occurs. As such, the uncertainty conveyed in 'semblait' and 'comme si' would then be accepted as non-transgressive evidence of Malivert's limited privilege. He is not sure what really happens and tries to approximate the movement of his hand to a more familiar state of affairs. However, the presence of Malivert's perspective is dismissed outright by the definitive assertion that he writes the note 'absolument sans conscience'. This assertion must logically be provided by the narrator; because he is unconscious, the protagonist could not provide it. So, the modalization of 'semblait' and 'comme si' must be attributed to the heterodiegetic narrator and it is this which poses a problem for the reader.

The actual state of affairs in this passage is that Guy de Malivert did write a letter of nine or ten lines; it exists as proof of his actions. However, his unconsciousness makes this fact inexplicable according to the rational rules which have been shown to pertain in the fictional world. A different order of the real or the rational is therefore introduced to explain this fact. This order is signified by a shift in the transitivity pattern of the verbs contained in these lines. In the nocturnal visit extract from *The Queen of Spades*, passive and reflexive verbal forms are accounted for by the restricted point of view of the protagonist. Here, the passive and intransitive verbs function differently: they signal that a different nature of reality is now governing events. The protagonist's body 'se fût ennuyé' ['was agitated'] by an unidentified agent and his fingers 'se détendaient et se repliaient' ['relaxed and contracted]'. The intransitive form suggests that the objects are themselves also the instigators of this movement. The rules of the rational world tell us that this cannot be the case because movement must generally be consciously controlled. Hesitation is provoked here because it is suggested that this is no longer the case. They are now able to move of their own accord. What is more, far from being resolved, this hesitation is compounded if it is now accepted that the modalization stems from the narrator's perspective. This situation represents a fundamental shift from numerous passages elsewhere in the novella where the narrator provides no commentary whatsoever upon the apparently supernatural. This modalizing syntax is employed by the narrator in an effort to explain this 'other', irrational order. The protagonist's hand moves of its own accord because it 'seems' to be trying to function without having been told to do so. The protagonist's body is moved by some unidentified force 'as if' it is waiting for the next words to come. Therefore, these elements show the narrator's uncertainty when trying to explain actions which have already made the reader hesitate because of their 'otherness'. By including the definitive 'entirely unconsciously' indicating the absence of Malivert's perspective, the narrator denies himself the possibility of justifying the modalization. The presence of modalizers in the narrator's perspective calls his previously established authority and competence into question in a manner which transgresses textual decorum. Gautier ensures that the interpretation of a key event is ambiguous by unexpectedly manipulating the authority possessed by the narrator. Where he has previously been shown to be all-knowing, he now appears to be susceptible to human frailties and as incapable as the protagonist of accounting for the seemingly supernatural. The reader is bewildered by this shift which leaves her unable to attribute a stable degree of authority to this figure; this inability ensures the presence of hesitation.

A very similar combination of techniques harnessed to similar effect can be found in a passage from the second chapter of *The Queen of Spades*. Here, the reader is told that Tomskii's anecdote about the gambling formula has produced a profound effect upon Germann's imagination. He spends the entire day after the card party wondering how he might convince the countess to reveal the winning formula to him. The reader is then informed how: 'рассуждая таким образом, очутился он в одной из главных улиц Петербурга, перед домом старинной архитектуры' ['reasoning thus, he suddenly found himself in one of the main streets of Petersburg, in front of a house of old-fashioned architecture'] (Q 331). Germann is shocked to discover that the house belongs to the countess ★★★. In bed that night, he dreams of playing cards, winning repeatedly and pocketing the gold, but then: 'проснувшись уже поздно, он вздохнул о потере своего фантастического богатства, пошел опять бродить по городу и опять очутился перед домом графини ★★★' ['waking when it was already late, he sighed over the loss of his fantastic wealth, and then, setting out again to wander around the city, he once more suddenly found himself in front of countess ★★★'s house'] (Q 332). The key point of interest here is the repetition of the verb 'очутиться' ['suddenly to find oneself'], used in its standard reflexive form. Just as with Malivert writing his letter, this intransitive form suggests that Germann is not actively or consciously walking to the countess's house. He is not, as reason ought to dictate, the active subject executing this movement. A potential, though irrational, explanation is provided for the second of these seemingly agentless actions when it is revealed that: 'неведомая сила, казалось, привлекала его к нему' ['an unknown force, it seemed, was drawing him to it']. If this situation could be established unambiguously, hesitation would be resolved and the story could be classified as 'merveilleux'. However, this is not to be. The modalizing 'казалось' ['it seemed'] undermines the statement's validity from within: it only 'seemed' that an unknown force was acting upon the protagonist.

As in *Spirite*, the ambiguity concerning the existence of this 'unknown force' is exacerbated and problematized if the source of the modal verb is considered. The reader is confronted by another instance of interference between perspectives which means that the modalization could be attributed to either the protagonist or the narrator. The statement could equally validly be the narrator's reaction or an instance of free indirect speech expressing the thoughts of Germann. The confusion arises from the lack of an attributing 'ему' ['to him'] alongside 'it seemed' which would have placed it clearly within the latter's perspective. Such attribution *is* present in the description of the countess winking at Germann from the coffin. So its absence in this example should be read as an intentional device. The confusion provoked by this device is recognized by Gei (1983, 185) when he asks:

> Кому это «казалось»? Случайному наблюдателю, персонажу или самому повествователю? Собственно говоря, эта многогранность и воссоздает нефиксированную систему отношений разных компонентов внутри художественного мира и во вне его.

> [To whom does this 'it seemed' belong? A chance observer, the protagonist or the narrator himself? Strictly speaking, this multifacetedness reconstructs a free system of relations between the different components both within and without the artistic world.]

As with the example from *Spirite*, because its source cannot be identified, the instance of this modalizer constitutes a more transgressive move than has been encountered elsewhere. This renders reader uncertainty both more acute and more unsettling. Ambiguity now revolves not simply around the possible existence of an 'unknown force' but also around the reader's ability to decide to whom such an opinion belongs. And it would not matter so much if the accusation did not pose such a significant threat to the rationality of the fictional world.

So, as my discussion of these two works has shown, heterodiegetic narrators need pose no fundamental problems to the practice of the fantastic. In fact, such narrators find themselves in a strong position when it comes to creating conditions of reliability and authority which help to persuade the reader of the 'realness' of the story world. Once this believability has been established, neither text has any difficulty in generating uncertainty. *Spirite* and *The Queen of Spades* offer multiple examples of the type of syntactic devices which can be employed to create interpretative ambiguity. What they also illustrate is that the convention within heterodiegetic texts is to justify such complicating verbal devices by means of a switch in the point of view of the narrative. By ceding his position to the less authoritative protagonist, the narrator makes way for instances of uncertain perception and interpretation. However, more fundamental challenges to the cognitive integrity of the text can also be offered by making the heterodiegetic narrator apparently responsible for such tentative descriptions. Coming full circle, such moments of narrator modalizing unsettle the reader profoundly because they undermine the notion of diegetic authority upon which the entire narrative has been founded. Heterodiegetic narratives might need to be more resourceful about crafting and justifying moments of hesitation, but they manage to do so in a way which means that they should be accorded their rightful place in the genre of the fantastic.

Notes to Chapter 1

1. Dostoevskii (1972, vol. 30, p. 192).
2. References to *Spirite* are taken from *L'Œuvre fantastique: Romans* (Paris: Bordas, 1992).
3. References to *The Queen of Spades* are taken from *Polnoe sobranie sochinenii v desiati tomakh*, vol. 6, Moscow: Akademiia Nauk, 1957.
4. For instance, in the second chapter of the novella, the baron de Féroë warns Guy de Malivert that the man who falls in love with Mme d'Ymbercourt will meet the fate of Nathaniel in Hoffmann's *Der Sandmann*.
5. Narrative concretization essentially consists in providing an alibi for the narrative. It is the convention whereby the author will delegate the whole or part of his text to a narrator-character; in its most explicit form, it sees a character accept the invitation to 'tell us your story'.
6. Genette's terms (1972, 252–53) stem from his dissatisfaction with the traditional labels of 'first-person' or 'third-person' narrator. He believes such labels insist upon an element which is actually invariable: the presence of the narrator in the discourse. His three new proposals are: *heterodiegetic* where the narrator is absent from the story he recounts; *homodiegetic* where the narrator is present in the story he tells; and *autodiegetic* where the narrator is also the hero of the story he relates. I restrict myself to the use of 'heterodiegetic' and 'homodiegetic'.
7. Borrowing from Genette, Lanser posits four categories of relationship between the time of the events and the time of narration: *posterior* where narration follows the completion of the events; *anterior* where the time of narration precedes events; *simultaneous* where the narration is contemporary with the action; and *interspersed* where narration occurs between the moments of action.
8. The terms 'fabula' and 'siuzhet' were first coined by the Russian Formalists; hence my decision here to employ the transliterated original forms. Put simply, the fabula consists of the events which took place; it provides the basic building blocks of the plot. Siuzhet, on the other hand, is the result of organizing, ordering, and presenting these events in the narrative; it is the presentation of the plot to the reader. Shlomith Rimmon (1977, 30) helps to explain the importance of these concepts to the authority associated with temporal stance when she says: 'from the point of view of artistic creation, the *fabula* precedes the *siuzhet*, the *fabula* being the raw material which can be artistically molded into various *siuzhets*' (original italics).

9. The work of Paul Simpson (1993), who draws up a modal grammar of point of view, provides further help in understanding the role of modalization in narrative. Todorov's concept of 'modalization' is developed into an epistemic modal system; using Simpson's terminology, 'it seemed to him', is an example of a modal lexical verb of perception.

10. This combination of protagonist modalization and narrator silence as a generator of hesitation can be noted in a later description of the baron de Féroë as he warns Guy de Malivert against terrestrial love affairs in case mistakes in this world are punished in the next:

Pendant que le jeune baron suédois disait cette phrase étrange, ses yeux, d'un bleu acier, brillaient singulièrement et lançaient des rayons dont Guy de Malivert crut sentir la chaleur à sa poitrine. Après les événements de la soirée, cette recommandation mystérieuse ne le trouva pas aussi incrédule qu'il l'eût été la veille. (*S* 216)

[As the young Swedish baron uttered this strange phrase, his eyes, of a steely blue, shone in a singular fashion and sent out rays, the warmth of which Guy de Malivert thought he could feel in his chest. After the events of the evening, this mysterious advice did not find him as disbelieving as he would have been the previous day.]

The modalizing 'crut sentir' belongs to the protagonist's perspective while the narrator provides no useful additional commentary which might confirm or disavow the validity of this impression of warmth.

11. This use of approximative adjectives echoes that found in Rabou's *Le ministère public* (1832) where Desalleux espies 'un object noirâtre' ['a blackish object'] in the corner of his room (1963, 109). This adjective likewise suggests a threshold existence given that the object is revealed as being the severed head of Pierre Leroux, a man wrongly executed on the strength of Desalleux's oratory.

12. This technique can be observed on two occasions in Rabou's *Le Ministère public*. The account of the appearance of Pierre Leroux's severed head is presaged by the detail: 'trois heures venaient de sonner' ['it had just struck three'] (1963, 108). In the subsequent description of Desalleux's wedding night, during the course of which the head reappears with murderous consequences, the reader is informed that the protagonist 'regardait de temps en temps la pendule qui marquait une heure trois quarts' ['from time to time looked at the clock which read a quarter to two'] (1963, 112). Abel Hugo in *L'Heure de la mort* (1833) favours the same proximity of temporal reference and apparently supernatural. The protagonist's entry into the church where he will encounter the vision of a priest is preceded by the description: 'Une horloge sonna l'heure. Albert écouta en frissonnant: douze coups tombèrent lentement sur le timbre argentin' ['A clock began to strike the hour. Albert shivered as he listened: twelve strokes fell slowly on the silvery bell'] (1963, 122).

13. Simpson divides his transitivity model (how meaning is represented in the clause) into three categories: material processes, verbalization processes, and mental processes. In material processes, he envisages the finer distinctions between action processes and event processes. The former are further divided into intention processes (where the actor performs the act voluntarily) and supervention processes (where the process just happens).

CHAPTER 2

Personality and Multiple Voice: Hesitation in Homodiegesis

Introduction

This second chapter investigates some of the ways in which homodiegetic narratives provoke hesitation. It is intended to operate very much in tandem with Chapter 1 in order that a broad picture of the devices generating ambiguity in the fantastic might be compiled. It begins with an investigation of the use of syntactic devices in first-person narratives. In revealing that a significant number of the same devices are used in both heterodiegesis and homodiegesis, it establishes these as essential tools in the genre. My discussion here also attempts to develop understanding about the fantastic and homodiegesis by analysing the role played by narrator personality. This aspect is viewed as the counterpart to the authority of the narrator in the heterodiegetic context. The traits and beliefs of the first-person narrator are considered from two principal angles: their role in the construction of an image of the narrator-protagonist as an essentially reasonable figure and the contrast this image offers to the nature of events being described. Both these factors entail significant consequences for the degree of hesitation experienced by the reader. The third part of this chapter builds upon the discussion of the role of switches in point of view conducted in Chapter 1. It analyses the contribution made by heteroglossia to the fantastic's signature uncertainty. The coexistence of multiple voices within a single narrative clearly suggests itself as a potential tool in the creation of ambiguity of interpretation. This multiplicity implies the possibility of moving away from the type of monosemy which would be fatal for the fantastic. Crucially, I will illustrate how the presence of even a single additional voice can be used to cast doubt upon the interpretation of events offered by the primary narrating voice. Although the introduction of heteroglossia is achieved in radically different ways in the texts to be discussed, similar fundamental questions are raised. Of central importance is the issue of how the reader arrives at an assessment of the relative authority of the various voices. With the conventional authority bestowed by omniscience upon the heterodiegetic voice removed, the question of the authority of the homodiegetic voice is problematized. Reference will therefore be made to the applicability and consequences of the concept of narrative levels in the analysis of which voice(s) and which interpretation(s) should be considered to be most trustworthy.

Prosper Mérimée's *La Vénus d'Ille* was first published in *La Revue des deux mondes* in 1837. Mérimée (1803–70) began his career as a writer in the 1820s with works in a number of different genres: the dramas *Le Théâtre de Clara Gazul* (1825) and *La Jacquerie* (1828); the historical novel *Chronique du règne de Charles IX* (1829); and the short story *Mateo Falcone* (also 1829). It is in this latter genre that Mérimée excelled at a time when the short story was in its earliest stages of development in France. In 1831, he became a civil servant and was then named General Inspector of Historic Monuments in 1834. Despite this seeming change of career, he continued to write, short stories for the most part, at a leisurely pace until 1846. A twenty-year hiatus in his fictional output then ensued whilst he concentrated upon historical writing until the appearance of *Lokis* in 1868. Mérimée enjoys a relatively modest reputation both in France and abroad. He has been described as lacking in originality and his cold, detached writing style is certainly not to everybody's taste. Nevertheless, in *La Vénus d'Ille*, he has produced an adroit and interesting example of the fantastic.

The story, recounting the apparent animation of a statue of Venus with fatal consequences, draws upon a particularly potent image from literary history.[1] It is narrated by an archaeologist-historian who, whilst on a field trip, calls in on an amateur antiquarian, M. de Peyrehorade, who has promised to show him the local sights. In return, M. de Peyrehorade asks the narrator for advice regarding the inscriptions on a statue of Venus which he has recently unearthed. The village of Ille is in festive mood because only a couple of days remain before the marriage of M. de Peyrehorade's son, Alphonse, to a local girl. On the morning of the wedding, Alphonse places the ring intended for his fiancée on the statue's finger as he plays real tennis. He forgets to retrieve it before the ceremony and so has to present Mlle de Puygarrig with a substitute ring. On the morning after the wedding, Alphonse is found crushed to death in the marital bed. The statue is accused as it is alleged that the Venus entered the house in order to claim the man her ring indicates is her groom. The essentially linear temporal structure of *La Vénus d'Ille* is underpinned by a complex system of interwoven themes and motifs. This drives a constant movement of echoing and foreshadowing which gains a particular resonance when the role played by the narrator is considered. Upon the discovery of Alphonse's death, the narrator becomes the embodiment of the rational as he begins to conduct himself like a detective searching for proof. In view of this mutation of the narrator's role, the pattern of repeated motifs can reasonably be considered to become a web of clues leading to the perpetrator of the crime. The story thus comes to represent an early example of the 'whodunnit' in a manner indicative of the similarities Todorov recognizes between the fantastic and detective fiction (*F* 95). The key to the hesitation generated in *La Vénus d'Ille* is the fact that the narrator-detective's quest for a rational explanation ultimately argues for the acceptance of the irrational. Mérimée ironically has the rational act par excellence, detection, work towards providing definitive proof of supernatural intervention. One of the most significant factors in the failure of the narrator's rational undertaking is the presence of alternative voices in the text which provide contradictory interpretations of events.

Vladimir Odoevskii's *Сильфида* (*The Sylph*) was also first published in 1837 in the journal *Современник* (*The Contemporary*). The reputation of Odoevskii (1804–69) is far stronger in Russia than it is in the West, where he remains a relatively neglected figure. He was an extremely active and important member of Russian cultural society and his interests were numerous and eclectic. In addition to pursuing a literary career, Odoevskii was also a public servant (he became a Moscow senator), a leading musicologist, an amateur scientist and harboured desires to become historian to the royal court. He was acquainted with virtually all of the leading cultural lights of his age, including Griboedov, Pushkin, Gogol, Turgenev, Tolstoi, and Tchaikovskii. Many of the most significant writers of the time influenced Odoevskii and were, in their turn, influenced by him. However, perhaps precisely because of the breadth of his interests outside literature, the reputation he deserved eluded him during his lifetime. This was partially corrected at the beginning of the twentieth century and, by the end of the Soviet period, his popularity in Russia had been confirmed.

In spite of the improved fortunes of Odoevskii's reputation, *The Sylph* remains a story which has not, to date, received the in-depth critical attention it merits. It is most frequently classified alongside his other stories, *The Cosmorama* (1840) and *The Salamander* (1841), as an example of his philosophical or mystical concerns. It has also been compared thematically to Hoffmann's *The Golden Pot*. However, as references to the story in Izmailov (1973, 165) and Cornwell (1990, 65) suggest, *The Sylph* can justifiably be seen as an embodiment of the fantastic. The story presents an initial homodiegetic narrator who, bored with life on his late uncle's estate, begins to experiment with sunlight and water after reading a collection of alchemical and cabbalistic books. He chooses the simplest experiment he can find which tells him to place a signet ring in a glass of water and to position the glass so that it will be illuminated by the sun. His initial scepticism begins to be overcome when this ring is apparently transformed into a rose which, in turn, reveals a water sylph. This creature subsequently initiates the narrator into a higher, more poetic realm where he wishes to remain. Despite the description he provides of this 'other' world, doubts surrounding the actual existence of this realm persist. A friend visits and, with the help of a doctor, cures him of his 'madness'. However, the narrator is anything but grateful for having been rescued, accusing his friend of denying him the greatest happiness he had ever known.

Of particular interest to my investigation of hesitation here is the fact that *The Sylph* is a mixed-format text presenting a variety of narrative voices. The first half of the story consists of eight letters composed by two voices: the first seven by the narrator-experimenter, Mikhail Platonovich, and the eighth by his neighbour, Gavril Rezhenskii. The second half is presented as the account of a third voice, Mikhail Platonovich's friend, and includes extracts from the experimenter's journal. Just as in *La Vénus d'Ille*, the hesitation between natural and supernatural interpretations can be accounted for, primarily, by the incompatibility of the views expressed by the different voices. Specifically, the second and third voices overtly contradict the claims made by Mikhail Platonovich as to the existence of the supernatural. The difficulty in establishing any clear hierarchy of authority between these various voices only serves to accentuate the consequent ambiguity. Finally, the incursion of the apparently supernatural is magnified owing to the fact that all the narrating voices display, at least at the outset, rational personalities unpredisposed to a belief in anything other than the natural world.

Part 1: Hesitating Syntax in the Homodiegetic Context

Theories of discourse conventionally view heterodiegetic and homodiegetic narratives as presenting quite distinct storytelling frameworks. However, by illustrating how heterodiegesis can still generate the ambiguity necessary to the fantastic, I hope to have shown an affinity between it and the homodiegetic context championed by Todorov. This basic similarity is reinforced when the syntactic devices designed to foster uncertainty in *La Vénus d'Ille* are considered. The narrative situations in Mérimée's story where hesitation occurs closely mirror the episode of the dead countess's nocturnal visit in *The Queen of Spades*. The experiencing personae generally resort to terms of indefinite description only when, like Germann, their visual perspective is somehow restricted. The recurrence of this combination of techniques suggests it as a staple of the fantastic genre. In the case of the archaeologist-historian narrator, particularly, the circumstances which delineate this syntactic usage offer preliminary clues as to his personality. As I will discuss in more detail later, his reluctance to employ modalization in situations other than those of restricted perspective reveals much about his supposedly informed and reasoning personality. It becomes clear, therefore, that a discussion of syntax functions as an effective introduction to the subsequent discussion of personality. The most persuasive illustration of the use of indefinite syntax in Mérimée can be achieved by examining two episodes from the later stages of *La Vénus d'Ille*. These two descriptions actually refer to the same period of time although they are narrated from two distinct perspectives. Both are of fundamental importance to the interpretation of the story because they relate to events which occur just prior to the death of Alphonse.

The first description is provided by the homodiegetic narrator and concerns the various comings and goings in the de Peyrehorade house on the night of the wedding. The narrator's visual perspective during this description is confined to his bedroom. However, the events he describes occur on the other side of a closed door. This obliges him to rely exclusively on his aural faculties. The reader recognizes that the quality of information which can be received aurally is inferior to that offered by visual perception and this arguably primes her for scepticism. In the tentativeness it conveys, the syntax used during this account faithfully reflects the constraints placed on observation:

> j'avais entendu force allées et venues dans la maison, les portes s'ouvrir et se fermer, des voitures partir; puis il me semblait avoir entendu sur l'escalier les pas légers de plusieurs femmes se dirigeant vers l'extrémité du corridor opposée à ma chambre. C'était probablement le cortège de la mariée qu'on menait au lit. Ensuite on avait redescendu l'escalier. (*V* 461)[2]

> [I had heard numerous comings and goings in the house, doors opening and closing, carriages leaving; then it seemed to me that I had heard the light footsteps of several women on the staircase heading towards the opposite end of the corridor from where my room was situated. It was probably the bride's cortege being brought to bed. Then they went back down the stairs.]

With the modal lexical verb of perception, 'il me semblait', the narrator acknowledges not only that he cannot see any of these events, but that he cannot even be sure of what he thinks he hears. This modal verb is reinforced by the presence of two verbs in the reflexive form ('s'ouvrir' and 'se fermer') which illustrate material processes of supervention. As the equivalent of the Russian 'дверь отворилась' ['the door opened'], these reflexive verbs most obviously indicate the similarity between this scene and the nocturnal visit episode in Pushkin. In *La Vénus d'Ille*, ambiguity is introduced because, whilst the reader recognizes that doors do not open and close themselves, supervention leaves the performer(s) of these actions unidentified. This failure to identify agents, which pertains throughout the description, is further revealed by the use of the indefinite pronoun 'on' (the quasi-equivalent of 'кто-то' ['someone'] in Russian). Mérimée's narrator is certain that he hears someone going down the stairs but is unable to tell the reader who this person is. The combination of these three devices (modal verb, reflexive verb, and indefinite pronoun) ensures that the description is as uncertain as the limited visual perspective informing it suggests it should be. Multiple elements are open to interpretation and the reader has little choice but to hesitate about the actual nature of events.

The second description of events during this crucial period is informed by the perspective of Alphonse's bride. Her account is reported indirectly by the intermediary voice of the king's procurator who has recorded her testimony as part of the official investigation. The opening section of this description bears a striking resemblance to that provided by the narrator because it too is guided by a limited visual perspective. Although her position inside the marital bedroom means that Mme Alphonse is situated much closer to the action, she is unable to provide a direct eyewitness account because 'elle était couchée [...] depuis quelques minutes, les rideaux tirés' ['she had been in bed [...] for several minutes with the curtains drawn around it'] (*V* 464). These curtains fulfil a similar function to the narrator's bedroom door by preventing unfettered observation and an exhaustive description. The account continues:

> la porte de sa chambre s'ouvrit, et quelqu'un entra. [...] Au bout d'un instant, le lit cria comme s'il était chargé d'un poids énorme. Elle eut grand'peur, mais n'osa pas tourner la tête. Cinq minutes, dix minutes peut-être... elle ne peut se rendre compte du temps, se passèrent de la sorte. Puis elle fit un mouvement involontaire, ou bien la personne qui était dans le lit en fit un, et elle sentit le contact de quelque chose de froid comme la glace [...]. Peu après, la porte s'ouvrit une seconde fois, et quelqu'un entra, qui dit: 'Bonsoir, ma petite femme.' Bientôt après, on tira les rideaux. Elle entendit un cri étouffé. La personne qui était dans le lit, à côté d'elle, se leva sur son séant et parut étendre les bras en avant. (ibid.)

> [her bedroom door opened and someone came in. [...] A moment later, the bed creaked as if under a heavy weight. She was extremely frightened, but did not dare turn round. Five minutes, ten minutes perhaps, she cannot say how long, passed in this way. Then she made an involuntary movement, or rather the person in the bed made one, and she felt the touch of something cold, like ice [...]. Shortly thereafter, the door opened for a second time, and someone came in and said: 'Good evening, my little wife.' Soon afterwards, the curtains were drawn. She heard a muffled cry. The person who was next to her in bed sat up and appeared to stretch their arms out in front of them.]

There are multiple syntactic echoes between this passage and both the extract considered above and the passage from *The Queen of Spades*. The reader confronts two instances of the verb 'to open' in the reflexive form where the identity of the agent is suppressed. Equally, the three examples of indefinite pronouns (two 'quelqu'un' and one 'quelque chose') prevent the reader from ascertaining who it is that enters the bedroom or what it is that Mme Alphonse feels next to her. The use of the enigmatic 'quelqu'un' is reinforced by two references to 'la personne', a noun which (despite its inherently feminine grammatical gender) is equally uninformative. As in the first account, this lack of identification is sustained as the person who pulls the curtains around the bed is simply referred to as 'on'. The status of this description becomes even more tentative thanks to the use of the comparator 'comme si' as Mme Alphonse approximates her experience to a more familiar circumstance. The syntax of the clause leaves the reader to ask whether the bed creaks because of an actual heavy load or because of something which merely resembles a heavy load. The modal adverb 'peut-être' indicates that Mme Alphonse has become unaware of that rational organizer, time. In a manner which recalls Malivert's unconscious writing of the letter in *Spirite*, the inconclusive relative conjunction 'ou bien' reveals that she struggles to decide whether actions are performed by her or by another. The uncertainty in her perceptions could scarcely be more profound. Finally, the modal verb, 'paraître', is employed once again to mitigate the narrating perspective's suggestion that the figure in the bed stretched out its arms. This passage of description is impressive in terms of the sheer number and variety of syntactic devices which betray the perceiver's uncertainty and which problematize the reader's appreciation of the scene. Based on this description alone, it is out of the question that the reader will construct a clear picture of the events which lead to the death of Alphonse. Retrospectively, of course, the ambiguity generated during these lines gains even greater importance when Mme Alphonse alleges that the figure who enters the bedroom and kills her husband is, in fact, the statue of Venus.

Limited visual perspective to produce incomplete and ambiguous descriptions is not a technique employed by Odoevskii in *The Sylph*. This does not imply, however, that attenuated description is absent as a feature of the story. Similar syntactic devices are indeed present but, rather than indicating information gaps caused by visual impediment, they express the narrator's struggle to describe phenomena which he witnesses directly and unhindered. Description is problematic because the perceived events or objects challenge the norms operating in the natural world to such an extent that human language is incapable of rendering them satisfactorily. The type and effect of linguistic devices employed in *The Sylph* is, therefore, far closer to those encountered in the passage in *Spirite* which describes the appearance of the face in the mirror.

These devices are particularly prevalent in the sixth and seventh letters where Mikhail Platonovich claims that his cabbalistic experiments have come to fruition. In letter six, he describes the first stages of the apparently supernatural transformation which his signet ring undergoes:

> Вчера вечером, подошел к вазе, я заметил в моем перстне какое-то движение. Сначала я подумал, что это был оптический обман и, чтоб удостовериться, взял вазу в руки; но едва я сделал малейшее движение, как мой перстень рассыпался на мелкие голубые и золотые искры, они потянулись по воде тонкими нитями и скоро совсем исчезли, лишь вода сделалась вся золотою с голубыми отливами. Я поставил вазу на прежнее место, и снова мой перстень слился на дне ее. (*Sy* 115)[3]

[Last night I walked up to the vase and noticed some sort of movement in my signet-ring. At first I thought it was an optical illusion and, to make sure, I picked the vase up; but I had hardly caused the slightest movement, when my signet ring disintegrated into small blue and gold sparks that spread out through the water in thin threads and soon disappeared altogether, except that the water all turned gold, shot with blue. I put the vase back down and my ring coagulated again on the bottom.]

Two particular syntactic devices call the reliability of this description into question. Firstly, the indefinite adjective 'какое-то' ['some sort of'] qualifying 'movement' suggests that, although the narrator does not doubt the existence of the movement, difficulties arise when he attempts to define its nature. This adjectival form is the Russian equivalent of the 'une sorte de' which Guy de Malivert employs to describe the image appearing in the mirror. And the same phrase is used again by Platonovich in the opening lines of the seventh letter. Secondly, reader uncertainty is reinforced by the modal lexical verb 'подумал' ['thought']. This is the only example here of syntax calling into question the reality of what Platonovich witnesses. Interestingly though, it is used to attenuate the proposal of a more rational explanation for the transformation of the ring: at first, Platonovich thinks it is nothing more than 'an optical illusion'. However, both the modal formulation of the clause and the temporal adverb 'at first' indicate that he no longer believes that the mutation can be attributed to anything so rational.

The sole occurrence of such a modal verb is explained by the fact that, when he composes his seventh letter, Platonovich does not doubt the reality of his experiment's results. Uncertainty, however, persists. In the opening lines of this letter, this is due, in part, to the presence of approximative adjectives. Both the colour of the water in the vase and of the waves permeating this water are described as 'зеленоватый' ['greenish']; the rays meanwhile are 'опаловый' ['opalescent'] (*Sy* 116). These more tentative formulations of colour adjectives suggest a sense of the inadequacy of language to render faithfully what Platonovich witnesses: the water is not green but some colour which is most closely comparable to green. Not only that, this device (as has been noted in relation to the baron de Féroë in *Spirite*) also suggests the advent of a phenomenon which interrogates the boundaries between the natural and the supernatural. Platonovich's efforts to equate what he witnesses to phenomena in the natural world continue as he describes there being 'как будто солнечное сияние' ['a radiance as if of the sun'] (ibid.) in the water. The 'как будто' ['as if'] indicates that it is not actually a radiance from the sun and, as such, performs the same attenuating function as the 'comme si' encountered repeatedly in both *Spirite* and *La Vénus d'Ille*.

The climax in the transformation of the signet ring is described in the second half of the seventh letter. The account is worth reproducing at some length because of the evidence it provides of three syntactic devices discussed previously:

Сегодня я подошел к моей розе и в середине ее заметил что-то новое... [...] в средине его что-то мелькало: листы растворились мало-помалу, и — я не верил глазам моим! — между оранжевыми тычинками покоилось — поверишь ли ты мне? — покоилось существо удивительное, невыразимое, неимоверное — словом, женщина, едва приметная глазу! Как описать мне тебе восторг, смешанный с ужасом, который я почувствовал в эту минуту. [...] Она, казалось, была погружена в глубокий сон [...]. (*Sy* 117)

[Today I walked up to my rose and in the middle of it I noticed something new...
[...] in the middle of it something flashed: the leaves unfurled little by little and
— I couldn't believe my eyes — between the orange stamens there reposed
— will you believe me? — there reposed an amazing, indescribable, unbelievable
creature: in a word, a woman, barely visible to the eye! How can I describe to you
the delight, mixed with horror, which I felt at that moment? [...] She, it seemed,
was immersed in a deep sleep [...].]

Mikhail Platonovich's inability either to recognize or to comprehend fully the
events occurring in the vase is illustrated by two instances of the indefinite pronoun
'что-то' ['something']. However, its use in this context is quite distinct from that
encountered in *La Vénus d'Ille* and *The Queen of Spades*. The non-identification of the
object in the vase is not now the result of obscured observation; it is representative
of a more fundamental failure. Physically, nothing prevents the narrator from gaining
a clear view of the object, and yet he is still incapable of providing a satisfactory
description of it. He does not *not* name it because he cannot see it; he simply cannot
name it. This situation is therefore suggestive of a more profound breakdown in the
narrator-protagonist's experience of the world. His difficulties are further incarnated
in a technique identified in *Spirite* as a favourite of the fantastic: multiple adjectives.
The creature revealed as the petals slowly open is described as 'удивительное,
невыразимое, неимоверное' ['amazing, indescribable, unbelievable']. The semantics
of each of these adjectives is adroitly reinforced by the structure of the clause itself.
The creature is so amazing that three adjectives are needed to qualify the single noun.
This is strongly reminiscent of the terms in which Spirite is described in Gautier's
novella. In both cases, this verbal structure gives the reader the impression that the
witness is unable to give a single definitive description of the emerging creature.
In *The Sylph*, the uncertainty is further accentuated by the semantics of the final
adjective: 'unbelievable' clearly indicates the challenge the creature in the rose offers
to the rules of the natural world. Finally, the extract offers one instance of a modal
lexical verb of perception: the woman in the middle of the rose 'it seemed' was fast
asleep. Again, however, this modal verb does not throw doubt upon the existence of
the sylph *per se*, but rather questions whether she is sleeping or not. This device is
indicative of the role assigned to ambiguous syntax throughout this passage. Mikhail
Platonovich does not employ attenuation to bring the reality of the supernatural into
question; rather, it betrays the difficulties he encounters in ascertaining and expressing
the form that this otherworldly intervention takes. This modal verb sums up, therefore,
the fundamental distinction between the target of the ambiguity present in the
passages from *The Sylph* and *La Vénus d'Ille*. In Mérimée's story, the witnesses cannot
be sure whether what they believed they witnessed actually took place or not. In the
case of Odoevskii's text, Mikhail Platonovich is convinced he sees a sylph; he merely
struggles to find satisfactory terms in which to describe it.

Part 2: The Role of Narrator Personality

According to Todorov, homodiegesis is better suited to the fantastic than heterodiegesis
because it facilitates identification between the narrator and the reader. Discussing
Charles Nodier's *Inès de Las Sierras* (1837), he claims that the suspense experienced

in this story is a result of its narrator being a man like any other: 'les événements sont surnaturels, le narrateur est naturel' ['the events are supernatural, the narrator is natural'] (F 89). The manner in which Todorov formulates this claim suggests that the qualities of the narrator are actually of greater importance than the reader's sympathy with this figure. Taking this to be so, it is the salient characteristics of the narrator's personality which can be seen to exert a fundamental influence upon the reader's experience of the supernatural. In the discussion that follows, this personality will be considered not in the light of embodying the reader within the text but in terms of the contrast it offers with the nature of events being depicted.

In the context of heterodiegesis, the mimetic and diegetic authority of the narrative voice has been shown to be of paramount importance to the experience of hesitation. Such issues of authority are also pertinent in the homodiegetic situation. However, here, the question of personality is arguably deserving of even greater attention. We talk of the attributes of a heterodiegetic voice, but can reasonably discuss the personality of a homodiegetic voice because, as Franz Stanzel remarks (1984, 201), this figure can 'take on a more strongly marked personal and physical presence in the fictional world'. As such, the character traits, attitudes, or habits displayed by the homodiegetic voice are more easily recoverable by the reader. *La Vénus d'Ille* and *The Sylph* can be used to investigate in the first instance the contribution that this display of attitudes and beliefs makes to the narrators' authority and reliability. Specifically, I will argue that the narrators in both stories earn a significant degree of authentication authority by espousing reasonable beliefs. This rationalizing tendency influences the uncertainty felt by the reader in response to the supernatural in two contradictory ways. On the one hand, hesitation is supplemented by doubts arising from the marked contrast between the reasonable personality displayed previously and the unreasonable nature of events subsequently reported. The reader experiences both surprise and uncertainty because of the stark contrast which exists between the characteristics of the narrator and those of the fictional event. Yet, at the same time, presentation of the supernatural by this voice signals to the reader that the previously established beliefs must now be under threat. She is confronted by the difficulty of reconciling the question of how the reasonable can come to present the unreasonable. Finally, these narrative voices prove to be susceptible to subtle changes in their essential rationality; the basically common-sense personalities are gradually threatened by the apparent incursion of the supernatural.

The figure of the narrator in *La Vénus d'Ille* has already aroused a considerable amount of critical interest and a consensus exists regarding his personality. Anthony Pilkington (1975–76, 24) sums up both this view and the disparity between the personality and the nature of certain events occurring in the fictional world when he describes him as:

> a level-headed man, a sober academic, sceptical about mystery and superstition, unlikely to be given to romance [...] the fact that he is not a neutral and uninvolved observer but a character in his own right with the attitudes defined above, guarantees his reliability and authenticates his account of a series of events which might in themselves strain the credulity of the reader.

This narrator's personality is sketched in two principal ways: by contrasting him with other characters and by recording his reactions to a number of key events. The contrastive method of characterization is first evident during a conversation he has with his Catalan guide even before arriving in Ille. The subject is a bronze statue which the guide has helped find on M. de Peyrehorade's land. The juxtaposition of the narrator with an easily excitable Catalan who is more than ready to allege the existence of the supernatural helps to depict the former as calm, knowledgeable, and reasoning. The essentially *in medias res* opening of the story, which provides geographical information but no biographical details for the narrator, lends the ensuing conversation with the guide greater importance. Their conversation appears to act out, on a surface level, Jean Bellemin-Noël's claim (1971, 111) that every fantastic text is composed of two distinct discourses:

> d'un côté un discours raisonneur, celui du témoin ou de la conscience lucide, qui s'efforce d'avérer un référentiel; de l'autre côté, le discours de l'inexplicable, de l'activité délirante ou de la perception hallucinatoire.

> [on the one hand, a reasoning discourse, that of the witness or of the lucid mind, which endeavours to confirm a referential; on the other, the discourse of the inexplicable, of the delirious activity or of the hallucinatory perception.]

The guide's tendency towards easy excitability and credulity is betrayed by his insistence upon using the historic present tense to narrate a discovery made two weeks earlier:

> Voilà donc qu'en travaillant, Jean Coll, qui y allait de tout cœur, il donne un coup de pioche, et j'entends bimm... comme s'il avait tapé sur une cloche. [...] Nous piochons toujours, nous piochons, et voilà qu'il paraît une main noire, qui semblait la main d'un mort qui sortait de terre. Moi, la peur me prend. Je m'en vais à monsieur, et je lui dis: 'Des morts, notre maître, qui sont sous l'olivier.' (*V* 440)

> [So as he's working away at full whack, Jean Coll, he swings his mattock and I hear bimm... as if he had hit a bell. [...] We carry on mattocking, we mattock, and then this black hand appears, which seemed like the hand of a corpse coming out of the ground. Me, I get frightened. I take myself off to the master and tell him: 'Dead people, master, under the olive tree.']

The guide's fear at what they find stems from his difficulty in correctly identifying the object in the ground and this is betrayed by the modal verb 'sembler' ['to seem']. His readiness to imagine the object to be a corpse's hand suggests his fanciful personality.

His association of the statue with a living person intensifies a few lines later as the guide claims it possesses animate powers:

> C'est une idole, vous dis-je: on le voit bien à son air. Elle vous fixe avec ses grands yeux blancs... On dirait qu'elle vous dévisage. On baisse les yeux, oui, en la regardant. (*V* 440–41)

> [It's an idol, I tell you: you can see it in its eyes. She fixes you with her big white eyes... You'd say she was staring at you. You lower your gaze, so you do, looking at her.]

Although this initial claim as to the animate nature of the statue is attenuated at one point by the conditional 'on dirait que', it remains a clear indication of the guide's belief-system. Crucially, it also represents the first invocation of the animate/inanimate dichotomy which proves to be fundamental to the interpretation of the story as a whole. The guide is far from being alone in granting animate powers to the statue. Indeed, characters in the story can broadly be divided into two categories: those who believe in its animation and those who deny it. The guide reinforces his first accusation when he recounts how Jean Coll is injured as the statue falls on his leg. Although he does not explicitly claim that the fall is an active gesture made by the statue, the violence of his reaction suggests he does not believe it to be simply an unfortunate accident either. He blames the statue in a manner more appropriately directed towards an active perpetrator: 'Pécaïre! quand j'ai vu cela, moi, j'étais furieux. Je voulais défoncer l'idole à coups de pioche, mais monsieur de Peyrehorade m'a retenu' ['Curses! When I saw that, me, I was furious. I wanted to smash the idol with the mattock, but monsieur de Peyrehorade held me back'] (*V* 441).

Faced with these claims, the narrator remains calm and eminently reasonable, providing rational interpretations to challenge each one of the guide's allegations. For example, his reaction to the first episode of the discovery is a simple, 'Et enfin que trouvâtes-vous?' ['And in the end what did you find?'] (*V* 440), whilst to the claim that the statue must date from Charlemagne's time, he calmly retorts: 'Je vois ce que c'est... Quelque bonne Vierge en bronze d'un couvent détruit' ['I see what it is... Some nice bronze Virgin from a destroyed convent'] (ibid.). In terms of its illustration of his unimpressionable and rationalizing personality, his response to the suggestion that the statue stares at people is even more revealing. He counters it with an explanation which, the reader is invited to assume, stems from his knowledge of the subject: 'Des yeux blancs? Sans doute ils sont incrustés dans le bronze. Ce sera peut-être quelque statue romaine' ['White eyes? They are no doubt set in the bronze. It is perhaps some Roman statue'] (*V* 441). This series of well-informed and analytical responses clearly characterizes the narrator as 'level-headed' and 'sober'.[4] Although he is careful not to dismiss overtly the guide's contentions, his reasonable interpretations of the discovery paint him as unpredisposed to a belief in the irrational. This implicit characterization of the narrator is then made more explicit as the guide calls him 'un savant comme [M. de Peyrehorade]' ['a learned man like [M. de Peyrehorade]'].

The more informative contrast in terms of characterization is drawn between the narrator and M. de Peyrehorade. At dinner on the first evening, he echoes the guide's assessment of the narrator. Whilst he is merely 'un vieil antiquaire de province' ['an old provincial antiquarian'], the narrator is 'un savant de Paris'. Complementing the rational vs. irrational conflict already noted, this comparison introduces two further dichotomies of knowledge vs. ignorance and Paris vs. provinces. The debate between the two men regarding the inscriptions on the statue neatly plays out these contrasts. The superiority of the narrator is largely established by means of the irony with which he views M. de Peyrehorade's inventive suggestions regarding the meaning of the inscriptions. The narrator's reactions during this extended discussion essentially echo the character traits he has displayed during his earlier conversation with the guide. However, the contrast in approach and personality between the narrator and M. de Peyrehorade is more clearly underlined in this scene because he does now judge his host's suggestions overtly.

Whilst acknowledging the ambiguity of the words 'Cave Amantem' ['Beware the lover'] on the statue's plinth, the narrator opts for the more grammatically likely of two potential renderings: 'Prends garde à toi si *elle* t'aime' ['Take care if *she* loves you'] (*V* 449; original italics). In contrast, M. de Peyrehorade embellishes the inscription with reference to Venus's lover and arrives at a very different translation: 'Malgré toute ta beauté, ton air dédaigneux, tu auras un forgeron, un vilain boiteux pour amant' ['Despite all your beauty, your disdainful air, you will have a blacksmith, a limping villain as a lover']. Even to a reader with no knowledge of Latin, the narrator's more succinct translation suggests itself as the more probable version. In fact, the narrator actively and explicitly establishes his superiority by remarking with regard to M. de Peyrehorade's attempt: 'Je ne pus m'empêcher de sourire, tant l'explication me parut tirée par les cheveux' ['I could not suppress a smile, so outlandish did the explanation seem to me'] (ibid.). The gentle mocking of M. de Peyrehorade for his tendency to over-interpret continues as the two men discuss the partly erased lines found on the statue's arm. The narrator admits to being troubled by the incomplete 'Turbul', but decides that 'Turbulenta' ('qui trouble, qui agite' ['which troubles, which agitates']) is the most likely form. M. de Peyrehorade is unimpressed and suggests that the full inscription should be 'Turbulneræ'. Whilst the reader is unable to judge which of these complete inscriptions is the more likely, the provincial host's recourse to obscure details of local geography and to dubious modifications of Latin pronunciation in order to justify his version makes it less convincing. Just as before, the narrator ensures that the reader recognizes the misguided nature of M. de Peyrehorade's efforts by commenting: 'Je parvins à réprimer une forte envie de rire' ['I managed to stifle a strong desire to laugh'] (*V* 451). This condescending attitude is reiterated as he explains that his reluctance to continue arguing with M. de Peyrehorade stems from a personal conviction: 'M'étant fait une loi de ne jamais contredire à outrance les antiquaires entêtés, je baissai la tête d'un air convaincu en disant: "C'est un admirable morceau"' ['Having given myself the rule never to contradict excessively stubborn antiquarians, I lowered my head as if convinced, saying: "It is a fine piece"'] (*V* 452). The narrator's conversations with both the Catalan guide and M. de Peyrehorade succeed in characterizing him as a reasonable man upon whom the reader can rely.

This impression is developed by the narrator's reactions to a number of events or reports which hint at the existence of the supernatural. This can be clearly illustrated by considering three passages from *La Vénus d'Ille*. The first describes the incident, witnessed by the narrator from his bedroom window, in which two local troublemakers throw stones at the statue of Venus. During this episode the narrator enjoys only a limited visual perspective as his window is over one hundred feet away and he acknowledges: 'à la distance où j'étais, il m'était difficile de distinguer l'attitude de la statue; je ne pouvais juger que de sa hauteur' ['from this distance, it was difficult to make out the statue's bearing; I could only tell how tall it was'] (*V* 446). The two attackers share the Catalan guide's impulse to animate the statue by calling their stone-throwing a punishment for Jean Coll's injury: 'C'est donc toi qui as cassé la jambe' ['So it was you who broke his leg']. This attitude is confirmed by the difference in the reactions of the troublemakers and the narrator in the development of this confrontation:

[Le plus grand des apprentis] se baissa, et probablement ramassa une pierre. Je le vis déployer le bras, lancer quelque chose, et aussitôt un coup sonore retentit sur le bronze. Au même instant l'apprenti porta la main à sa tête en poussant un cri de douleur.

'Elle me l'a rejetée!' s'écria-t-il.

Et mes deux polissons prirent la fuite à toutes jambes. Il était évident que la pierre avait rebondi sur le métal, et avait puni ce drôle de l'outrage qu'il faisait à la déesse.

Je fermai la fenêtre en riant de bon cœur. (*V* 446)

[[The taller of the apprentices] bent down and probably picked up a stone. I saw him extend his arm, throw something, and a moment later a sound rang out from the bronze. At the same time, the apprentice put his hand to his head and cried out in pain.

'She threw it back at me!' he shouted.

And my two apprentices ran off as fast as they could. It was clear that the stone had rebounded on the metal and had punished this joker for the insult he had made to the goddess.

I closed the window, laughing heartily.]

The apprentice's accusation that the statue has thrown the object back at him has the potential to introduce a degree of uncertainty into the narrative. However, this is counterbalanced by two interpretations from the narrator which betray his rational character. Firstly, the narrator attempts to fill the information gap which arises from his limited visual perspective by making an assumption. The indefinite 'something' which the man throws at the statue is identified as 'probably' being a stone. The epistemic modal adverb signals that the narrator is supplementing the facts he can actually observe with information he feels he can safely presume. Such a reflex betrays his dissatisfaction with missing information and his desire to resolve any uncertainty which may result from it by imposing a reasonable solution. This characterization of the narrator as a deductive reasoner is more obvious in his reaction to the apprentice's accusation. His confident statement that the stone must have rebounded off the statue re-imposes the rational. Whilst not definitive, the modal adjective, 'évident', makes a stronger argument than the earlier 'probablement' that a rational explanation for the event exists. His laugh displays the same superior attitude towards the apprentices as he has displayed towards his host.

This rationalizing tendency is of crucial importance in developments during the description of the wedding reception. A considerable degree of the hesitation experienced by the reader during the remainder of *La Vénus d'Ille* stems from the narrator's reaction to claims made by Alphonse regarding the statue and his wedding ring. The narrator is repeatedly unwilling to grant credence to irrational claims. However, ultimately, it is a failure on his part which permits the possibility of the irrational, and with it acute uncertainty, to persist. The spectre of the supernatural raises its head when, following a brief absence from the reception, Alphonse asks the narrator for help because 'je suis ensorcelé! le diable m'emporte!' ['I am bewitched! The devil take me!'] (*V* 460). The narrator immediately attributes this outlandish exclamation to Alphonse having had too much to drink. This dismissal is repeated as, even before the groom has had time to explain his problem fully, the narrator states matter-of-factly: 'je le crus tout à fait ivre' ['I thought him completely drunk'] (ibid.).

When Alphonse persists and informs the narrator that he cannot remove the diamond ring from the statue's hand, this complaint is countered with the straightforward explanation: 'vous n'avez pas tiré assez fort' ['you haven't pulled hard enough'] (ibid.). Alphonse rejects this and his claims take a more serious turn as he alleges: 'mais la Vénus... elle a serré le doigt' ['but the Venus... she has bent her finger'] (ibid.). Again, the narrator is sceptical and insists quite logically that he must have pushed the ring on too firmly. He reassures Alphonse: 'Demain vous l'aurez avec des tenailles' ['you'll get it off tomorrow with some pliers'].

Alphonse is not to be pacified so easily, however, and finally lays his most troublesome charge against the statue. In a move which aligns him with those characters who allege that the statue is animate and which introduces a central ambiguity into the text, he states:

> Le doigt de la Vénus est retiré, reployé; elle serre la main, m'entendez-vous?... C'est ma femme, apparemment, puisque je lui ai donné mon anneau... Elle ne veut plus le rendre. (ibid.)

> [The Venus's finger is bent, pulled in; she is clenching her hand, do you understand me?... She is my wife, apparently, seeing as I gave her my ring... She does not want to give it back.]

Momentarily, the uncertainty prompted by this claim is allowed to stand as the narrator admits to feeling a sudden shiver run down his back. However, his rationalizing instinct quickly reasserts itself as he recalls: 'Puis, un grand soupir qu'il fit m'envoya une bouffée de vin, et toute émotion disparut. Le misérable, pensai-je, est complètement ivre' ['Then, a big sigh he let out sent me a cloud of wine fumes, and all my emotion disappeared. The wretch, I thought, is completely drunk'] (ibid.). The reader nevertheless senses here that the gravity of Alphonse's allegation renders such a simple verbal dismissal inadequate. The fact that the description of the statue's clenched hand is indirect means that any hesitation could potentially be resolved by a direct visual report from the narrator. Indeed, the narrator appears to acknowledge this as he initially agrees to go and inspect the statue for himself. However, this potential for quick resolution is snatched away when, because of the rain and the damage such a move might make to his reputation, he decides against it:

> Je serais un bien grand sot [...] d'aller vérifier ce que m'a dit un homme ivre! Peut-être, d'ailleurs, a-t-il voulu me faire quelque méchante plaisanterie pour apprêter à rire à ces honnêtes provinciaux [...]. (V 461)

> [I would be a complete fool [...] to go and check what a drunken man has said to me. Anyway, perhaps he wanted to play a trick on me so that these honest provincials could have a laugh at my expense [...].]

This constitutes an important turning point in the impact of the narrator's reasoning instincts. Up until this point, these have attempted to counter uncertainty by providing rational explanations. Now though they serve as an impediment to that same act of resolution. The narrator's desire to protect his reputation as the erudite and reasonable Parisian means, ironically, that he fails to live up to this reputation by allowing an information gap to stand. This is arguably the first step in the development highlighted by Laurence Porter (1982, 270) whereby the reasonable and supposedly reliable narrator becomes unreliable. It is also one of the events which Frank Bowman believes (1960, 480) 'endows [him] with a certain responsibility in the disaster'.

The paradox of having the narrator's reasonable personality contribute towards his unreliability is further constructed during his description of events occurring on the wedding night. Part 1 of this chapter has shown how his limited visual perspective impacts upon the syntax employed in his account. For instance, his typical desire to fill information gaps with deduction is obvious when he describes: 'C'était probablement le cortège de la mariée qu'on menait au lit' ['It was probably the bride's cortege being brought to bed'] (*V* 461). Such gap-filling is quite acceptable here as the modal adverb honestly reflects the narrator's speech situation: he cannot actually see what is happening and so he surmises that this is 'probably' the case. However, the impact of his need to rationalize becomes more serious, and potentially more disruptive, when subsequent deductions lack explicit indicators of their conjectural status. For example, when he describes the sounds he hears on the staircase later on the wedding night and early the next morning, he displays a rational, but unreliable, reflex:

> Le silence régnait depuis quelque temps lorsqu'il fut troublé par des pas lourds qui montaient l'escalier. Les marches de bois craquèrent fortement.
> 'Quel butor!' m'écriai-je. [...]
> Le jour allait se lever. Alors j'entendis distinctement les mêmes pas lourds, le même craquement de l'escalier que j'avais entendu avant de m'endormir. Cela me parut singulier. J'essayai, en bâillant, de deviner pourquoi M. Alphonse se levait si matin. (*V* 462)

> [Silence had reigned for some time when it was disturbed by heavy footsteps going up the staircase. The wooden steps creaked loudly.
> 'What a boor!' I exclaimed. [...]
> Day was about to break. Then I distinctly heard the same heavy footsteps, the same creaking of the staircase as I had heard before I had fallen asleep. This seemed strange to me. I tried, yawning, to work out why M. Alphonse was getting up so early.]

The narrator's previous descriptions of Alphonse leave the reader in no doubt that he is the character implied by the epithet 'butor'. However, neither here nor in the penultimate line of the extract does the narrator overtly acknowledge that he is only hypothesizing that the footsteps on the stairs belong to the bridegroom. Still enjoying only limited visual perspective, he cannot be sure that it is Alphonse on the staircase. If the narrator was faithfully respecting these restrictions, the statements regarding the footsteps should be modalized, thereby identifying them as suppositions. He arguably chooses not to do so in an effort to minimize uncertainty. However, the failure to acknowledge the compromised nature of this information must raise further queries about his reliability. Both here and in the earlier wedding reception scene, therefore, the irony is that it is precisely those elements which characterize the narrator as a reasonable man unwilling to countenance the existence of the supernatural which raise doubts regarding the degree of trust which should be granted to his interpretation of events.

This potential weakness assumes an even greater importance when, following the discovery of Alphonse's death, the narrator expands his role as the voice of reason to become a detective searching for an explanation for this crime.[5] Given that the detective's task involves using available proof to arrive at a persuasive and rational explanation for events, the narrator would appear to be well suited to this role. However, the denouement of *La Vénus d'Ille* illustrates how, perversely, this search for a reasonable explanation effectively rules out the possibility of accounting for the death rationally. The ambiguity which persists at the close of the narrative is therefore far more resonant because it is perpetuated by efforts to resolve it. The narrator is typically forthright in his declaration, upon the discovery of Alphonse's body, that the death must have a rational explanation:

> Il ne me paraissait pas douteux que M. Alphonse n'eût été victime d'un assassinat dont les auteurs avaient trouvé moyen de s'introduire la nuit dans la chambre de la mariée. (*V* 463)

> [It did not seem to me to be in any doubt that M. Alphonse had been the victim of a murder, the perpetrators of which had found a way of getting into the marital suite during the night.]

The skill of the narrator as detective must, even at this early stage, be questioned because his declaration is made whilst ignoring the importance of a fact which he, himself, records. As he examines Alphonse's body on the bed, he notes, but does not pursue, what should be recognized as a potential clue to the identity of the murderer: 'Mon pied posa sur quelque chose de dur qui se trouvait sur le tapis; je me baissai et vis la bague de diamants' ['I stepped on something hard which was lying on the carpet; I bent down and saw the diamond ring'] (ibid.). This line encourages the reader to adopt an active role in reconstructing the text's implied meaning: she should equate this ring with the one which Alphonse has earlier claimed to be unable to remove from the statue's finger. However, it is as if the narrator's haste to impose a rational interpretation upon events leads him to ignore a clue which indicates a very different solution. Ideal detectives should not be so selective.

The narrator's suspicions instead fall unimaginatively upon the Aragonais muleteer whom Alphonse has beaten at real tennis on his wedding morning. He justifies this by arguing that the strange circular marks on Alphonse's chest could have been inflicted by the type of long leather sacks filled with sand which, so he has heard, are used as murder weapons in Valencia. Moreover, he recalls the threat issued by the muleteer upon losing the game: 'Me lo pagarás' (Spanish for 'you will pay for that') (*V* 457). Neither of these justifications for suspecting the man from Aragon stand up to scrutiny, however. In the case of the latter, the narrator himself admits his reluctance to interpret the mule-driver's light-hearted words in such a threatening manner. In the former, the narrator's skill as a detective is called into question by means of a reversal of roles. In the impression it gives of being 'tiré par les cheveux', the theory of death having been caused by a Valencian weapon recalls M. de Peyrehorade's suggestions regarding the statue's inscriptions.

In spite of the disdain with which this suggests the narrator ought to consider his own accusation, he refuses to relinquish it. He thereby breaks the golden rule of detection by searching for clues to fit an already identified perpetrator rather than allowing the clues to speak for themselves. Hints at the ultimate failure of his rational quest appear from an early stage, as the narrator records:

> J'allais dans la maison, cherchant partout des traces d'effraction, et n'en trouvant nulle part. Je descendis dans le jardin pour voir si les assassins avaient pu s'introduire de ce côté; mais je ne trouvai aucun indice certain. (*V* 463)

[I walked through the house looking everywhere for signs of breaking and entering but found none anywhere. I went down into the garden to see if the murderers had managed to get in from there; but I could find no irrefutable clue.]

More disruptive than the lack of definitive proof of the rational, however, is the fact that his search actually unearths details which suggest a diametrically opposed interpretation of the crime. For instance, when a set of deeply imprinted footprints is found which lead to and from the statue, the narrator hypothesizes:

> Ce pouvaient être les pas de M. Alphonse lorsqu'il était allé chercher son anneau au doigt de la statue. D'un autre côté, la haie, en cet endroit, étant moins fourrée qu'ailleurs, ce devait être sur ce point que les meurtriers l'auraient franchie. (ibid.)

[These could be the footsteps of M. Alphonse as he went to fetch his ring from the statue's finger. On the other side, the hedge at this spot was less bushy than elsewhere; this must be the point where the murderers climbed over it.]

Both of these facts, however, simultaneously support Mme Alphonse's subsequent claim that it is the statue who is her husband's killer. Whilst it might be argued that such clues only make themselves felt retrospectively, the animate/inanimate dichotomy introduced from the outset sensitizes the active reader to their potential significance. The ambiguity in Mérimée's story is skilfully maintained by having all the clues, which the narrator interprets rationally, indicate equally validly the possibility of the irrational. And yet, in spite of his privileged temporal position, apart from the occasional use of an imperfect tense, the narrator declines to show any appreciation of this fact.

The likelihood that the narrator will succeed in imposing his rational explanation begins to recede with the report that, under interrogation, the muleteer defends himself stoutly and convincingly. His claims of innocence are subsequently supported by the revelation that, when compared with the footprints in the garden, the Aragonais's boots are found to be far too big. Pilkington (1975–76, 27) argues in some detail that this discovery stands as further proof of the narrator's failure as a detective. The final step in this apparent defeat of the rationalizing mind involves reference back to the first potential clue: the diamond ring. The narrator interrogates the last servant to have seen Alphonse alive and asks him, specifically, whether the groom had the diamond ring in his possession as he climbed the stairs to the bedroom:

> Il dit qu'il ne le croyait pas, qu'il n'y avait fait au reste aucune attention.
>   'S'il avait eu cette bague au doigt', ajouta-t-il [...], 'je l'aurais sans doute remarquée, car je croyais qu'il l'avait donnée à madame Alphonse.' (*V* 466)

[He said that he did not think so, that besides he had not paid any particular attention to it. 'If he had had this ring on his finger,' he added [...], 'I would have noticed it without doubt, because I thought that he had given it to Madame Alphonse.']

This response clearly contradicts the narrator's earlier assumption that the groom had collected his ring from the statue and subsequently dropped it on the bedroom floor. Although the narrator does not pose it directly in the text, the reader is left to contemplate the question of how the ring could have found its way onto the bedroom floor if Alphonse had not brought it there.

Thus the clues which the narrator cites in his attempt to account rationally for Alphonse's death are all revealed to be red herrings. Each one in turn is dismissed and shown, in fact, to suggest the potential involvement of the statue: each thereby serves to make the irrational seem distinctly possible. And yet, equally, those clues which point to a potentially irrational explanation do not amount to a wholly convincing account of affairs either. Defeat of the rational does not have as its direct consequence victory of the irrational. A partial explanation for the lack of a definitive resolution is the narrator's precipitate departure from the village following Alphonse's funeral. He abruptly abdicates the responsibility which he has previously claimed for himself as amateur detective and refuses to pursue the mystery any further. In so doing, the narrator's behaviour recalls the failure of the heterodiegetic narrators in *Spirite* and *The Queen of Spades* to provide commentary upon the irrational. Mérimée's narrator simply reports: 'Depuis mon départ je n'ai point appris que quelque jour nouveau soit venu éclairer cette mystérieuse catastrophe' ['Since my departure I have not learned that any new light has been cast upon this mysterious catastrophe'] (*V* 466). Therefore, given that neither the rational nor the irrational definitively gains the upper hand, there can be no resolution of the hesitation experienced by the reader. I will return to a discussion of how the irrational gains particular currency in the closing stages of *La Vénus d'Ille* in Part 3 of this chapter.

I would first like to turn my attention to a discussion of the portrayal and impact of the narrator personality in *The Sylph*. This discussion will focus upon the initial narrator, Mikhail Platonovich, who is the author of the first seven letters in the story. Certain consequences which the epistolary format imposes upon the portrayal of personality mean that two important preliminary remarks should be made. The first concerns the relative authority implied by this narrator's temporal stance. The three works discussed so far have all presented narrators who occupy a stable, temporally posterior position in relation to events. They have, therefore, been expected to possess relatively full access to information and elevated authority. The epistolary format of *The Sylph* means that its opening section departs from this pattern by presenting an interspersed narration of events. By its very nature, interspersed narration deprives itself of the aspect which imbues posterior temporal stance with authority: the fact that all action is completed before narration begins. Genette signals the potential problems associated with interspersed narration when he notes (1972, 229) that, in this category of temporality, it is conceivable that the 'fabula' and the 'siuzhet' will interfere with each other because they exist in a state of relative simultaneity.[6] Seymour Chatman (1978, 170) indicates how the interspersed narration typical of epistolary texts affects the degree of knowledge attributed to the narrator:

> unlike genuine narrators, the correspondent or diarist cannot know how things will ultimately turn out. Nor can he know whether something is important or not. He can only recount the story's past, not its future. He can only have apprehensions or make predictions. Suspense derives from our curiosity about whether or not his hopes or fears materialise.

Consequently, the reader does not automatically bestow as great a degree of authority upon Mikhail Platonovich in *The Sylph* as he does upon the archaeologist-historian in *La Vénus d'Ille*. Secondly, the epistolary format nevertheless creates circumstances which, to a certain degree, counterbalance any loss of authority stemming from interspersed temporality. It enables a direct 'я–ты' ['I–you'] form of address to be established in the narrative's opening lines: 'Пишу к тебе, сидя в огромных дедовских креслах' ['I am writing to you whilst sitting in my grandfather's huge armchair'] (*Sy* 106). Although the extrafictional reader clearly cannot be the intended recipient of the letters, the use of the personal pronoun, 'ты' ('you'), and its related forms, nevertheless creates the impression that she is being directly addressed. This encourages an even greater degree of narrator–reader identification than is envisaged by Todorov as essential to the fantastic. The reader is given the impression of enjoying intimate contact with the narrator and is also encouraged to identify with the addressee of the letters who is the real 'ты'. As I will show, this comes to be of crucial significance in the later stages of the story. This model of direct address therefore encourages the reader to grant a greater degree of credence to Mikhail Platonovich than might otherwise be the case.

The initial epistolary format of Odoevskii's story means that the methods available for depicting narrator personality are less complex than in *La Vénus d'Ille*. To a certain extent, characterization is achieved directly by the narrator himself as his letters set forth an account of his beliefs and attitudes. The type of depiction through contrast with other characters observed in Mérimée's story is theoretically ruled out by the indirect and one-sided nature of Mikhail Platonovich's letter-writing. Nevertheless, this method does still operate as the reader learns about Mikhail Platonovich thanks, in part, to his reports of interaction with other characters. Furthermore, as in Mérimée, the depiction of this narrator as an essentially reasonable man relies upon reference to a series of underlying dichotomies.

A degree of the authority granted to the archaeologist-historian narrator in Mérimée's story can be attributed to the fact that he is an educated urban visitor to a provincial community. Mikhail Platonovich is cast in broadly the same role with similar consequences. The major caveat to this symmetry is that Odoevskii's narrator has been sent to the countryside, not in search of knowledge, but to recover from a bout of spleen; and this perhaps foreshadows the distinctions between the narrators of the two stories. Still, his first letter sets out his urban credentials and illustrates his unfamiliarity with his new surroundings, which he uses to establish superiority over his rural neighbours:

> я, как новый помещик, сделал визиты всем моим соседям, которых, к счастию, немного; говорил с ними об охоте, который терпеть не могу, о земледелии, которого не понимаю, и об их родных, о которых сроду не слыхивал. (*Sy* 107)

> [As the new landowner, I have called in on all my neighbours, of whom thankfully there are few; I have talked to them about hunting, which I can't stand, about farming, which I don't understand, and about their families, of whom I have never heard in my life.]

Mikhail Platonovich's early attitude appears to be somewhat less reasonable than might generically be expected as he advocates that the ignorance in which these characters live is blissful. He declares himself attracted by their 'полное равнодушное невежество' ['completely indifferent ignorance'] (ibid.) and attempts to ingratiate himself by dismissing the value of knowledge:

> я им высказал, что, по моему мнению, лучше ничего не знать, нежели знать столько, сколько знают наши ученые, что ничто столько не противно счастию человека, как много знать, и что невежество никогда еще не мешало пищеварению.

> [I told them that, in my opinion, it was better to know nothing than to know as much as our scientists know, that nothing was more contrary to human happiness than being knowledgeable, and that ignorance had never yet hindered digestion.]
> (*Sy* 107–08)

In spite of these claims, Mikhail Platonovich never abandons the condescending tone which typifies his commentary upon his new rural surroundings. It comes as little surprise, therefore, when, in the following letter, he changes tack and acknowledges his praise of ignorance to have been ironic. Mikhail Platonovich begins his second letter with the complaint that his neighbours are boring him to death and confidently states: 'я уверился, мой друг: невежество не спасение' ['I am convinced, my friend: ignorance is not salvation'] (*Sy* 109). He reveals that all the same vices exist in his provincial neighbours as are to be found in educated society, the sole difference being that they are exacerbated by ignorance. Close observation of their behaviour has made the narrator realize 'отчего безнравственность так тесно соедина с невежеством, а невежество с несчастием' ['why immorality is so closely linked to ignorance, and ignorance to unhappiness'] (*Sy* 110). Having initially attempted to fit in with his neighbours by affecting a regard for ignorance, Mikhail Platonovich now violently condemns the existence of the uneducated man. By chronicling the various vices and shortcomings of the uneducated rural type, and distancing himself from them, the narrator implicitly characterizes himself as possessing the contrary and, consequently, positive traits. By the same token, he persuades the reader to regard him as a reasonable and authoritative voice.

Just as has been seen to be the case in *La Vénus d'Ille*, the fundamental benchmark against which the narrator's reliability is measured in *The Sylph* is the rational/irrational dichotomy. The irony which sees the narrator's rationality become the key to the introduction of the irrational in Mérimée is also replicated in Odoevskii. Mikhail Platonovich's sense of intellectual and moral distance from his rural neighbours takes on physical form when he decides to lock himself away on his estate. However, his desire to avoid ignorance leads him to discover the very element which will oblige him to challenge his previous convictions about the nature of the world: the cabbalistic books. To break the monotony of his self-imposed exile and despite his previously stated loathing for books, the narrator reluctantly asks whether the house contains a library. His steward's reply hints at the potentially malefic character of what the shelves contain: 'по смерти дядюшки вашего тетушка изволила запечатать эти шкафы и отнюдь не приказывала никому трогать' ['after your uncle died, your aunt went and sealed the cupboards and ordered that henceforth no one was to touch them'] (*Sy* 111). Mikhail Platonovich shows himself to be entirely unimpressed by this veiled warning when he seeks no further details and simply asks that the cupboards be opened. The warning pre-emptively casts the cabbalistic books in a negative light and, by defying it, the narrator displays his refusal to be intimidated by superstition.

The account of Mikhail Platonovich's initial experience of these books further promotes his characterization as a reasonable man in the unenlightened provinces. Towards the close of the second letter, he acknowledges the incongruity of his reading this type of book:

> и теперь, вообрази себе меня, человека в XIX-м веке, сидящего над огромными фолиантами и со всеусердием читающего рассуждение: о первой материи, о всеобщем электре, о душе солнца, о северной влажности, о звездных духах и о прочем тому подобном. (*Sy* 111)

> [and now, imagine me, a man of the nineteenth century, sitting studying huge folios and assiduously reading their argument: on prime matter, on elemental electricity, on the soul of the sun, on northern humidity, on stellar spirits, and all manner of things like that.]

His unmistakable implication is that a man of his time, steeped in rational knowledge, has no business indulging in writings which discuss such fanciful topics. Although he does not explicitly dismiss their contents out of hand, his qualification of reading them as 'смешно, и скучно, и любопытно' ('amusing, and tedious, and interesting') (ibid.) rings with the type of superiority displayed by Mérimée's narrator towards his hosts. It is hardly the reaction of a man predisposed to a belief in the irrational and supernatural. In fact, the early failure of Mikhail Platonovich to be swayed by the cabbalistic books is effectively illustrated by the fact that he abandons discussion of their contents to concentrate upon a topic of more immediate interest: his pretty neighbour, Katia.

From the closing paragraphs of this second letter until the fifth, the narrator's experiment with cabbalism is contrasted with his nascent romantic relationship with Katia. Where cabbalism represents the supernatural, the natural is embodied by the planned nuptials between Mikhail Platonovich and his neighbour. Although these two occupations incarnate opposing values and vie for attention in the narrator's letters, both, in their own way, portray him as a predominantly reasonable and practical man. Mikhail Platonovich's early reactions to the cabbalistic books are characterized by an ironic scepticism which undermines any expectation of the supernatural being realized. Typical is his argument that the decision to experiment with alchemy is motivated by a desire to escape boredom: 'чего не выдумает безделие!' ['what idleness won't think up!'] (*Sy* 111). The narrator does not blindly believe in the experiments but rather finds many of the formulae 'смешны до крайности' ['funny in the extreme'] (ibid.). This matter-of-fact, seemingly underwhelmed approach to cabbalism is sustained as he explains why he chooses to carry out an experiment with sunlight and water. His choice is not predicated on any deep-seated desire to conjure up a water sylph; rather it is determined by the fact that the ingredients are easy to come by. The initial failure of the experiment prompts a further debasing of the supernatural through irony. Although a water sylph has not yet appeared, he says that drinking the water in the vase has meant that 'сон мой сделался спокойнее' ['my sleep has become calmer'] (*Sy* 112). Such remarks succeed in distinguishing Mikhail Platonovich from the type of credulous characters who might be thought to experiment in such fields.

This debasement of the supernatural is mirrored by Mikhail Platonovich's light-hearted and distinctly unromantic approach to his relationship with Katia. This is evident as early as the first letter when, philosophizing over the relative merits of knowledge and ignorance, he is led to mention her thanks to an unfortunate association of ideas:

> Но к черту философия! она умеет вмешаться в мысли самого животного человека... Кстати о животных: у иных из моих соседей есть прехорошенькие дочки (...). У одного из ближайших моих соседей, очень богатого человека, есть дочь, которую, кажется, зовут Катенькой (...). (*Sy* 108)

> [But to hell with philosophy! It can interfere with the thoughts of the most bestial of men.... Speaking of the bestial, some of my neighbours have the most attractive daughters [...]. One of my nearest neighbours, a very rich man, has a daughter whom it seems is called Katenka [...].]

The irony of being prompted to make a first mention of his future wife by the adjective 'bestial' is impossible to miss.[7] What is more, Mikhail Platonovich's mention of Katia's father's wealth hints at a somewhat mercenary attitude. The motif of financial gain is reiterated when he reveals the reasons for his interest in Katia: 'все, что я ни слышу об ней, все показывает, что она, как называли в старину, предостойная девица, т.е. имеет большое приданое' ['everything that I hear about her, everything shows that she is what used to be called in the old days a good match, that is to say she has a large dowry'] (*Sy* 111). In the fourth letter, Mikhail Platonovich informs his correspondent that Katia is 'head over heels' in love with him, and yet, still, his consideration of a possible union is dominated by practical matters. The idea of marriage is suggested by Katia's father who hints that it could resolve an outstanding feud over disputed woodland. The narrator is far more inclined to consider making a proposal because of these business, and other selfish, considerations than because of Katia's charms:

> женившись на ней, я кончу глупую тяжбу и сделаю хоть одно доброе дело в жизни: упрочу благосостояние людей, мне подвластных; одним словом, мне очень хочется жениться на Кате, зажить степенным помещиком, поручить жене управление всеми делами, а самому по целым дням молчать и курить трубку. (*Sy* 114)

> [by marrying her I would put an end to this stupid lawsuit and do at least one good deed in my life: I would guarantee the welfare of the people dependent on me. In a word, I would really like to marry Katia, start living like a sedate landowner, hand over the running of everything to my wife, and myself keep silent for days on end, smoking my pipe.]

Such comments achieve a characterization of Mikhail Platonovich which is very similar to that created by his discussion of cabbalism. Here is a man with few romantic sentiments who prefers the practical, uncomplicated side of life.[8] The views he espouses during these early stages, however, do not remain unaltered as the story progresses.

Just as Mikhail Platonovich's opinions on the benefits of ignorance have wavered, so his judgement upon cabbalism also changes. In the latter half of the third letter, he begins to suggest that the contents of the manuscripts should not be dismissed out of hand:

> Посреди разных глупостей, показывающих младенчество физики, я нашел много мыслей глубоких; многие из этих мыслей могли казаться ложными в XVIII-м веке, но теперь большая часть из них находит себе подтверждение в новых открытиях. [...] Словом, смейся надо мною как хочешь, но я тебе повторяю, что эти позабытые люди достойны нашего внимания. (*Sу* 113)

> [Among the various silly ideas demonstrating the infancy of physics, I have found many profound thoughts; many of these thoughts may have seemed false in the eighteenth century, but now most of them are finding confirmation in the new discoveries. [...] In a word, laugh at me as you wish, but I repeat to you that these forgotten men are worthy of our attention.]

The narrator characterizes himself as a nineteenth-century positivist who, far from indulging in irrational flights of fancy, is interested in proving the scientific logic of the cabbalists' thoughts and rediscovering 'знан[ия] которые теперь потерялись' ['the knowledge we have now lost'] (ibid.). Therefore, while Mikhail Platonovich's initial tendency to debase the books' contents recedes, he retains a certain critical detachment from the ideas they contain. He persists in pleading for a consideration of their contents from a scientific rather than a sentimental standpoint. This overwhelmingly positivist and practical approach to radically different aspects of life greatly contributes to the evaluation of Mikhail Platonovich as a reliable voice. This conferring of authority is of crucial importance to the reader's interpretation of descriptions contained in the sixth and seventh letters when the narrator's assessment of the validity of cabbalistic beliefs shifts fundamentally.

In the run-up to this eventual introduction of the supernatural, the depiction of Mikhail Platonovich as a reasonable man is thrust to the fore. In letters four and five, discussion of the benefits of marriage preclude any mention of the progress of the cabbalistic experiment. The apparent victory of the worldly realm signified by such focus ensures maximum shock value for the subsequent introduction of the supernatural in letter six. My discussion in Part 1 of this chapter has shown how the ambiguous syntax in these descriptions is focused on the form taken by the supernatural, rather than on its actual existence. By looking in more detail at Mikhail Platonovich's beliefs, it is possible, on the one hand, to understand why this should be the case and, on the other, to appreciate the role played in the experience of hesitation by contradictory expectations.

The fifth letter closes with a confident invitation from Mikhail Platonovich to his correspondent to come and visit the happy couple. The hesitant tone in the opening lines of the sixth could not be more different. He opens with the disclaimer, 'ты меня почтешь сумасшедшим' ['you will think I am mad'] (*Sу* 115), to show his awareness that the description which follows might not be believed. However, in a statement which illustrates the fundamental shift in his opinions, the narrator declares his belief in the changes occurring in his vase of water: 'я не могу сомневаться в том, что я видел и что вижу всякий день собственными глазами' ['I cannot doubt what I have seen and what I see every day with my own eyes'] (ibid.). Part of the reader's hesitation at this juncture comes from the difficulty she has in reconciling these new beliefs in the transformation of a signet ring with the previously espoused, eminently practical ones. Between the close of the fifth letter and the opening of the sixth, therefore, the reader is transported from the apparent victory of the rational to the entirely contrary position. Now a belief in the irrational events occurring in the vase has the upper hand. If the narrator had previously displayed an ill-considered predisposition to believe unquestioningly in the claims of the cabbalists, the accounts contained in these letters would provoke no such ambiguity of interpretation. It is precisely the initial characterization of this narrator as a reasonable and unromantic figure which guarantees the reader's uncertainty. Conversely, the portrayal of this narrator as an essentially reasonable character lends his voice a reliability, which means that his claims cannot simply be dismissed out of hand. Earlier, he has assessed the cabbalists' theories analytically; this makes it less likely that the apparently irrational descriptions now encountered will be explained away as nothing more than a hallucination, for example. This likelihood is further reduced by the fact that this analytical approach remains evident in the quasi-scientific manner in which Mikhail Platonovich examines the vase:

я долго повторял свой опыт, размышляя над этим странным явлением. — Я несколько раз переливал воду из одной вазы в другую: всякий раз то же явление повторялось с удивительною точностию — и между тем оно не изъяснимо никакими физическими законами. (*Sy* 116)

[I repeated my experiment for a long time, reflecting upon this strange phenomenon. Several times I poured the water from one vase into another: every time the same phenomenon recurred with a surprising exactness — and at the same time it was inexplicable by any law of physics.]

It is the narrator's measured and reasonable observation of disturbing phenomena which encourages the reader to confer upon his descriptions a certain degree of credence and not simply to dismiss them as the ravings of a deranged mind.

In fact, it is feasible to argue that, over the course of letters six and seven, the nature of the narrator's claims is such that the reader might seriously consider granting them full credence. That is, the reader could resolve her hesitation by admitting that the rules governing the fictional world are not those which operate in the rational, actual world. Crucial to this possibility is the fact that the various syntactic devices which allow interpretative ambiguity to exist elsewhere in these two letters are entirely absent from the final paragraph of the seventh. This is explained because Mikhail Platonovich's own initial uncertainty evaporates, his earlier confidence returns, and he categorically declares:

О, теперь я верю кабалистам; я удивляюсь даже, как прежде я смотрел на них с насмешкою недоверчивости. Нет, если существует истина на сем свете, то она существует только в их творениях. (*Sy* 117)

[Oh, now I believe the cabbalists; I am even surprised that before I should have looked upon them with derision and mistrust. No, if a truth does exist in this world, then it exists only in their works.]

Such a direct and explicit declaration of belief in the supernatural illustrates how, at the close of the seventh letter, this initially reasonable personality with his practical and financial preoccupations has undergone fundamental changes. This direct claim, coupled with the reliability granted to the narrator's voice in view of previously expressed opinions, should be sufficient to persuade the reader to respect his interpretation and resolve hesitation by believing in the reality of the water sylph's existence.

Part 3: Narrative Levels and Relative Authority

Any inclination towards such a resolution of hesitation in *The Sylph* is forcibly denied by a two-step transition effected in the structure of the text. For the duration of the opening seven letters, the text has presented the reader with a single narrative voice. Although the views of this voice have not remained static, they have been able to stand unchallenged owing to the monophonic nature of the text. This status quo is disrupted and the irrational version of events which has steadily been gaining ground is challenged by the introduction of two additional voices. What can be considered to be the second half of *The Sylph* is constituted by one letter from Mikhail Platonovich's neighbour to the same addressee and by extracts from the 'рассказ' ['account'] of this addressee. This change in narrative format introduces heteroglossia into the text and drastically modifies the reader's experience and interpretation of fictional events.

Purely on the basis of the four texts discussed so far in this study, it is possible to see that the presence of a multiplicity of voices is a convention of literary narratives. Discourse theorists commonly interrogate such a multiplicity by mapping the different voices onto a framework of narrative levels. For Genette, Abbé Prévost's *Manon Lescaut* (1731), in which the hero's act of narration is contained within a discourse performed by the marquis de Renoncour, provides the perfect paradigm for a discussion of how such levels function. He offers the following definition (1972, 238) of the distinction between the various narrative levels operating within a text: 'tout événement raconté par un récit est à un niveau diégétique immédiatement supérieur à celui où se situe l'acte narratif producteur de ce récit' ['each event recounted by a narrative is at a diegetic level immediately superior to that in which the narrative act producing the account is situated']. Genette posits the existence of three possible narrative levels within any given text: the 'extradiegetic level' is located at a position immediately superior to the main narrative and is concerned with its narration; the 'diegetic level' is represented by events narrated by the extradiegetic level; while the 'metadiegetic level' involves stories told by the fictional characters. The visualization of the various voices operating within a given narrative as forming different strata indicates the underlying concept of a hierarchy of voices. Lanser (1981, 136) acknowledges the importance of this idea of hierarchy to the reader's reaction to the text: 'The concept of narrative levels is structurally significant because it signals differences among narrative voices that must be clarified if we are to recognise the relations of subordination and authority generated by a given text'. Mieke Bal makes these relations explicit when she comments (1997, 52) that 'the dependence of the actor's text with regard to the narrator's text should be seen as the dependence of a subordinate clause to a main clause'. Most important for the purposes of this discussion is the convention that states that any (metadiegetic) act of narration embedded in the diegetic level enjoys a lesser degree of authority because it depends for its existence upon that diegetic narrative. In *La Vénus d'Ille*, the failure of the archaeologist-historian's attempts definitively to impose a rational explanation for Alphonse's death is ensured by the appearance of an alternative voice which, albeit indirectly, challenges his interpretation. Consideration of this voice's position in the hierarchy of levels suggests that the reader should grant the account it gives less authority than that accorded to the narrator. However, as will be illustrated in the second half of this section, the exploitation of an additional narrative technique counteracts the inferiority dictated by the hierarchy of levels. Similarly in *The Sylph*, uncertainty is sustained because the two later voices make claims regarding the interpretation of events which overtly contradict those made by Mikhail Platonovich. However, in the case of Odoevskii's story, the mixed narrative format renders the conventional notion of levels and the relative authority of voices inapplicable. It is, in large part, the disruption of this model which explains the reader's inability to resolve her uncertainty.

The first signal that *The Sylph* disrupts the conventional system of narrative levels is the fact that the act of narration constituted by the eighth letter does not depend for its existence upon the voice of Mikhail Platonovich. Because it is not embedded in the account of this first narrator, it is difficult to attribute it a lesser degree of authority. Indeed, this has to be the case in epistolary narratives where the various speech acts stand independently from one another.[9] The subsequent appearance of extracts from the journal account of a third voice further complicates the situation. Given its appearance within a journal, this third narrating voice, like the second, cannot be considered to rely on the first for its existence and so should not be subordinate to it. The lack of interdependence between these three voices makes it difficult to establish a clear hierarchy of authority amongst them. In fact, initially, the unexpected replacement of Mikhail Platonovich's voice creates confusion regarding the identity of the other two voices. While the title to the eighth letter names the sender as Gavril Sofronovich Rezhenskii and the recipient as 'издатель' ['publisher'], the reader cannot immediately equate either figure to characters already known in the fictional world. However, when Rezhenskii reveals that he has been engaged in a lawsuit with Mikhail Platonovich and that the addressee of his letter is a close friend of Platonovich's, the cognitive gap can be filled. By mapping these details back onto information already provided, the reader is able to recognize the author of this eighth letter as Katia's father, and its publisher recipient as the addressee of Mikhail Platonovich's letters.

The uncertainty, which had seemed as if it might be resolved by Platonovich's declarations in the seventh letter, is reintroduced when Rezhenskii offers quite different opinions upon events. His rational personality is evident when he declares that he believed his prospective son-in-law's withdrawal from society to be due to reasons of 'ill-health' and that later '[он] полагал, что он хочет завести поташный завод' ['[he] supposed that he wanted to set up a potash factory'] (*Sy* 118). This latter supposition mirrors the juxtaposition constructed in the opening letters between the marvellous realm of the cabbalists' beliefs and the banal everyday reality of the landowner. However, it is ironically undermined owing to its status as a passage of repeated temporality: the period of time being accounted for here by Rezhenskii has previously been described at first hand by Mikhail Platonovich.[10] The reader enjoys superiority over Rezhenskii because the earlier letters have provided her with information he does not possess. Consequently, the reader can be quite sure that building a potash factory is not what prevents Mikhail Platonovich from visiting his prospective father-in-law. The rationalizing effort is thus mocked from the outset. Rezhenskii himself recognizes the fallacy of his initial suspicion in the second half of his letter and suggests that, like his late uncle before him, Mikhail Platonovich may have become involved in cabbalistic pursuits. The challenge offered to the initial narrator by this second voice is clearly established as Rezhenskii categorically states that 'чернокнижию не верю' ['I don't believe in black magic'] (ibid.). This summary dismissal of the otherworldly is reinforced by Rezhenskii's request to the publisher: 'поспешить вашим сюда приездом для вразумления Михаила Платоновича' ['hasten your arrival here so as to bring Mikhail Platonovich to his senses'] (*Sy* 119). The plea from Rezhenskii to bring his daughter's suitor 'to his senses' implicitly challenges Mikhail Platonovich's claims regarding the existence of a supernatural, 'other' realm. It suggests rather that he has become the victim of madness.

The autonomy of the voices of Mikhail Platonovich and Rezhenskii theoretically gives each the same degree of diegetic authority. The two versions of events they offer could, therefore, be taken to be equally valid. In practice, however, it is evidently not the case that Rezhenskii's suggestions convince the reader that Mikhail Platonovich hallucinates the creation of a water sylph. The influence which this second epistolary voice is capable of exerting upon the reader's interpretation of events is restricted by the brevity of its presence: its only appearance is in this eighth letter. Minimal presence is not the only reason, however. The reader's scepticism is also triggered by the quality of information provided by Rezhenskii. He restricts himself to sweeping dismissals of events which he has not witnessed at first hand: he admits that the allegation of Mikhail Platonovich staring into a carafe of water is no more than rumour, for instance. Such indirect access must restrict the authority which can be attributed to his voice. Nevertheless, its mere appearance plays a significant role, breaking the monopoly enjoyed thus far by Mikhail Platonovich and proposing as it does an alternative version of events. It also functions as an important intermediary stage which prepares the ground for the appearance of the third voice and the more forceful proposition of a rational explanation it offers.

A full understanding of the part played in the provocation of hesitation by this third voice necessitates a brief discussion of the personality it displays. At the point when the publisher's voice makes its first direct appearance in the narrative, the reader is not entirely ignorant of its characteristics. Information contained within the preceding eight letters has served to create an image of him as a rational and knowledgeable man. The simple fact that Rezhenskii asks him to try to make Mikhail Platonovich see sense gives an indication of the regard in which he is held. This characterization has, in fact, begun during the first seven letters as Mikhail Platonovich addresses his correspondent as a friend whom he holds in high regard and whose advice he seeks on certain matters. For instance, the reversal in his attitude towards the ignorance of his neighbours owes something to the advice of the publisher, as he acknowledges:

правду ты мне писал, что я напрасно сообщаю им мои иронические замечания об ученых и что мои слова, возвышая их глупое самолюбие, еще больше сбивают их с толка. (*Sy* 109)

[you rightly wrote that I was wrong to share with them my ironic remarks about learned people and that my words, by raising their stupid pride, would only confuse them even more.]

The reader can infer additional details regarding the publisher's personality thanks to references which Mikhail Platonovich makes to his friend's views on his marriage to Katia. In the closing lines of the fourth letter, he has asked the publisher whether he is fit to be a husband, whether his marriage will cure his bout of spleen, or whether he should wait longer. At the beginning of the next letter, Mikhail Platonovich thanks his correspondent for his 'решительность, [...] советы и [...] благословление' ['decisiveness, [...] advice and [...] blessing'] (*Sy* 114) and promptly gallops off to make his proposal.

Remarks made by Mikhail Platonovich during the crucial sixth and seventh letters go further in casting the publisher as a figure embodying reason. His admission that the publisher might think him mad when he recounts the occurrences in the vase has been noted earlier. This is reinforced when he suggests at the same time, 'ты будешь смеяться, бранить меня...' ['you will laugh at me and rebuke me...'] (*Sy* 115). It is clear that Mikhail Platonovich does not expect his correspondent to be sympathetic to his supernatural claims. The opening lines of the seventh letter oblige the reader to infer the publisher's response on the evidence of Mikhail Platonovich's words:

Нет, мой друг, ты ошибся и я также. Я предопределен быть свидетелем великого таинства природы и возвестить его людям, напомнить им о той чудесной силе, которая находится в их власти и о которой они забыли. (*Sy* 116)

[No, my friend, you were mistaken and so was I. I am predestined to be the witness of a great mystery of nature and to proclaim it to people, to remind them of the wondrous force that is within their power and which they have forgotten.]

The first line above clearly invites the reader to imagine that the publisher has somehow attempted to contradict Mikhail Platonovich's unlikely claims. Taken together, these comments and the inferences which they encourage characterize the third narrative voice as belonging to a reasonable man whose advice is worth seeking and who is unwilling to relinquish his belief in the rational. The declaration in the lines above not only illustrates Mikhail Platonovich's convictions but effectively establishes a contrast between these and the beliefs of the publisher. It is this conflict which proves to be the central driving force behind the ambiguity in the second half of the story.

Personality makes an unmistakable contribution to the degree of authority bestowed upon the voice of the publisher, but it is not the only factor. The responsibility which this figure possesses for the presentation of the narrative as a whole also needs to be taken into account. The problems posed to the conventional hierarchy of authority between voices in *The Sylph* are exacerbated by the identification of the third voice as that of the publisher. Although not conventionally embedded in it, the two voices in the letters might therefore be considered to be subordinate to this figure's account.

He is the recipient of all eight letters and, as publisher, is responsible for presenting them to the reader in the form in which they appear. And this responsibility implies authority. Recognition of the publisher figure as a fictional construct not responsible for the publication of the story in the actual world does not negate the question of relative authority. For the purposes of this discussion, it is sufficient to state that the third voice in the narrative enjoys at least as much authority as has been bestowed upon the initial narrating voice.[11] Thanks to the diametrically opposed views offered by Mikhail Platonovich and the publisher, this equality of authority will be seen to play a central role in sustaining hesitation. One final remark concerning the authority and impact of this third narrating voice needs to be made. As I have noted earlier, the direct 'I–you' address generated by the epistolary format invites the reader to place herself in the position of the recipient of the eight letters. This narrative situation assumes far greater significance when the recipient of the letters, the 'you' the reader has identified with, steps directly into the text as the publisher. The degree of authority granted by the reader to the claims made by this third voice will undoubtedly be elevated as a consequence of the sense of identification encouraged between her and the narrator. Whilst this narrative situation may not guarantee that the reader will give full credence to the rational claims made by the publisher, it unquestionably results in the bestowal of a degree of authority which is not solely dependent upon the validity of his views.

The hesitation generated during the journal section of *The Sylph* is a consequence of the publisher interpreting Mikhail Platonovich's opinions and behaviour in a rational manner. This authoritative figure directly challenges the earlier supernatural claims with an insistence that these are nothing more than the beliefs of a madman. The interpretative difficulties provoked by these contradictory views are compounded by the fact that neither voice, upon the evidence of the text, can exploit superior authority in order to prevail. The rational approach of the publisher is revealed when his first course of action involves seeking the advice of a doctor. In the fantastic, doctors stand as the embodiment of rational, scientific knowledge, the enemy of the supernatural.[12] *The Sylph* aligns itself with this convention when the publisher's counsellor reacts to being shown Mikhail Platonovich's letters by saying: 'все это очень понятно, [...] и совсем не ново для медика... Ваш приятель просто с ума сошел...' ['all this is quite understandable, [...] and absolutely nothing new to a medical man... Your friend has simply gone mad...'] (*Sy* 119). This statement is the first explicit refutation of the supernatural based on direct evidence provided in the story: Mikhail Platonovich's interpretation of events should not be believed because it is the product of an unstable mind. Whilst it might be tempting to assign lesser authority to the doctor's diagnosis because of its indirect nature, it must be remembered that it is based on the same evidence as has been presented to the reader: Mikhail Platonovich's letters. The publisher proves his reliable credentials, and distinguishes himself from the excessively rational narrator in *La Vénus d'Ille*, by refusing to give premature credence to the doctor's conclusion:

> Но перечтите его письма, [...] есть ли в них малейший признак сумасшествия? отложите в сторону странный предмет их, и они покажутся хладнокровным описанием физического явления... (*Sy* 119)

[But read his letters again, [...] is there in them even the slightest sign of madness? Put to one side their strange subject matter and they seem like a cold-blooded description of a physical phenomenon...]

These rational and irrational interpretations are then brought into closer proximity when extracts from Mikhail Platonovich's journal are presented within the publisher's own account. Arriving at his friend's estate, the publisher espies pages covered with writing lying on a table and records what he is able to make out. In its description of how Mikhail Platonovich, accompanied by the water sylph, leaves the human world to enter a new, harmonious realm of eternal light, this passage represents a prime example of Odoevskii's metaphysical thought. It also offers clear evidence of the influence of the occult tradition and German Romantic models upon the story. Whilst these 'отрывки' ['fragments'] have interested critics as an example both of the author's philosophical thought and his esoteric sources, they make no real contribution to my analysis of hesitation. What is worth stating, however, is that their direct presentation clearly serves as a reminder to the reader of Mikhail Platonovich's supernatural claims and beliefs. In its description of two interlinked universes and of the ability to travel through time and space with no regard for the rational rules governing these phenomena, the fragments challenge the perceived functioning of the natural world. The absence of syntactic devices betraying uncertainty illustrates, just as in the seventh letter, that these apparently irrational possibilities are granted full belief by their original narrating voice.

The reliability of this description is called into question, however, by the terms in which the publisher both introduces and reacts to it. Both before and after the passage is presented, he echoes the sentiments of the doctor by implying that Mikhail Platonovich is not in full possession of his rational capacities. Elements within the publisher's account of the scene which greets him and his doctor companion as they arrive at Mikhail Platonovich's house suggest he has been swayed by the diagnosis of insanity: 'когда мы подошли, он не узнал нас, хотя глаза его были открыты; в них горел какой-то дикий огонь; на все наши слова он не отвечал нам ни слова' ['when we approached, he did not recognize us, although his eyes were open: in them blazed some sort of wild light; he did not reply to anything we said'] (Sy 120). While the opinion is not expressed overtly here, motifs such as the 'wild light' in his friend's eyes make it quite clear that the publisher considers Mikhail Platonovich to have lost his grip on reason. Prefacing the extracts of the journal with such a prejudicial description ensures that their validity is called into question even before they can produce their full impact. Similarly, the publisher's account of the nature of the final lines of the fragments casts further doubt upon their trustworthiness:

Дальше почти невозможно было ничего разобрать; то были несвязные, разнородные слова: «любовь... растение... электричество... человек... дух». Наконец, последние строки были написаны какими-то странными неизвестными мне буквами и прерывались на каждой странице... (Sy 123)

[Further on it was almost impossible to make anything out; there were only disconnected, mixed-up words: 'love... plant... electricity... human being... spirit'. Finally, the last lines were written in some strange kind of letters that I did not know and which broke off on every page...]

By highlighting the journal's eventual descent into illegibility, its inclusion of confused words and its switch to an unknown language, the publisher openly questions the degree of credibility which can be attributed to beliefs expressed throughout it. It is as if he were attempting to convince the reader not to believe in the existence of the other world described by the journal because, ultimately, the account of it proves indecipherable even to a man of his talents.

The conflict between the opposing interpretations of events reaches its climax in the publisher's description of his efforts to help Mikhail Platonovich. He appears to accept the doctor's diagnosis of madness and treats his friend as a patient in need of a cure. This rational, quasi-scientific approach to the problem of insanity, in which it is treated as little more than a physical ailment, is neatly illustrated in the description of the publisher and doctor's first actions: 'запрятив подальше все эти бредни, мы приступили к делу и начали с того, что посадили нашего мечтателя в бульонную ванну' ['having cleared all these ravings out of the way, we got down to business and started off by sitting our dreamer in a bouillon bath'] (ibid.). The publisher further undermines the validity of Mikhail Platonovich's account by referring to him not simply as a 'dreamer' but also as a 'чудак' ['crank'] and, on five occasions, as 'больной' ['the patient']. He is repeatedly subjected to bouillon baths and fed medicine in an attempt to force him out of his torpor (*Sy* 123–24). In contrast, the publisher characterizes his ministerings to Mikhail Platonovich as 'благоразумн[ые] попечени[я]' ['reasonable care'] and congratulates himself on being 'человек аккуратный' ['a conscientious man'] (*Sy* 124). The rational/irrational contrast constructed between the voices of the publisher and Mikhail Platonovich could hardly be more evident. The publisher's efforts to turn his friend's attention away from thoughts of a higher, poetic realm and towards 'вещи основательные и полезные' ['basic and useful things'] appear to be successful. This is indicated by the gradual shift in epithets he uses to refer to Mikhail Platonovich away from the negative 'patient' and toward more frequent references to him as a 'friend'. It is as if the condition for him being considered a friend is that he recovers his sanity. The publisher's apparent victory in curing Mikhail Platonovich is symbolized by an echo back to a dichotomy which has operated during the first half of *The Sylph*. The combined effect of medicine, wine, and roast beef is sufficient to lead Mikhail Platonovich to the church where he marries Katia. With this act, the conflict between cabbalism and terrestrial romantic matters, which have battled for supremacy over the course of the first seven letters, is seemingly resolved with the latter winning out.

However, these claims for the victory of the rational are not allowed to stand unchallenged. The publisher's self-congratulatory attitude towards his success is repudiated strongly by the reappearance in the narrative of the voice of Mikhail Platonovich. During the description of the cure, his voice has been suppressed, being only indirectly reported by the publisher. In the closing pages of the story, however, the publisher directly reports a conversation he has with Mikhail Platonovich a few months after the wedding. In its revelation of how both men remain faithful to their opposing beliefs, this dialogue powerfully illustrates the impossibility of finding a resolution between the two interpretations of events. When the publisher asks Mikhail Platonovich, 'ну, что, несчастлив ты, брат?' ['well then, brother, aren't you happy?'] (*Sy* 124), he evidently expects his friend to be grateful for his salvation and return to the rational world. Mikhail Platonovich proves to be nothing of the sort and refuses to renounce his beliefs. Instead, he ironizes both the publisher's rational attempts to cure him and the self-satisfaction he feels at his success. He goes on to express his own sense of frustration, loss, and sadness:

я с отчаянием вспоминаю то время, когда, по твоему мнению, я находился в сумасшествии, когда прелестное существо слетало ко мне из невидимого мира, когда оно открывало мне таинства, которых теперь я и выразить не умею, но которые были мне понятны... где это счастие? – возврати мне его! (*Sy* 125)

[I recall with despair that time when, in your opinion, I was mad, when a charming creature flew down to me from the invisible world, and when it opened to me secrets which now I cannot even express, but which were comprehensible to me then... where is that happiness? Give it back to me!]

It is clear from these lines that Mikhail Platonovich still believes that he was visited by a water sylph who initiated him into an alternative realm and who showed him true happiness. For him, the cure does not symbolize a thankful return to the rational world but rather represents the loss of higher knowledge and the sense of joy which came with it. It is these lines that lead certain critics to consider the ending of *The Sylph* as essentially pessimistic and, as such, distinguished from the work of E. T. A. Hoffmann.[13]

This final plea for a belief in the existence of a supernatural realm does not sway the rational publisher in the slightest. He rather views it as a temporary return to former insanity, 'это был его последний припадок' ['this was his last attack'], and moves on to praise his friend for subsequently becoming 'совершенно порядочный человек' ['a thoroughly respectable man'] (*Sy* 126). Once again, the proof the publisher cites for this return to normality refers back to elements which have embodied practical concerns during the first eight letters: he sets up a potash factory, he introduces crop rotation, and wins several lawsuits concerning property. The publisher attempts to seal the victory of his rational beliefs by proclaiming: 'по крайней мере он теперь человек, как другие' ['at least now he is a man like the others'] (ibid.). However, the coexistence of these two voices during the dialogue on the story's final page, and their sustained espousal of contradictory beliefs, ensures that the reader is unable to follow the publisher's confident example. Neither voice wins out in the battle to establish a greater sense of reliability for its account. The reader is thus left, at the close of *The Sylph*, with two equally convinced accounts of two irreconcilable realities.

As I have shown earlier, in *La Vénus d'Ille*, the narrator's investigations in his adopted role as amateur detective lead to a series of defeats for the rational. His repeated failure to find reasonable proof to support his intruder theory allows the possibility of an irrational explanation, and consequently the hesitation of the reader, to persist. It is the introduction of an alternative voice into the narrative which sees the undermining of his rational efforts reach its climax. The natural interpretation of the death offered by the narrator is overtly challenged by the indirectly reported account of the wedding night given by Mme Alphonse. A decision to give credence to her claims that the statue of Venus is responsible for her husband's murder would lead to a classification of Mérimée's story as 'fantastique-merveilleux'. Such a move is impossible, however, in view of the contradictory claims surrounding this account's reliability. As my discussion in Part I of this chapter has shown, a measure of the ambiguity experienced during this passage stems from syntactic devices triggered by limited perspective. But these two factors do not tell the whole story. Neither is it sufficient to account for reader uncertainty simply by pointing to the passage's status as a contradictory version of events. Reader hesitation is generated by two further narrative techniques, each of which problematizes the question of the relative authority and reliability of this alternate voice.

The first of these concerns the relationship between the voice of the narrator and that of Mme Alphonse. The format of Mérimée's story means that the introduction of multiple voice is constructed according to a far more conventional model of narrative levels than is the case in *The Sylph*. Bowman (1960, 479) argues that the homodiegetic voice in *La Vénus d'Ille* represents an extreme point in the type of narrators employed by Mérimée's because:

> from an expository point of view, all he doesn't see directly is told to him, he is our only source for the tale [...]. The ideas and reactions of others are only presented through dialogue with him. He thus occupies a much more important place in the tale than does the narrator in any other of the stories.

There can be little argument that the voice of the narrator is, indeed, the most dominant in Mérimée's story. Only his voice has the ability to penetrate the boundaries of the fictional world in order to address the reader; the other characters can only address their textual counterparts. However, from the very outset, *La Vénus d'Ille* has contained other voices, presented directly, which have repeatedly suggested the possible existence of the supernatural. The less reasonable voices of the Catalan guide, Mme de Peyrehorade, and Alphonse find their strongest echo in the voice of Mme Alphonse. The impact of alternative voice, which has been an important feature throughout the text, is at its most forceful in this particular passage.

Directly contradicting the narrator's claim that Alphonse is murdered by vengeful intruders, Mme Alphonse alleges that she sees 'son mari à genoux auprès du lit, la tête à la hauteur de l'oreiller, entre les bras d'une espèce de géant verdâtre qui l'étreignait avec force' ['her husband kneeling next to the bed with his head at the same height as the pillow, in the arms of a kind of greenish giant which was forcefully embracing him'] (*V* 464). Mme Alphonse identifies this 'greenish giant' as the statue of Venus and thereby argues for a supernatural interpretation of the murder. The reader is entitled to question the reliability of Mme Alphonse's account of events because it exists on a narrative level which is, in fact, doubly subordinate to that of the narrator: it is reported by the narrator who, in turn, hears the account through the intermediary of the king's procurator of Perpignan. Therefore, existing at a metadiegetic narrative level, the accusation of the statue as Alphonse's murderer enjoys a lesser degree of authority and reliability.

The indirect reporting of Mme Alphonse's accusations justifies the procurator's repeated use of dialogue tags such as 'elle dit' or 'dit-elle'. However, these tags are employed with notably greater frequency as the account moves towards an identification of the culprit. In so doing, the procurator's desire appears to be to distance himself from Mme Alphonse's claims. He uses the tags as a means of reminding his audience that none of these far-fetched accusations are his own. Therefore, this supernatural account battles not only against the scepticism of the rational narrator, but against the incredulity of the procurator. Furthermore, mirroring the example of Mikhail Platonovich's journal extracts in *The Sylph*, the persuasive strength of Mme Alphonse's account is pre-emptively undermined by the subjective introduction it receives: 'cette malheureuse jeune personne est devenue folle [...]. Folle! tout à fait folle' ['this unfortunate young woman has gone mad [...]. Mad! Absolutely mad'] (ibid.). By means of this unequivocal declaration, the procurator clearly aligns himself with the rationalist camp and its principal adherent, the narrator, who has earlier dismissed Alphonse's accusations as drunken ravings. This is underlined by the fact that, despite reporting that Mme Alphonse repeats her accusation 'vingt fois', the procurator persists in referring to her as 'pauvre femme' and 'la malheureuse jeune personne' (ibid.).

The combination of the embedded status of this supernatural allegation and the lack of belief displayed by the diegetically superior voice permits the existence of one further narrative feature which undermines Mme Alphonse's claims. The indirect nature of the account allows the voice of the procurator to entangle itself with that of Alphonse's widow. The procurator fails to do everything that he could in order to insure that his scepticism does not contaminate the version of events supplied by Mme Alphonse. Rather, he allows his own interpretation to coexist alongside hers:

> Revenue à elle, elle revit le fantôme, ou la statue, comme elle dit toujours, immobile, les jambes et le bas du corps dans le lit, le buste et les bras étendus en avant, et entre ses bras son mari, sans mouvement. (*V* 465)

> [Having come to, she saw the ghost, or the statue, as she keeps saying, unmoving, its legs and the lower half of its body in the bed, its bust and its arms stretched out in front, and between its arms her husband, motionless.]

The parenthetical interjection suggesting that the figure Mme Alphonse witnesses at her bedside is not the statue but a ghost is clearly not her own; she never wavers from her version of events. The lack of compatibility between these two versions indicates that the former originates with the procurator and is evidence of his efforts to interpret Mme Alphonse's account in a slightly more rational manner. However, the procurator's failure to acknowledge explicitly that this suggestion has its source in his consciousness and not hers means that it appears to offer a challenge to the statue interpretation from within. Mme Alphonse's account is successfully undermined, as a consequence, both explicitly and implicitly.

Given these various factors, why then is it not possible to dismiss out of hand the claims made by Mme Alphonse? I would like to suggest that one narrative device in particular makes corroboration of her supernatural version of events eminently possible. It is, equally, this device which ensures that her voice offers a strong challenge to the dominant, rational voice of the archaeologist-historian. Up until the point at which Mme Alphonse's account of events is reported, the narrative in *La Vénus d'Ille* has been presented in a linear chronological order: the description of events in the 'siuzhet' follows the order in which events forming the 'fabula' take place. However, Mme Alphonse's testimony disrupts this linearity by being a section of repeated temporality. It is, in fact, an action replay of events that have already been presented to the reader by the narrator. The story has proceeded from the account of events on the wedding night, to the report of the discovery of Alphonse's dead body the next morning, to the description of the narrator's investigations during the following day. With the introduction of Mme Alphonse's testimony, the narrative takes a leap back in time to the wedding night.

The most overt signal that this passage replays narrative time appears in the line in Mme Alphonse's account which records how 'un coq chanta' ['a cock crowed'] (*V* 465). This line refers the reader back to the narrator's earlier account where he states:

> Il pouvait être cinq heures du matin, et j'étais éveillé depuis plus de vingt minutes, lorsque le coq chanta. Le jour allait se lever. Alors j'entendis distinctement les mêmes pas lourds, le même craquement de l'escalier que j'avais entendu avant de m'endormir. (*V* 462)

> [It might have been five o'clock in the morning, and I had been awake for more than twenty minutes, when the cock crowed. The day was about to break. Just then I distinctly heard the same heavy footsteps, the same creaking of the staircase that I had heard before falling asleep.]

The symmetry of references to the cock crow in both accounts serves as an implicit invitation to the reader to superimpose the details provided by Mme Alphonse onto those previously supplied in the narrator's description.[14] Such a mapping back of details onto this pre-existing account will see Mme Alphonse's claims gain greatly in validity. For instance, the footsteps that the narrator reports hearing on the staircase just after the cock crows correspond to the apparent departure of the statue from the bedroom as described by Alphonse's bride: 'alors la statue sortit du lit, laissa tomber le cadavre et sortit. Mme Alphonse se pendit à la sonnette' ['then the statue got out of bed, dropped the corpse, and walked out. Mme Alphonse started ringing the bell'] (*V* 465). Mme Alphonse's actions following the departure of the statue now explain the 'tintement des sonnettes' ['ringing of bells'] which prevents the narrator from falling back to sleep having heard the footsteps. His assumption that the footsteps in the morning belong to Alphonse has previously been undermined by the discovery of his dead body: it would have been almost impossible for Alphonse to have gone downstairs if he is found murdered soon afterwards in the bedroom. This part of his rationalizing attempt is now further challenged by the information contained in Mme Alphonse's account. The narrator has stated that the footsteps he hears in the morning precisely resemble those which he heard as the second set on the staircase just before falling asleep on the wedding night. Mme Alphonse's description reveals that this second set of footsteps could not have belonged to Alphonse because he was the third, and not the second, person to enter the bedroom. In her account, the second set of footsteps belongs to the statue of Venus. Indeed, the reader is led to believe that the narrator must have fallen asleep before Alphonse enters the bedroom, because he hears only two sets of footsteps whereas Mme Alphonse suggests that there should have been three. The difficulty for the reader is that this lack of coincidence in the number of footsteps might also justifiably be interpreted to indicate the contrary situation. The narrator's report of two sets of footsteps challenges Mme Alphonse's contention that the statue was the third figure in the bedroom that night.

Given that she and her husband were definitely there, if there were only two sets of footsteps, the statue of Venus could not have joined them. This passage of repeated temporality causes the reader untold problems of comprehension because it demands not only a retrospective reading but also a prospective one. The process of deciphering information moves from a linear model to one which is circular and which leaves the reader in an ontological impasse.

The introduction of Mme Alphonse's testimony into the narrative makes it possible to identify several factors which plant hesitation in the mind of the reader. The narrator's faltering rational explanation for the murder is further challenged by the voice of another character who claims the involvement of the apparently inanimate statue of Venus. If she is to resolve this uncertainty, the reader must decide to which of these versions of events she will grant credence. Belief in Mme Alphonse's version is problematized by the fact that her account exists on a narrative level twice removed from the authority of the narrator. Its reliability is further questioned owing to the fact that the voice which recounts her accusation overtly qualifies it as the result of unreason. However, simple dismissal of this description is ruled out by the correspondences revealed by the technique of repeated temporality. As noted earlier, the close of the narrative following Mme Alphonse's account does nothing to permit the resolution of hesitation, as the narrator's interpretation is further undermined by the Aragonais's alibi and the revelations concerning the diamond ring.

In its discussion of homodiegetic narratives, this second chapter has shown how the device of ambiguous syntax enjoys universal application in the fantastic. By examining narrative voices which display very different reactions to the supernatural, an appreciation of how such syntax can be used to portray a variety of perceptual situations can be reached. In *La Vénus d'Ille*, modalization is most often justified as being the consequence of limited visual perspective. In *The Sylph*, on the other hand, it is employed because Mikhail Platonovich struggles to find appropriate terms to describe what he witnesses. Although the modalization in these two works may refer to two different situations for the speaker, its result, the provocation of hesitation, remains broadly the same. My discussion of the impact of narrator personality in the homodiegetic fantastic builds upon Todorov's claims regarding the role of narrator–reader sympathy. Just as the creation of a verisimilar world with an authoritative narrative voice is of crucial importance in the heterodiegetic context, so it appears that the essential role of personality in homodiegesis is to guarantee the reliability of the narrating voice. This reliability is then exploited in two quite different ways to create uncertainty about the interpretation of events. In *La Vénus d'Ille*, it is the reasoning narrator's insistence upon the rational seemingly at all costs that actually makes the irrational appear to be the more likely state of affairs. In *The Sylph*, Mikhail Platonovich's early practical and materialistic concerns make it more difficult for the reader to dismiss his subsequent claims that the supernatural exists. However, the exploitation of narrator personality alone in homodiegetic texts is not enough to create the sustained hesitation necessary to the fantastic. In both of the texts discussed, the most interesting contribution made to ambiguous interpretation is the manipulation of multiple voices. This narrative technique can be seen to mirror the device of switches in point of view which is so effective in the heterodiegetic context. Heteroglossia refuses the imposition of a single version of events which would be likely to resolve reader uncertainty. In the fantastic, it is necessary for the additional voice(s) to contradict the interpretation being championed by the initial narrator. Not only that, optimum conditions for the genre are created when, thanks to a variety of constructions, it is impossible for the reader to grant definitively superior knowledge to any one of these voices. In these conditions, the fantastic flourishes.

Notes to Chapter 2

1. The pervasive presence of this theme in Western literary history explains why critics have had difficulty identifying the sources for Mérimée's story; see Decottignies (1962, 453–61). Ziolkowski (1977, 18–77) traces the first appearance of stories involving Venus and a ring back to c.1125 in William of Malmesbury's *Chronicle of the Kings of England*, and notes (1977, 27):

   [the figure of Venus] underwent the same process of demonisation that transformed all the classical deities during the twelfth and thirteenth centuries. Rather than ignoring or denying the existence of the classical gods, the Church found it more expedient to declare that they were nothing but devils. Venus is no longer a symbol of the classical joy of life: she has become the devil incarnate, or at least his principal agent of temptation.

   The nineteenth-century audience would have been resensitivized to this theme by the production in 1787 of Mozart's *Don Giovanni*.

2. References to *La Vénus d'Ille* are taken from the Pléiade edition of *Romans et nouvelles*, Paris: Gallimard, 1951.

3. References to *The Sylph* are taken from *Sochinenie v dvukh tomakh*, vol. 2, Moscow: Khudozhestvennaia literatura, 1981. Translation of the extracts is my own but based upon *The Salamander and Other Gothic Tales*, trans. by Neil Cornwell, London: Bristol Classical Press, 1992.

4. This technique of characterizing the homodiegetic narrator by contrasting him with other characters who display very different traits is effectively employed in Nodier's *Inès de Las Sierras*. The narrator displays a personality and belief-system which stands as a median point between that of his two friends, Sergy and Boutraix. While Sergy has 'une organisation délicate et nerveuse, [...] [une] âme ardente, [...] beaucoup de penchant pour le merveilleux' ['a delicate and nervous constitution, [...] an ardent soul, [...] a penchant for the marvellous'], Boutraix (1961, 662) adopts a policy of denying everything: 'à toutes les inductions tirées de la foi ou du sentiment, il répondait par deux mots sacramentels, accompagnés d'un haussement d'épaule: *fanatisme* et *préjugé*' ['to all those inductions informed by faith or feeling, he responded with two ritualistic words accompanied by a shrug of his shoulders: *fanaticism* and *prejudice*'] (original italics). Although the narrator does not overtly characterize himself here, his ability to critique the excesses of his friends suggests he sees himself somewhere between the two.

5. While the role of detective becomes most obvious following the death, the posterior temporality of the narrative, which creates a dual perspective, can be seen to cast the narrator into this role from the very outset of the story. The temporal stance implies that the narrator is aware of Alphonse's death before he begins to recount his narrative. Consequently, the narrative can be considered as a report of the facts leading up to this death whose organization is determined by this event. The narrator therefore describes his own efforts at detection in a text which is itself an effort to throw new light on the mystery.

6. Just such a case of interference can be noted at one point in *The Sylph* when Mikhail Platonovich writes a letter (ostensibly an element of the 'siuzhet') asking for advice concerning his engagement to Katia and it is the reply to this letter which spurs him to make a proposal (an element of 'fabula').

7. In *La Vénus d'Ille*, Alphonse is also characterized ironically thanks to the link he draws between animals and his fiancée: 'Enfin [Alphonse] en vint à me parler de sa future, par la transition d'une jument grise qu'il lui destinait' ['Finally [Alphonse] started to talk to me about his intended by means of a mention of a grey mare he was going to give her'] (*V* 452).

8. Similar attitudes to women and marriage are displayed by the eponymous hero in Rabou's *Le Ministère public*. Desalleux only begins to frequent female company on the advice of his doctor who recommends that social distractions might mitigate against his tendency to overwork which, in turn, produces his nocturnal visions. His positivist and self-serving approach to life means that love will play little or no part in his choice of a wife.

9. This said, a notion of the model of narrative levels can continue to exist. Lanser (1981, 135–36) cites the example of Choderlos de Laclos's *Les Liaisons dangereuses* in which the text's editor-figure occupies the first diegetic level of narration whilst the various correspondents all occupy the same metadiegetic level.

10. A similar instance of repeated temporality associated with a switch in point of view can be observed in *The Queen of Spades*, where the switch is from the heterodiegetic narrator to Germann (Q 332). When Germann is drawn, for a second time, to the countess's house he notices a woman sitting in the window but is unable to identify her. This information is possessed by the reader, however, because this same scene has already been narrated from the perspective of Lizaveta, who is the woman who notices the young man under her window.

11. The identification of the third narrating voice as belonging to the 'publisher' invites the reader to perform a further reconstruction of the narrative situation relevant to the characterization of this voice. If the third narrating voice is responsible for publishing the story, the subtitle 'из записок благоразумного человека' ['from the notes of a reasonable man'] must refer to him and his 'account' must be these notes.

12. Rabou's *Le Ministère public* provides a particularly clear example of this convention. Following his first confrontation with the severed head of Pierre Leroux, Desalleux seeks the advice of a doctor and recounts his experience. The matter-of-fact reaction he receives is quite typical (1963, 110):

Le docteur, qui, à force de regarder dans les cerveaux sans découvrir la moindre trace de quelque chose qui ressemblât à une âme, était arrivé à une savante conviction de matérialisme, ne manqua point de rire aux éclats en écoutant le récit de la vision nocturne. [...] Il ne fut pas d'ailleurs, comme on s'en doute, fort embarrassé d'expliquer à M. Desalleux son hallucination par un excès de tension de la fibre cérébrale, suivie d'une congestion et d'une évacuation sanguine, qui avait fait justement qu'il avait vu ce qu'il n'avait pas vu.

[The doctor who, by dint of looking into brains without finding the least trace of anything resembling a soul, had come to an informed conviction of materialism, did not miss the opportunity of bursting out laughing upon hearing the tale of the nocturnal vision. [...] Furthermore, he showed no embarrassment, as might be expected, in explaining M. Desalleux's hallucination by an excess of cerebral tension, followed by a congestion and release of blood which made him see what he did not see.]

13. Norman Ingham (1974, 185) considers the distinction between the two authors in the following terms:

We cannot overlook the fact that, while Hoffmann's heroes actually attain the magic world and receive immortality, Mikhail Platonovich is called back from it by 'rational' men. This reflects a certain pessimistic strain which runs all through Odoevskii's works.

14. The selection of a cock crow as the motif which most clearly signals the temporal duplication in these scenes might also be considered to have a symbolic value. In Potocki's *The Manuscript Found in Saragossa*, the story recounted by Emina and Zubeida, who claim to be the protagonist's cousins and who display numerous signs of potential otherworldliness, is abruptly interrupted by the first cock crow: 'At that moment we heard a cock crow and Emina stopped talking. The cock crowed a second time and a superstitious man might have expected the two beautiful girls to fly away up the chimney' (Potocki 1996, 21–22). In fantastic narratives, cock crows frequently signal the end of the supernatural's period of dominion.

CHAPTER 3

Madness and Narrative Disintegration: Hesitation and Coherence

Introduction

Madness has featured as a potentially rational explanation for the supernatural in each of the four works discussed so far. In *Spirite*, having unconsciously written the letter to Mme d'Ymbercourt, Guy de Malivert asks himself whether he is 'fou ou somnambule?' ['mad or somnambulist?']. In *The Queen of Spades*, the shock Germann receives when the countess apparently winks out at him from the losing card sends him 'out of his mind'. Both the king's procurator in *La Vénus d'Ille* and the publisher in *The Sylph* exploit madness as a means of undermining the supernatural allegations made by other characters. Each of these examples corresponds closely to the role which Todorov assigns to insanity in the genre of the fantastic. In his discussion of the 'étrange-fantastique' ['uncanny-fantastic'] sub-genre, he identifies madness as one of a number of potential elements which can reduce the supernatural and resolve hesitation:

> il y a d'abord le hasard, les coïncidences [...]; viennent ensuite le rêve [...], l'influence des drogues [...], les supercheries, les jeux truqués [...], l'illusion des sens [...], enfin la folie [...]. (*F* 50)

> [first of all there is chance, coincidences [...]; then comes the dream [...], the influence of drugs [...], tricks, fixed cards [...], the illusion of the senses [...], and finally madness [...].]

Madness, along with dreams and drugs, is labelled a 'real-imaginary' explanation. In such situations, the potential for a supernatural explanation of events is ruled out because, in reality, no event has actually taken place. It is nothing more than the product of a deranged mind.

It is undeniably the case that certain texts use madness to explain away the supernatural and to dismiss hesitation. However, Todorov's claim that madness always succeeds in reducing the supernatural to the natural is itself reductive. What I would like to argue is that there also exists a category of texts, equally belonging to the fantastic, in which madness serves no such purpose of disambiguation. Here, it is rather the case that the coincidence of madness and the supernatural renders the uncertainty characteristic of the genre more profound and more pervasive. This exacerbated hesitation is largely the result of the presence of a narrative voice which manifests deteriorating lucidity. The questionable mental state of the experiencing persona, be it narrator or protagonist, threatens the coherent quality of the discourse and the stability of the fictional world. The key factor in explaining how such perceptual unreliability leads to discursive incoherence is the existence, either actual or manufactured, of a single, isolated voice providing the reader with her information.

With its reading of Guy de Maupassant's *Le Horla* (*The Horla*) and Fedor Dostoevskii's *Двойник* (*The Double*), this chapter investigates the techniques used to create such sustained ambiguity in texts of different diegetic modes. Maupassant (1850–93) is frequently championed as the father of the modern short story in France. As well as being an accomplished exponent of the realist story, he also published over thirty 'contes fantastiques' between 1877 and 1890. In May 1887, Ollendorff published the second version of a story, *Le Horla*, which had first appeared under the same title a year earlier.[1] This 1887 version presents a diary-form homodiegetic narrative in which the narrator recounts the apparent invasion of his house and, eventually, his own self by an invisible creature. In her summary of Maupassant's story, B. E. Fitz (1972, 954) implicitly indicates its credentials as an example of the fantastic:

> Two apparently contradictory readings of *Le Horla* are suggested by the anonymous author's frequent questioning of his own sanity: 1) The first reading would assume the author to be sane and to remain sane while he becomes the slave of a foreign will. [...] 2) The second reading would assume the author to be insane, and to become increasingly alienated as he records in his journal the so-called events, which are actually hallucinations arising from his deranged faculties of perception. The equal credibility of these two readings comes from a carefully constructed ambiguity in the tale.

The homodiegetic presentation of this narrative produces what Jacques Finné (1980, 73) labels a 'du-dedans' ['from within'] record of madness in which 'le narrateur, dément lui-même, peint sa réalité' ['the narrator, himself the madman, paints his reality']. The coincidence of the roles of madman and narrator leads the reader to expect that the effects of mental disorder will make themselves felt on a discourse level. The first half of *Le Horla* depicts the narrator's struggle to comprehend a series of events which challenge the laws of the rational world. At this stage, the provocation of ambiguity is achieved through relatively conventional practice although the spectre of madness as a potential explanation looms larger than has been the case in the works discussed earlier. As *Le Horla* develops, however, the narrator's attempts to decide whether or not he is insane peter out as he becomes increasingly persuaded that he is possessed by an invisible assailant. At the same time, his ability to impose the rational falters seriously and the consequent disintegration in his discourse confronts the reader with increasing interpretative difficulties.

Fedor Dostoevskii (1821–81) is best known for the major novels written during the second half of his career, following his return from exile in Siberia. He had, however, already announced himself as a notable new talent on the St Petersburg literary scene in the years before 1849. His second novella, *The Double*, was published in February 1846, a matter of only weeks after the successful appearance of his first, *Poor Folk*. Despite the high hopes which Dostoevskii harboured for it, *The Double* met with a hostile critical reaction. Arguably, it was his belief that the execution of this project did not match the quality of the central idea, which prompted Dostoevskii to revise *The Double* repeatedly.[2] Accounts of the interpretative problems posed by the novella, such as that proposed by Victor Terras (1985, 103), make it clear why *The Double* can be considered to provoke the hesitation necessary to the fantastic:

> *The Double* showed Dostoevsky mastering that technique in E.T.A. Hoffmann's tales which makes the reader search among conflicting data with increasing frustration in an effort to decide whether the events are the fantasies of an unbalanced character or the presentation of the supernatural as real. In *The Double*, the morbidly sentimental and pretentious clerk, Golyadkin, already clinically deranged by the social pressures of his office, is finally driven to a madhouse by a series of encounters with a being who is sometimes clearly his own reflection in a glass, sometimes the embodiment of his own aggressive fantasies, sometimes an unpleasant ordinary mortal who happens to have the same name and appearance, and sometimes, in some supernatural way, himself. The massing of irreconcilable data leads the reader into a state of mind not unlike Golyadkin's.

On the one hand, the depiction of a protagonist encountering a figure who is apparently his double arouses uncertainty because it clearly contravenes the laws operating in the rational world. On the other hand, as hinted by Terras's reference to the 'clinically deranged' state of the protagonist, the difficulties faced by the reader because of this supernatural dimension are augmented by the significantly disruptive role which madness plays.

As a heterodiegetic narrative, *The Double* constructs a clear contrast to *Le Horla* in terms of the manner in which madness is likely to be depicted. Primarily, heterodiegesis implies a 'du-dehors' ['from without'] account of madness in which the narrator, acting as a discursive filter, keeps the disconcerting experiences of the unstable protagonist at a safe distance from the reader. In actual fact, the hesitation experienced by the reader of *The Double* proves to be the consequence, in large part, of the narrator's failure to play this role effectively. Dostoevskii employs a variety of techniques to ensure that the unreliable perceptual abilities of the protagonist, Goliadkin, remain unsupplemented by any other perspective, including that of the heterodiegetic voice. The comparison of the impact of madness in *Le Horla* and *The Double* undertaken in this chapter therefore reveals a striking irony. Contrary to expectations, it is, in fact, Dostoevskii's ostensibly heterodiegetic text which provides the more extreme illustration of the consequences of a single, restricted voice. The failure of his narrator to fulfil the role conventionally assigned to it results in a disintegration of the stability of the fictional world which is more acute than that encountered in *Le Horla*. It is arguably this more transgressive non-fulfilment of expectations which accounts for the criticism frequently levelled at Dostoevskii's novella. Ronald Hingley (1962, 10), for instance, contends that: 'though the ideas of "The Double" are original and foreshadow much of his later work, the execution of those ideas is not impressive. The defects of the novel are repetitiveness and lack of clarity'. Craig Cravens (2000, 66) even permits himself to offer advice on how the novella might have been improved: 'we might speculate that had Dostoevskii chosen a different narrative form, the first person for example, his idea might have emerged more clearly'. Such charges may refer accurately to stylistic features of *The Double*. However, they need not be viewed in a negative light. What I would like to argue is that the novella's narrative form, its repetitiveness, and its lack of clarity all make of it an unsettling, but highly successful, account of madness in which hesitation persists.

Part 1: Unstable Openings

In the two previous chapters, I have argued that the portrayal of a stable, mimetic fictional world and the presence of a reliable, reasonable narrative voice represent important preliminary steps in the provocation of hesitation. The introduction of the supernatural into such conditions is likely to cause uncertainty because it disrupts the prevailing sense of rational normality. However, this reliability and rationality is rarely maintained uniformly in the fantastic. In *Le Horla* and *The Double*, the disruption of this status quo is far more radical than has been seen elsewhere. Honouring the convention of fantastic stories noted particularly in Chapter 2, both of these works set up a tension between the dichotomies of reliable/unreliable and rational/irrational from the outset. However, the reader is unsettled by a series of contradictory indicators regarding the authority and beliefs of the narrating voice and the nature of the fictional world. These signals effectively foreshadow the struggle which will ensue in the texts between control and disintegration of the discourse.

The most notable of the changes effected to *Le Horla* between its 1886 and 1887 publications is the shift from a framed story in which an initial heterodiegetic voice introduces an embedded homodiegetic voice to a narrative presented in diary format. This second version comprises forty entries beginning on 8 May and concluding on 10 September in an undisclosed year. The crucial consequence of this distinction in narrative mode concerns the degree of authority which can be attributed to the narrator and his speech act in each case. The non-journal format of the first version permits the direct presence of additional voices including, in particular, that of the respected doctor Marrande, which verify the truth of the supernatural claims made by the narrator. These voices counteract the lesser degree of authority which might be granted to this account because of its existence at an embedded narrative level. In the 1887 version, the journal format effectively imposes the presence of a sole homodiegetic voice — that of the diarist. Consequently, the prospect of external validation for any irrational claims is removed and the reliability of the account must come under greater scrutiny. Jacques Neefs (1980, 234–35) offers the following comparison of the two versions:

> Quand le récit a pour seul garant le sujet narrateur, il doit conjurer la possibilité d'illusion qui l'affecte par le recours à des témoins. C'est d'une certaine manière, ce que refuse la seconde version, plus ouverte à l'indétermination. Dans la première version du *Horla*, le récit interne se raccroche à son récit introducteur comme à sa preuve externe. [...] Dans l'écriture du journal, la conjonction des rôles (héros/observateur, personnage/narrateur) resserre la complexité [...].

> [When the account has as its sole guarantor the narrating subject, it must ward off the possibility of illusion which affects it by means of recourse to witnesses. This is, in a sense, what is refused by the second version, which is more open to indetermination. In the first version of *Le Horla*, the embedded narrative clings on to the narrative that introduces it as if to external proof. [...] In the writing of a journal, the coincidence of roles (hero/observer, character/narrator) increases the complexity [...].]

The frame narrative of the first version acts as a guarantor for the embedded account because, by underlining the eminence of doctor Marrande and identifying the metadiegetic narrator as one of his patients, it invites the reader to grant credence to this narrator's account. The diary format of the second version deprives it of such a guarantor.

The degree of reliability enjoyed by the narrator's voice in the 1887 version is also determined by the temporal stance implied by the format. Keeping a diary involves recording events at regular intervals, usually not long after the moment(s) at which these events have taken place. *Le Horla* therefore offers a more sustained example of the type of interspersed narration encountered during the epistolary section of *The Sylph*. By recording events at regular intervals, almost as they happen, the narrator in *Le Horla* guarantees 'une violence performative à l'énonciation de l'événement' ['a performative violence to the enunciation of the event'] (Neefs 1980, 235). Simultaneously, however, it is deprived of the benefits of temporally complete information and hindsight. The impact of interspersed narration in *Le Horla* can be clearly appreciated if it is compared to the posterior temporality employed in another account of madness, Gérard de Nerval's *Aurélia ou le Rêve et la vie* (1855). Nerval's story also features a homodiegetic narrator but its temporal stance leads Shoshana Felman (1978, 67) to distinguish between the two roles played by the voice: narrator and protagonist. Her assessment of the consequences of this division are particularly revealing for the case of *Le Horla*:

> Le héros est un 'fou'; le narrateur, un homme qui a recouvré sa 'raison' [...]. Le héros vit la folie au présent; le narrateur la raconte après coup, il est décalé du héros dans le temps.
>
> [The hero is a 'madman'; the narrator, a man who has regained his 'reason' [...]. The hero lives his madness in the present; the narrator recounts it after the fact; he is removed from the hero in time.]

The interspersed temporal stance of Maupassant's narrator means that he has not regained his reason before beginning his speech act and so his reliability can legitimately be questioned.

Whilst epistolary and journal–format narratives commonly imply a similarity of temporal stance, they are differentiated by their intended audience. This is a difference which entails negative consequences for *Le Horla* in terms of reliability, as Chatman (1978, 172) explains:

> The narratee of a letter is the addressed correspondent; the narratee of a private diary is usually the writer himself, though the diary may ultimately be intended for someone else's eyes [...]. The diarist may narrate events for his own edification and memory. But he may also be working out his problems on paper. Still, he is talking to himself.

The private act of narration implied by the diary format of *Le Horla* poses potential reliability problems because it excuses the narrator from the responsibilities that come from having an external audience. The fact that the narrative is intended ostensibly for no one but its author sets up the possibility that elements which lead to confusion or ambiguity might not receive the clarification they would in the context of a more conventional, public narrative. In a sense, the narrator has to think of no one but himself and this will impact upon the quality of the information he provides.

Putting these considerations to one side for a moment, the format of *Le Horla* does not have uniquely negative consequences upon the authority attributed to the narrative voice. Factors exist which implicitly persuade the reader to recognize the reliability of the account being given. The first of these is the referential status typically associated with the diary format, that is the claims it makes to be a factual account of events. Lanser (1981, 163) contends that, while the reader may conventionally recognize that all fictions are 'inventions', greater or lesser efforts can be made to convince her of the truthfulness of the narrator's account. She measures the referential status of a text against a sliding scale of report/invention where: 'the mode closest to the axis of report is the fictional text that insists on its historical truth by claiming to be a factual document, a biography, or an eyewitness account'. Although Lanser does not specifically cite the example of the diary-format narrative, it should be considered as figuring alongside those which make strong claims for their factual referential status. While, on the one hand, the fact that the narrator is his own interlocutor leads to worries about his reliability, it might equally be seen to persuade the reader of the honesty of his narrative act. The narrator commits his account to paper, not for the purpose of entertainment, but in order to leave a faithful account of what he experiences. Therefore, any temptation towards embellishment to impress an audience is curtailed, and the impression of honesty and reliability is created.

In a similar vein, the diary format encourages the reader to grant credence to its claims simply because the act of recording events in a diary constitutes a rational undertaking. Keeping a journal entails organizing time and passages of existence into structured and comprehensible slots: the author records events and, as Chatman suggests, by writing them down and reflecting upon them, he attempts to arrive at a deeper understanding of their significance. In *Le Horla*, this attempt to take stock of and rationalize events stands in stark contrast to the nature of some of the events which the narrator experiences. Indeed, in the fantastic, where protagonists necessarily experience events which challenge the natural order of the world, this act of trying to make sense of existence through writing assumes a heightened symbolic resonance. It can be noted in *The Queen of Spades* where, following his nocturnal visitation, Germann substitutes the legitimizing act of speaking to his sleeping servant with that of writing: '[он] засветил свечку и записал свое видение' ['[he] lit a candle and began to write down his vision'] (Q 350). Gwenhaël Ponnau confirms the rationalizing implications of keeping a diary when he contends (1997, 96) that writing constitutes 'le seul acte de résistance possible face aux manifestations bouleversantes du surnaturel' ['the only act of resistance possible in the face of the bewildering occurrences of the supernatural']. Hence, even before the beginning of the narrative proper, Maupassant's story creates contrasting expectations in the mind of the reader concerning the reliability of the discourse it will present.

These expectations are reinforced by the marked distinction in tone and content between the first two diary entries in *Le Horla*. This contrast announces the delicate balance which is established between structured control of the discourse and a tendency towards greater incoherence. The first entry aligns itself with the expectations of a reliable narrative thanks, in part, to its provision of more information than might seem usual for a diary. The private nature of this narrative act leads the reader to anticipate an *in medias res* opening, given that spatial, temporal, and character orientation are surplus to the narrator as interlocutor's requirements. However, this proves not to be the case as the opening entry provides a brief geographical orientation:

> De mes fenêtres, je vois la Seine qui coule, le long de mon jardin, derrière la route, presque chez moi, la grande et large Seine, qui va de Rouen au Havre, couverte de bateaux qui passent. A gauche, là-bas, Rouen, la vaste ville aux toits bleus, sous le peuple pointu des clochers gothiques. (*H* 913)[3]

> [From my windows, I can see the Seine which flows, for the length of my garden, behind the road, almost on my land, the long and wide Seine, which goes from Rouen to Le Havre, covered in passing ships. To the left, over there, Rouen, the vast town with its blue roofs, watched over by the population of pointed gothic bell towers.]

These lines are, in fact, typical of this entry in which the emphasis falls clearly upon the description of external physical phenomena. The narrator goes on to give further details of Rouen's bell towers, the boats which sail up the river past his house, and the tree he has lain under earlier that day. Whilst these references to physical surroundings may not be as sustained as those encountered in *Spirite*, for example, they nevertheless create a sense of the existence of a 'vraisemblable' fictional world. The air of stability lent to the discourse by geographical reference is reinforced by the balanced use of past and present tenses in this first entry. For instance, alongside descriptions in the past tense of events which have taken place over the course of the day, 'vers onze heures, un long convoi de navires [...] défila devant ma grille' ['at about eleven o'clock, a long convoy of ships [...] sailed past my gate'] (*H* 913), are generalized expressions of emotion in the present tense: 'J'aime ce pays, et j'aime y vivre parce que j'y ai mes racines' ['I love this country, and I love living here because my roots are here'] (ibid.). The equilibrium achieved between these tenses is important because it announces that this diary will not be entirely devoted to inward-looking philosophizing, the relevance of which might prove difficult for the reader to follow. Although both past and present tenses continue to be employed throughout this narrative, the pre-eminence of the latter during certain passages will be shown to contribute to the impression of a loss of control.

The reader's evaluation of the reliability of this narrative voice is also likely to be influenced by the overwhelming sense of contentment expressed in this first entry. On six occasions during his account of 8 May, the narrator expresses either affection for a particular element or pleasure at an incident or state of affairs. The tone for the entry is set by the opening sentence when he exclaims 'Quelle journée admirable!' and is developed through such statements as: 'j'aime ma maison où j'ai grandi' ['I love the house where I grew up'] and 'comme il faisait bon ce matin!' ['what nice weather we had this morning!'] (ibid.). The favourable emotional disposition at this point is worthy of note because it will be thrown into sharp relief by subsequent developments in the story. Whilst this narrator may not explicitly display the strong rationalizing tendencies of the archaeologist-historian in *La Vénus d'Ille*, for instance, he is nevertheless depicted as being a reasonable and contented man. Finné (1980, 74) is just one of a number of commentators to remark upon this when he states that *Le Horla*'s narrator 'semble parfaitement normal'. Particularly crucial to the subsequent provocation of hesitation is the fact that he does not show himself to be noticeably predisposed to hallucinations or mental illness.

The calm, stable, and reasonable impression created by this first entry is abruptly undermined in the second, which displays few, if any, of the same reassuring features. Description of the external physical world is now reduced to an absolute minimum as the narrator fails to describe a single action which he has performed on that day. Rather, the entry is entirely devoted to internal reflection, a shift which explains the overwhelming use of the present tense to the virtual exclusion of the past. This loss of balance in the narrator's focus is apparently triggered by a similar shift in mood. The contentment of four days earlier has evaporated as the narrator declares that he feels feverish and sad. In place of happiness and satisfaction, uncertainty and mystery dominate this second entry. And this change is clearly discernible in the syntactic elements employed. The narrator opens the entry with a hesitant statement betraying his inability to characterize the nature of his affliction definitively: 'je me sens souffrant, ou plutôt je me sens triste' ['I feel unwell, or rather I feel sad'] (*H* 914). The ambiguity of this sentence is produced by the relative conjunction, 'ou plutôt', which admits the possible existence of two different states of affairs. This device also suggests that the narrator struggles to find the best terms in which to describe his ailment, in a manner reminiscent of that we have seen in Chapter 2. This is reinforced in the second paragraph of the entry by the repeated recourse to questions. The narrator poses a total of seven, all of which interrogate the cause or nature of his illness. Two of these are simply 'pourquoi?', and none of the seven receive anything more than a hypothetical response:

> D'où viennent ces influences mystérieuses qui changent en découragement notre bonheur et notre confiance en détresse? On dirait que l'air, l'air invisible est plein d'inconnaissables Puissances, dont nous subissons les voisinages mystérieux. Je m'éveille plein de gaieté, avec des envies de chanter dans la gorge. — Pourquoi? — Je descends le long de l'eau; et soudain, après une courte promenade, je rentre désolé, comme si quelque malheur m'attendait chez moi. — Pourquoi? (ibid.)

> [Where do these mysterious influences which change our happiness into despondency and our confidence into distress come from? One might say that the air, the invisible air, is full of unknowable Powers whose mysterious proximity we endure. I wake up full of joy, with the desire to sing in my throat. — Why? — I walk alongside the river; and suddenly, after a short walk, I return home in distress, as if some misfortune were awaiting me there. — Why?]

With their reference to mysterious powers and their revelation of a predominantly melancholic state, these interrogatives and hypotheses form a telling contrast with the confidence of the first entry. The narrator now voices a sense of impotence and uncertainty where the opening entry expressed a sense of being securely rooted in the world. It is also interesting to note that these questions introduce a subsidiary dichotomy between the physical and psychic worlds which is clearly related to the central natural/supernatural dilemma.

The uncertainty prompted by multiple questions is heightened by the increased frequency with which extended sentences appear in this second entry. These create the impression of diminished control for the first time and, as such, effectively communicate the narrator's bewildered state. These sentences are divided into a myriad of clauses and subclauses which succeed in confusing the reader thanks to their repetition of similar linguistic constructions:

> Tout ce qui nous entoure, tout ce que nous voyons sans le regarder, tout ce que nous frôlons sans le connaître, tout ce que nous touchons sans le palper, tout ce que nous rencontrons sans le distinguer, a sur nous, sur nos organes et, par eux, sur nos idées, sur notre cœur lui-même, des effets rapides, surprenants et inexplicables? Comme il est profond, ce mystère de l'Invisible! Nous ne le pouvons sonder avec nos sens misérables, avec nos yeux qui ne savent apercevoir ni le trop petit, ni le trop grand, ni le trop près, ni le trop loin, ni les habitants d'une étoile, ni les habitants d'une goutte d'eau... avec nos oreilles qui nous trompent [...] ... avec notre odorat, plus faible que celui du chien... avec notre goût, qui peut à peine discerner l'âge d'un vin. (ibid.)

> [Everything which surrounds us, everything that we see without looking at it, everything that we brush against without knowing it, everything that we touch without feeling it, everything that we meet without making it out, exerts upon us, upon our organs and, through them, upon our ideas, upon our very hearts, rapid, surprising, and inexplicable effects? How profound it is, this mystery of the Invisible! We cannot probe it with our paltry senses, with our eyes which cannot perceive either the too small, or the too large, or the too near, or the too far, or the inhabitants of a star, or the inhabitants of a drop of water... with our ears which deceive us [...] ... with our sense of smell, weaker than a dog's... with our sense of taste which can only just judge the age of a wine.]

In the opening sentence above, the first five clauses all employ the 'tout ce' construction followed by a verbal clause which functions as either subject or object. All bar the first of these also build into the negative infinitive construct 'sans le...' which reinforces the repetition. Within this same sentence, repetition is then extended to the four indirect object phrases of the verbal constructs formed by the preposition 'sur...' and the possessive adjective. Even the only direct object of these verbal constructs, 'des effets', is qualified by three consecutive adjectives. The second sentence is similarly dominated by repetition with the sixfold use of the 'ni le...' construction and the listing of the inadequacies of four of the five senses.[4] The presence of extended sentences with repetitive structures effectively communicates the narrator's exasperation at man's relative weakness and his inability to comprehend fully the nature of the universe. Equally important is the sense it gives that the narrator's discourse is running away with him and that he no longer exerts as tight a control over it as during the opening entry. Matthew MacNamara (1986, 159) believes that such accumulative sentence structures are typical of the Maupassant narrator and that they 'reproduce the temporal and qualitative progression of his search for the expression that will ultimately satisfy him'. In the specific context of Le Horla, passages such as the one quoted above function as an important harbinger of the type of discursive difficulties that will assail the narrator at subsequent points of the story.

In Le Horla, therefore, the format of the discourse, the status of the narrative voice, and its temporal stance all conspire to create contradictory expectations regarding authority and reliability. The very first signals sent out by these same aspects in The Double could hardly be more reassuring for the reader. There is nothing exceptional about the novella's textual format. The opening sentence reveals a heterodiegetic narrative voice displaying a posterior temporal stance:

Было без малого восемь часов утра, когда титулярный советник Яков Петрович Голядкин очнулся после долгого сна, зевнул, потянулся и открыл наконец совершенно глаза свои. (*D* 109)[5]

[It was just before eight o'clock in the morning when Titular Councillor Iakov Petrovich Goliadkin woke from a long sleep, yawned, stretched, and finally opened his eyes completely.]

Providing as it does a specific time for the action, a full name for the protagonist and a matter-of-fact description of his actions, this sentence fulfils a number of the expectations associated with heterodiegesis. In fact, it is difficult to imagine how the opening line of a fictional narrative could seek to be more straightforwardly informative. The narrator also satisfies the reader's desire for spatial orientation when he offers a relatively detailed description of Goliadkin's room and the furniture to be found in it. The intended effect of this information is implied by the fact that the protagonist's own observation of his physical surroundings convinces him that:

он находится не в тридесятом царстве каком-нибудь, а в городе Петербурге, в столице, в Шестилавочной улице, в четвертом этаже одного весьма большого, капитального дома, в собственной квартире своей. (ibid.)

[he is not in some far-off realm but in the town of St Petersburg, in the capital, on Shestilavochnaia Street, on the fourth floor of one of the very large and imposing buildings, in his own flat.]

This suggests that, just as the protagonist's recognition of his flat satisfies him that he is no longer dreaming, the reader should allow this description to persuade her of the verisimilitude of the fictional world. The account of the location of Goliadkin's rooms is just the first in a series of references to actual geographical spaces in contemporary St Petersburg employed by Dostoevskii. Whilst acknowledging that such references help to create an air of reality, David Gasperetti (1989, 219) believes that they are also used to 'lull readers into a false sense of security and passivity'. This is exploited when Dostoevskii subsequently disrupts the spatial unity in the narrative, as I shall discuss later in this chapter.

The authority of the narrator of *The Double* is further established by his initially conventional exploitation of omniscient privilege. Although in the opening sentence this voice observes the protagonist's movements from an external perspective, he subsequently supplies details which could only be gained through direct access to Goliadkin's mind. For instance, he is able to record his sensations as he wakes up: 'вскоре, однако ж, чувства господина Голядкина стали яснее и отчетливее принимать свои привычные, обыденные впечатления' ['soon, however, Mr. Goliadkin's senses began to receive more clearly and distinctly their ordinary, everyday impressions'] (*D* 109). The narrator is equally capable of reporting the inner speech or thoughts of this fictional character: '"однако что же это такое?" подумал господин Голядкин, "да где же Петрушка?"' ['"however, what on earth is this?" thought Mr. Goliadkin; "where is Petrushka?"'] (*D* 110). The narrator reinforces the impression created by such omniscience when he demonstrates temporally extensive knowledge concerning situations and characters. For example, with reference to a bundle of banknotes lying on the table, the narrator is able to describe that Goliadkin 'в сотый раз, впрочем, считая со вчерашнего дня, начал пересчитывать их' ['for the

hundredth time, though, since the previous day began to count them over'] (ibid.).
This is just one of a number of examples which demonstrate that the narrator's
acquaintance with the fictional world extends back to a point prior to the beginning
of the narrative. Along with the omniscience and informative approach, this indication
of an extensive knowledge of the subject encourages the reader to view the heterodiegetic narrator as a reliable voice describing a mimetic fictional world.

However, just as the expectations aroused in the first entry of *Le Horla* are
undermined by the tone of the second, so the assessment of *The Double* as presenting
a straightforward and reliable narrative proves to be premature. Interwoven with
the examples highlighted above are numerous instances where the actual degree of
diegetic authority possessed by the narrative voice is called into question. Concerns
about his reliability centre, particularly, upon his failure to display a uniform degree
of omniscience. Alongside apparent proof of his access to the inner thoughts of
Goliadkin are descriptions in which the narrator appears to do no more than deduce
information on the basis of external observation. For instance, he describes the hero's
reaction to the servants crowding around Petrushka as follows: 'по-видимому, ни
тема разговора, ни самый разговор не понравились господину Голядкину'
['apparently, neither the subject of the conversation, nor the conversation itself was
to Mr Goliadkin's liking'] (*D* 111). A similar example comes when the hero inspects
Petrushka all dressed up in his livery: 'господин Голядкин осмотрел Петрушку
кругом и, по-видимому, остался доволен' ['Mr Goliadkin inspected Petrushka
from all sides and, apparently, was happy'] (ibid.). The epistemic modal adverb,
'по-видимому' ['apparently'], is difficult to reconcile with the degree of access to
information which the narrator displays elsewhere in this first chapter. His omniscient
privilege should permit him to state confidently whether or not Goliadkin liked
the subject of the conversation or Petrushka's outfit; he should not need to deduce
this information. The recourse to such ambiguous syntax is unsettling not so much
because it allows uncertainty to surround these particular observations (which are
relatively inconsequential) but because it poses awkward questions regarding the true
nature of the narrator's authority.

The tell-tale modal adverb reappears in a description in which the narrator's
inconsistent access to information more seriously threatens the reader's ability to make
sense of events in the fictional world. In this example, however, not even the attempted
deduction signalled by the adverb is sufficient to compensate for the information gap
created by the inexplicably limited perspective. The narrator describes how, having
jumped out of bed, Goliadkin runs to the window of his apartment:

> и с большим участием начал что-то отыскивать глазами на дворе дома,
> на который выходили окна квартиры его. По-видимому, и то, что он
> отыскал на дворе, совершенно его удовлетворило; лицо его просияло
> самодовольной улыбкою. (*D* 110)

> [and with great concern began searching with his eyes for something in the
> courtyard of the building on which the windows of his apartment looked out.
> Apparently, what he was looking for in the courtyard completely satisfied him; his
> face lit up with a self-satisfied smile.]

The modal adverb is now accompanied by indefinite object and relative pronouns, 'что-то' ['something'] and 'то, что' ['what'] which unmistakably indicate that the narrator's perspective is located outside the consciousness of the protagonist. In the heterodiegetic context, indefinite pronouns conventionally indicate the advent of limited perspective as the point of view is moved away from the narrator and towards the less authoritative protagonist. This cannot be the case in the example above because, given that the obscured details are perceived by the protagonist, a shift to his perspective would not result in limited information. Therefore, the uncertainty created by these syntactic elements is not the result of the protagonist's limited powers but of the shortcoming in the narrator's ability to access this information. What is most unsettling is that the narrator's limitations on this occasion are almost impossible to reconcile with his apparent possession of omniscience.

The unreliable omniscience and perspective illustrated in these examples poses an important dilemma for the reader in terms of the interpretation of the narrator's performance. Two possible explanations for this inconsistent omniscience could be proposed, although both are equally disruptive to storytelling conventions. Firstly, there might exist areas of knowledge to which the narrator does not enjoy unlimited access. Or secondly, there might be certain, unpredictable junctures of the discourse where he deliberately chooses not to exploit his omniscient privilege. Obviously, even the most consistent exploitation of omniscient privilege implies selectivity; if this were not the case, texts would become a series of endless details about every thought and development occurring in the fictional world. However, the situation confronting the reader in *The Double* is one where the narrator is selective about exercising omniscient privilege within the sphere of a single character's consciousness. This is hardly tenable. There can be no acceptable justification for the narrator's ability to inform the reader of Goliadkin's thoughts at one moment and his failure to do so just a few lines later. It is not the case here that there are areas of Goliadkin's mind which remain obscured from the narrator. Rather, in line with the second explanation, the narrator chooses not to respect his own rules and abilities at certain unpredictable junctures.

The potential consequences of this inconsistency become a matter of greater concern to the reader when the personality of the fictional protagonist begins to be revealed. The personality of the hero obviously influences the interpretation of every fictional narrative. In *The Double*, the impact of Goliadkin's personality and attitudes is particularly forceful because, as I will discuss in more detail later, events are often presented from what appears to be his point of view. The initial impression created by Dostoevskii's protagonist is quite distinct from that encountered in the texts discussed in Chapters 1 and 2. Whilst these protagonists have been characterized as predominantly reasonable and sceptical men, Goliadkin manifests a tendency towards obsessiveness and paranoia where logical thought processes are in short supply. The account of his consultation with doctor Krest´ian Ivanovich Rutenshpits in the novella's second chapter provides a striking illustration of this problematic personality. The behaviour, ideas, and speech patterns on display during this scene alert the reader to his faltering mental state before any hint of the supernatural has even been introduced. Their discussion is recorded through a combination of direct speech, indirectly reported speech and free indirect discourse. Sufficient illustration of the hero's unusual personality can be obtained from a brief examination of the content and style of his direct discourse. During the early part of the consultation, the topic being discussed is relatively clear: Goliadkin's lifestyle and need for more human contact. Nevertheless, his frequent use of ellipsis and repetition clearly reveals an acute degree of hesitancy. For instance, his assessment of his character and approach to life is as follows:

> Да-с, Крестьян Иванович. Я Крестьян Иванович, хоть и смирный человек, как я уже вам, кажется, имел честь объяснить, но дорога моя отдельно идет, Крестьян Иванович. Путь жизни широк... Я хочу... я хочу, Крестьян Иванович, сказать этим... Извините меня, Крестьян Иванович, я не мастер красно говорить. (*D* 116)

> [Yes sir, Krest´ian Ivanovich. I, Krest´ian Ivanovich, am a humble man, as I have already, I think, had the honour of explaining to you. But I go my own way, Krest´ian Ivanovich. The road of life is broad... I want... I want, Krest´ian Ivanovich, to say this... Excuse me, Krest´ian Ivanovich, I am not a master of speaking eloquently.]

The elliptical points encountered here are just three instances of a punctuation feature which is widespread not only in this dialogue but throughout the novella as a whole. Goliadkin frequently exhibits an inability to complete sentences satisfactorily, either because he does not know what to say or because he cannot decide upon the best expression for his thoughts, leaving phrases simply to drift into non-existence. He also repeats the doctor's name in a mantra-like fashion as if it were a verbal crutch to support him while he searches for what it is he wishes to say. Furthermore, he insists on restating the obvious because, as if it were not sufficiently self-evident, he explains on three further occasions that he is 'не мастер красно говорить' ['not a master of speaking eloquently'] (*D* 116–17).

As the dialogue continues and Goliadkin begins to elaborate on his relationship with society, clues to his insecure grip on reality become ever more numerous. For example, he repeatedly employs metaphorical expressions whose significance is far from clear to the reader. He states that in society 'нужно уметь паркеты лощить сапогами' ['it is necessary to know how to polish the parquet with your shoes'] and, when emphasizing that he is a simple person, he informs Rutenshpits that: 'блеска наружного нет во мне [...] я полагаю оружие; я кладу его' ['I cannot shine in society [...] I lay down my weapons; I lower them'] (*D* 116). Goliadkin also repeatedly employs easy, clichéd expressions such as '[я] умываю руки' ['I wash my hands'] or 'я иду своей дорогой' ['I go my own way'], the meaning of which is equally difficult to decipher. This mystifying use of clichés is particularly disruptive because, conventionally, they are a linguistic device whose defining characteristic is a semantic clarity which stems from overuse. Yet in the context of *The Double*, they do nothing to promote intelligibility. Similarly, Goliadkin employs a number of proverbial or idiomatic expressions whose relevance is obscure. Apparently talking about people who are not always slaves to public opinion, he says that they know how 'поднести коку с соком' ['to serve an egg with sauce']. And of his supposed enemy, he remarks that 'лимон съел' ['he had bitten into a lemon'] (*D* 119–20). M. F. Lomagin (1971, 5) notes the manner in which these phrases do nothing more than further confuse the reader:

особенности речевой системы Голядкина свидетельствуют о хаотичности мышления, о неразвитости чувства языка, что наглядным образом проявляется в том, как герой деформирует русские пословицы и поговорки.

[the peculiarities of Goliadkin's speech system testify to his chaotic thought processes and to his underdeveloped feel for language, which manifests itself graphically in the way in which he deforms Russian proverbs and sayings.]

What is perhaps of even greater importance about Goliadkin's speech patterns is the way in which they serve to dehumanize him to some degree. As Terras (1969, 173) argues, it is creative speech which makes man appear human and the overall effect of Goliadkin's repetitions, malfunctioning clichés, and deformed proverbs is to strip him of his creativity and, thus, his humanity.

The consultation descends into almost complete non-significance from the point at which Goliadkin informs Krest´ian Ivanovich that he 'only put[s] on a mask at masked balls' and not in public every day. This observation prompts him into making a number of allusions to 'враги' ['enemies'], 'злые враги' ['evil enemies'], 'известный человек' ['a certain person'], and 'один из ваших коротких знакомых' ['one of your closest acquaintances'] (D 118–20) where the persons signified remain effectively unidentified. It is not at all obvious, indeed, whether the implication of these remarks is even clear to the doctor. The repetition of these allusions is sufficient to raise the reader's suspicions regarding Goliadkin's paranoia. The various linguistic traits he displays all hint at the same conclusion: there exists a fundamental gap between the protagonist's grasp of reality and that recognized by the reader. The devices favoured by Goliadkin, such as clichés and proverbs, are only effective if the frame of reference they exploit is shared by speaker and listener. This is the case neither for his interlocutor in the fictional world, Rutenshpits, nor for the actual, extrafictional reader. Therefore, when the narrator describes the doctor as being 'в крайнем изумлении' ['in extreme bewilderment'] (D 121) when Goliadkin leaves his office, this characterization can be seen to apply equally appropriately to the reader. Goliadkin's display of paranoia, his inability to structure his discourse logically, and his questionable grip on reality all suggest that he is unlikely to prove a reliable witness of events occurring in the fictional world.

Part 2: Homodiegetic Disintegration in *Le Horla*

Although there exists no formal division into parts in *Le Horla*, Hamon (1971, 36) proposes a useful tripartite structure for the story. The first part extends to the entry for 2 July, which describes the diarist's trip to Mont Saint-Michel; the second proceeds from here to the entry for 16 July recording the hypnosis incident in Paris; the third part covers those entries from 19 July when the diarist returns from Paris until the end of the narrative. The contradictory expectations and uncertainty aroused by the first two diary entries have been noted. The remainder of the first part of the story, charting the diarist's struggle to understand his mysterious affliction and to cope with its manifestation in nocturnal crises, builds upon this initial impression. However, the most revealing episodes for a discussion of narrative disintegration are to be found in the second and third parts of *Le Horla* following the first more overt appearance of the supernatural in the entry for 5 July. I would like to propose that the hesitation necessary to the fantastic is provoked in three stages in Maupassant's story. Firstly, during the early descriptions of the apparent manifestation of an otherworldly force, *Le Horla* displays a relatively conventional use of ambiguous syntax creating interpretative uncertainty. This is somewhat differentiated from the practice revealed in the texts discussed previously because it is constantly intertwined with the debate the narrator conducts about his own mental state. Secondly, from a certain point onwards, this accepted use of ambiguous syntax is developed to create a more disruptive situation in which the coherent quality of the discourse intermittently deteriorates to a more troublesome degree than is usual. During these passages, the reader's ability to make sense of the discourse is threatened by syntactic devices which, whilst similar to those encountered in the second diary entry, are now employed to a more exaggerated degree. Finally, in the latter stages of the story, the failure of attempts to rationalize experience through written discourse is signalled not simply through syntactic devices but also through narrative techniques. The trigger for this shift from a relatively conventional practice of the fantastic to a state of far greater incoherence is a development in the narrator's discussion of his madness. The evolution of this debate, the associated question of the narrator's belief in the existence of an invisible creature, and the impact of these factors upon the reader's interpretative abilities will be traced through the argument below.

The apparently supernatural makes its first appearances in *Le Horla* in the three diary entries dated 5, 6, and 10 July. For these days, the narrator reports how water and milk disappear from his bedside while he is alone, locked inside his bedroom. As far as he is consciously aware, he is not responsible for the consumption of these articles. The dilemma confronting the narrator is revealed by the question that opens the first of these three entries: 'Ai-je perdu la raison?' ['Have I lost my mind?'] (*H* 919). The syntactic devices employed in these entries reveal both the narrator's initially rational response to the disappearance and the subsequent direction in which his beliefs develop. In the 5 July entry, the narrator records that, before falling asleep, he noticed that the carafe of water beside his bed was full. However, when he awakens suddenly after a disturbed period of sleep, he finds it empty. His bewilderment at the water's disappearance is succinctly expressed by the five consecutive questions he employs to interrogate the identity of the culprit: 'On avait donc bu cette eau? Qui? Moi? moi, sans doute? Ce ne pouvait être que moi?' ['Someone has drunk this water then? Who? Me? Me, undoubtedly? It could only have been me?'] (*H* 919–20). These questions introduce a conflict between the personal pronouns 'on' and 'je' (or 'moi') which effectively embodies the narrator's confusion and which will be central to the progression of the story. His uncertainty regarding the identity of the water-drinker is betrayed by the use in the first of these questions of the indefinite pronoun 'on'. However, the choice of 'moi' in the final three illustrates the narrator's attempts to account for the disappearance of the water rationally. He concludes that he must be suffering from somnambulism in order to be able to drink from the carafe, and yet retain no recollection of doing so.

This rational conclusion is undermined in the entry for 6 July as the impersonal pronoun endeavours to reassert itself. The narrator is again confused, having noted the second instance of the water's disappearance: 'on a encore bu toute ma carafe cette nuit; — ou plutôt, je l'ai bue!' ['someone has drunk the entire carafe again during the night; — or rather, I have drunk it!'] (*H* 920). The pronouns, and the contradictory interpretations they imply, are now held in greater parity and are mediated by the inconclusive relative conjunction 'ou plutôt'. This conjunction is a recurrent verbal feature of *Le Horla* and can be seen to confirm Ross Chambers's assessment of the narrator as a voice which is 'incapable of deciding' and which takes 'an infinite pleasure in hesitating' (1980, 113). Although the narrator's refinement of this declaration favours the less ambiguous use of 'je', the attempt to impose the rational again proves unsuccessful. This is because the statement is followed by a series of interrogatives which call into question the appropriateness of the use of the first-person pronoun: 'Mais, est-ce moi? Est-ce moi? Qui serait-ce? Qui?' ['But, is it me? Is it me? Who could it be? Who?'] (*H* 920). The interdependent nature of questions concerning the identity of the culprit and the narrator's state of mental health is reiterated in this entry. Momentarily, the narrator states the case for his encroaching insanity with more conviction: the interrogative which opened the previous entry is replaced by the unequivocal statement 'je deviens fou' ['I am going mad']. Nevertheless, such confidence proves to be short-lived as the penultimate clause reverts to the initial interrogative form: 'je deviens fou?' ['am I going mad?'] (ibid.).

In the entry for 10 July, the narrator's rationalizing instincts are again to the fore as he summarizes the experiments he has undertaken in order to try to identify the agent of these irrational actions. The accounts reveal a telling syntactic shift. Initially, the struggle between 'on' and 'je' continues: 'on a bu — j'ai bu — toute l'eau, et un peu de lait' ['someone drank — I drank — all the water and a bit of milk'] (ibid.). However, as the report of the experiments progresses, the use of 'je' to refer to the consumer of the liquids is suppressed until it is entirely replaced by the more ambiguous 'on':

> on n'a touché ni au vin, ni au pain, ni aux fraises [...] on n'a touché à rien [...] on avait bu toute l'eau! on avait bu tout le lait! (ibid.)

> [neither the wine, nor the bread, nor the strawberries have been touched [...] nothing has been touched [...] all the water had been drunk! all the milk had been drunk!]

This quasi-identification of the perpetrator is seemingly justified by the fact that the narrator has established, by means of graphite powder and muslin, that he cannot be responsible. However, the nature of the experiments is such that, while they may serve to resolve the 'je'/'on' confusion, they also lend the latter pronoun an even greater power of suggestion. The possibility of employing an indefinite personal pronoun is called into question by the fact that the experiments seem to rule out the involvement of any type of human agency, not just the narrator's. The ramifications of the victory of the indefinite personal pronoun apparently begin to dawn on the narrator as he closes the account of the experiments with the exclamation: 'Ah! mon Dieu!...' (ibid.). The elliptical points that follow this reaction effectively communicate his inability to fathom fully the significance of his discovery. Ellipsis becomes a powerfully effective indicator of the narrator's failure to impose full significance upon his experience as his written account becomes increasingly compromised by such gaps.

While these three entries provide a more focused expression of the uncertainty which assails the narrator during his earlier nocturnal crises, they still record only an indirect experience of the supernatural. The narrator witnesses the results of apparent otherworldly intervention, not its actual occurrence. His return from Paris on 16 July signals a crucial development in the narrator's experiences as he subsequently records a number of face-to-face confrontations. A consideration of two of these episodes will provide sufficient illustration at this stage: the rose-picking incident reported on 6 August and the book-reading scene described on 17 August. An immediate consequence of the shift to a more direct experience of the supernatural is a further modification in the narrator's assessment of his sanity. His reaction to the evidence of his experiments on 10 July has been to declare: 'décidément, je suis fou!' ['decidedly, I am mad'] (*H* 920). Opening the entry for 6 August with a judgement upon the meaning of events yet to be recorded, the narrator confidently declares the entirely contrary situation: 'cette fois, je ne suis pas fou' ['this time, I am not mad'] (*H* 927). In the following lines, the conviction of this statement evaporates as the narrator proves incapable of naming what it is he has seen to make him change his mind. He repeatedly claims 'j'ai vu', and yet, on each occasion, the direct object of the verb is replaced by elliptical points. This ellipsis serves not only to provoke suspense but also hints at the particular difficulties which surround the question of vision and visibility in *Le Horla*. This hesitancy is reinforced by the ambiguity which permeates the narrator's account of what it is he has witnessed as he looks at a giant oleander in his rose garden. The generically conventional nature of this description is signalled by the presence of three verbs in the reflexive form:

> je vis, je vis distinctement, tout près de moi, la tige d'une de ces roses se plier, comme si une main invisible l'eût tordue, puis se casser, comme si cette main l'eût cueillie! Puis la fleur s'éleva, suivant la courbe qu'aurait décrite un bras en la portant vers une bouche, et elle resta suspendue dans l'air transparent [...]. (ibid.)

> [I saw, I distinctly saw, right next to me, the stem of one of these roses fold over, as if an invisible hand had bent it, then break, as if this hand had picked it! Then the flower rose up, following the trajectory which would have been traced by an arm carrying the flower towards a mouth, and it remained suspended in the transparent air [...].]

Each of the logically impossible movements depicted by these intransitive forms is complemented by a clause which compares it to a more acceptable state of affairs: the first two are formed by the comparator 'comme si' and the pluperfect subjunctive tense while the third simply employs the conditional perfect. The narrator attempts to understand these events by aligning them with examples of human agency. However, the combination of verbs representing material processes of supervention and the particular tense forms ensures that this approximation is unconvincing. The identity of the agent responsible for picking the rose and the explanation for how this is possible remains obscured.

The narrator's immediate reaction to the movement and subsequent disappearance of the rose is essentially rational. He becomes angry that 'un homme raisonnable et sérieux' such as he could fall victim to such 'hallucinations' (ibid.). However, the attempt to classify this scene as nothing more than a troubling illusion is thwarted by the discovery on the plant of a freshly cut stem. Such physical proof forces the narrator to recognize that the incident has indeed taken place and, therefore, to contemplate alternative explanations for it.[6] He does this almost immediately and his revision of the hallucination theory could hardly be more radical. In the closing paragraph of the entry, he alleges, with no little conviction, that an irrational state of affairs now prevails:

> je suis certain, maintenant, certain comme de l'alternance des jours et des nuits, qu'il existe près de moi un être invisible, qui se nourrit de lait et d'eau, qui peut toucher aux choses, les prendre et les changer de place, doué par conséquent d'une nature matérielle, bien qu'imperceptible pour nos sens, et qui habite comme moi, sous mon toit... (ibid.)

> [I am sure, now, as sure as day follows night, that an invisible creature exists close to me, which feeds on milk and water, which can touch things, take hold of them, move them, and that it is endowed consequently with a material nature, albeit imperceptible to our senses, and which lives like me, under my roof...]

While the narrator may now allege the existence of an invisible creature with some certainty, this confidence does not extend to the consequences of what such a belief might be. Echoing the close of the 10 July passage, this entry is denied definitive closure by elliptical points which effectively indicate the apprehension and confusion experienced by the narrator in response to his own statement.

Among the most notable consequences of the profession of belief in 'un être invisible' is a further shift in the use of personal pronouns. The earlier victory of 'on' over 'je' is now superseded in post-6 August entries by an identification of this performer of unusual events as 'il'. For instance, on 7 August, the narrator states that 'il a bu l'eau de ma carafe, mais n'a point troublé mon sommeil' ['he/it drank all of my carafe, but did not disturb my sleep at all'] (ibid.) while on the 8th he notes: 'il ne se manifeste plus, mais je le sens près de moi' ['he/it does not show itself anymore, but I can feel him/it close to me'] (H 929).[7] While this evolution may imply a diminution of ambiguity in one sense, the entry for 17 August, where the pages of a book are turned, proves that uncertainty remains as deeply ingrained as ever. In terms of the syntactic devices employed to arouse hesitation, this scene is strongly reminiscent of the rose garden incident. However, the fact that the page-turning incident occurs after a declaration of belief in the irrational creates a fundamental distinction between the two scenes. Most importantly, this poses questions about the narrator's ability to justify some of the syntactic elements he employs.

As in the first description of the disappearance of the water on 5 July, the narrator espies the pages of the book turning after he has awoken unexpectedly in the middle of the night. Ambiguity surrounds this account from the outset as the narrator's first claim is qualified by a modal lexical verb of perception: 'tout à coup, il me sembla qu'une page du livre resté ouvert sur ma table venait de tourner toute seule' ['all of a sudden, it seemed to me that a page of the book open on my table had just turned over of its own accord'] (H 931). Recalling the rose-picking entry, importance is assigned to the visual nature of the encounter as the narrator repeats the claim 'je vis', although the ellipsis of the earlier passage is now suppressed: 'je vis, je vis, oui, je vis de mes yeux une autre page se soulever et se rabattre sur la précédente, comme si un doigt l'eût feuilletée' ['I saw, I saw, yes, I saw with my own eyes another page rise up and turn over onto the preceding one, as if a finger had leafed it'] (*H* 932). Both this description and that of the narrator's futile attempts to capture the invisible creature display the combination of reflexive verbs, the comparator 'comme si', and the pluperfect subjunctive tense which has been noted in the entry for 6 August. In one sense, the coincidence of this triad of devices between the two entries is entirely acceptable. In both, they combine to express succinctly the doubts the narrator experiences as he witnesses actions which are apparently performed by an invisible agent. However, in the sense in which these devices, particularly the intransitive verbs, express an ignorance of identity or a lack of agency, their presence in the second passage must be considered to be more disruptive. Having seen a page turn for the second time, the narrator makes quite clear who he believes is responsible: 'mon fauteuil était vide, semblait vide; mais je compris qu'il était là, lui, assis à ma place, et qu'il lisait' ['my armchair was empty, seemed empty; but I understood that he/it was there, him/it, sitting in my place, and that he/it was reading'] (ibid.).[8] The masculine singular personal pronoun is intended to identify the figure reading over the narrator's shoulder as the invisible creature. In the light of this act of identification, the reflexive verbs expressing material processes of supervention in the latter part of this account ('se renversa', 's'éteignit', and 'se ferma') now appear less justifiable. Belief in the 'être invisible' as agent implies that the narrator recognizes that these processes are not supervented; therefore, the verbs could acceptably appear in their non-reflexive forms. The decision not to use them in this way, whilst questionable, cannot be considered transgressive, however. Ultimately, the invisible nature of the creature means that identifying it as 'il' makes virtually no headway in resolving ambiguity. Therefore, the continued use of reflexive forms is legitimate. Nevertheless, the complication of syntactic exploitation during what is a relatively conventional supernatural scene indicates the greater degree of hesitation which the reader will experience in the development of Maupassant's story.

The diarist's declaration of belief in 'un être invisible' on 6 August paves the way for an extended discussion of his mental state in the entry for the 7th. This represents the culmination of the narrator's oscillations during previous entries between a belief that he is mad and equally confident declarations that he is not. His straightforward announcement in the 7 August entry, 'je me demande si je suis fou' ['I wonder whether I am mad'] (*H* 927), proves to be the catalyst for a calm and reasonable discussion in which his attitude recalls his earlier decision to conduct experiments in order to resolve the mystery of the disappearing water. The scepticism with which he views the possibility of his madness is conveyed through the use of the conditional tense:

> Certes, je me croirais fou, absolument fou, si je n'étais conscient, si je ne connaissais parfaitement mon état, si je ne le sondais en l'analysant avec une complète lucidité. Je ne serais donc, en somme, qu'un halluciné raisonnant. (*H* 928)

> [Admittedly, I would believe myself mad, completely mad, if I was not conscious, if I did not perfectly know my state, if I did not probe it by analysing it with complete lucidity. All in all, I am therefore nothing more than a reasoning hallucinator.]

This tense is sustained as the narrator proposes quasi-scientific hypotheses to explain what has happened to his mind. He suggests he might be suffering from a cerebral problem which produces effects similar to those experienced during dreams, or that a key within his brain might have become paralysed. Such reasoned consideration of his own mental state arguably justifies Ponnau's (1997, 299) characterization of this narrator as displaying 'une remarquable lucidité'. Crucially, the dominant tone in this discussion is one of hypothesis; the narrator never quite succeeds in persuading himself that he is mad. His lucid analysis does not, however, prevent the return of his 'malaise inexplicable' and the closing lines of the entry record the narrator's unease as he awaits 'quelque vision fantastique' (H 928–29).

This discussion of madness marks a watershed in the development of *Le Horla*. At no point in the subsequent diary entries does the narrator reinterrogate his sanity; he makes no further mention of the words 'fou' or 'folie'. It is as if his extended consideration of the question only serves to convince him that he is the victim of supernatural intervention and not of madness. However, it is not the case that this decision resolves all aspects of his uncertainty. Rather the focus of his hesitation is shifted to the nature of his invisible assailant. For the reader, the madness/supernatural ambiguity is maintained and heightened by the quality of the discourse at certain junctures of the post-7 August narrative. Although the narrator no longer overtly discusses his sanity, the deterioration in the coherence of his discourse as he obsesses increasingly about the invisible creature keeps the spectre of madness in the forefront of the reader's mind. Indeed, the narrator's dismissal of a rational explanation sets in motion a process of growing ineffectiveness in his attempt to find salvation through his written record.

The first evidence of disintegration in the discourse is to be found in the entry for 14 August. In it, the narrator claims that control over his body and soul is being wrested from him as he comes to be governed by another power: he wants to go out but finds himself unable to leave his armchair. The sense of a loss of dominion has first been clearly expressed in the entry for 12 August when the narrator describes his inability to leave his house to go to Rouen. The sense of impotence is inscribed on a discourse level by the use of dashes or strong punctuation, which create a disjointed feel:

> Tout le jour j'ai voulu m'en aller; je n'ai pas pu. J'ai voulu accomplir cet acte de liberté si facile, si simple, — sortir — monter dans ma voiture pour gagner Rouen — je n'ai pas pu. Pourquoi? (H 929)

> [All day I wanted to leave; I could not. I wanted to accomplish this act of freedom, so easy and simple, — to go out — to get into my carriage to go to Rouen — I could not. Why?]

The narrator's impression of a disjunction between will and power in his conscious existence can be linked to the sense of paralysis he experiences at the height of his nocturnal crises. In the entry for 25 May, he describes a nightmare in which somebody or something climbs on his chest and attempts to strangle him. This account displays a similar use of disjointed discourse:

> je veux crier, — je ne peux pas; — je veux remuer, — je ne peux pas; — j'essaie, avec des efforts affreux, en haletant, de me tourner, de rejeter cet être qui m'écrase et qui m'étouffe, — je ne peux pas! (H 916)

[I want to cry out, — I can't; — I want to move, — I can't; — I try, with the most awful efforts, breathless, to turn over, to throw off this being which crushes and suffocates me, — I can't!]

The broken rhythm imposed by the use of abrupt clauses and strong punctuation is present in both of these passages and is indicative of a division between mind and body. In the 14 August entry, syntactic elements give expression to the diarist's opening claim, 'je suis perdu' ['I am lost'] (H 929), as his discursive control diminishes. In the entry's final paragraph, exaggerated repetition deprives the discourse of the sense of steady forward progress which conventionally marks rational speech. The narrator describes the manifestation of the loss of sovereignty over his own body in the following terms:

> tout d'un coup, il faut, il faut, il faut que j'aille au fond de mon jardin cueillir des fraises et les manger. Et j'y vais. Je cueille des fraises et je les mange! Oh! mon Dieu! Mon Dieu! Mon Dieu! Est-il un Dieu? S'il en est un, délivrez-moi, sauvez-moi! secourez-moi! Pardon! Pitié! Grâce! Sauvez-moi! Oh! quelle souffrance! quelle torture! quelle horreur! (H 930)

> [all of a sudden, I must, I must, I must go to the end of the garden to pick strawberries and eat them. And I go. I pick strawberries and I eat them! Oh my god! My god! My god! Is there a God? If there is one, deliver me, save me! Help me! Forgiveness! Pity! Grace! Save me! Oh, what suffering! What torture! What horror!]

The dominant feature of these lines is the ternary clause group comprising repetition of either individual words or structures. This form is to be found in the triple repetition of the modal verb, 'il faut', as well as in the two series of exclamations, the pleas in the imperative form, and the lamentations on his suffering which close the entry. The sheer accumulative effect of placing five such ternary repetitions within this short paragraph succeeds in creating the impression of diminished coherence.

These first hints of deterioration develop into a far stronger impression during the account for 19 August. Ironically, the entry which presents the most persuasive illustration of the loss of discursive control opens with the declaration: 'je sais... je sais... je sais tout!' ['I know... I know... I know everything!'] (H 932). This declaration reveals the narrator's conviction, after having read an extract from the *Revue du Monde scientifique*, that he has fallen victim to the same epidemic of madness which has ravaged Brazil. In anticipation of Michel Foucault's category of 'Stultifera Navis' as found in his *Histoire de la folie à l'âge classique* (1972), the diarist believes that the creature has jumped off a Brazilian ship passing on the Seine and now inhabits his house. This cognitive leap, which prompts Chambers (1980, 112) to accuse the diarist of 'boundless credulity', leads him to consider not simply that he has lost the ability for self-dominion but that, in a far wider sense, mankind has forfeited its control over the universe. It is perhaps this which best explains the more acute sense of incoherence experienced during this entry. The statement 'le règne de l'homme est fini' ['the reign of mankind is over'] (H 933) introduces an extended period of reflection during which clarity is drastically undermined.

This is first announced by the increased use of extended sentences which comprise a multitude of sub-clauses repeatedly employing the same construct. The first of these is divided into five sub-clauses and is dominated by the repetition of 'Celui que', used to refer to the creature which has apparently been sensed throughout history but has only now defeated man:

> Il est venu, Celui que redoutaient les premières terreurs des peuples naïfs, Celui qu'exorcisaient les prêtres inquiets, que les sorciers évoquaient par les nuits sombres, sans le voir apparaître encore, à qui les pressentiments des maîtres passagers du monde prêtèrent toutes les formes monstrueuses ou gracieuses des gnomes, des esprits, des génies, des fées, des farfadets. (*H* 933)

> [He/It has arrived, the One feared in the first terrors of the naïve races, the One who was exorcised by anxious priests, that sorcerers called up on dark nights, without seeing him/it appear, to whom the premonitions of the temporary masters of the world lent all the monstrous or gracious forms of gnomes, of spirits, of genies, of fairies, of elves.]

The sense of exaggerated repetition is achieved by the enumeration in the final clause of five consecutive types of mysterious forms attributed to this creature. The supremacy which the narrator grants to it is betrayed by the fact that his previous designations of 'on' and 'il' are now superseded by the quasi-reverential 'Celui'. The closing lines of this paragraph convey a powerful sense of hesitancy through eighteen instances of ellipsis used to prevent the successful completion of a series of clauses. This uncertainty is generated by the narrator's attempt to take the naming process even further: 'Il est venu, le... le... comment se nomme-t-il... le...' ['he/it has arrived, the... the... what is he/it called... the...'] (ibid.). These first four instances of ellipsis imply the difficulty the narrator encounters as he searches for an appropriate name for the creature. However, the following eight uses appear to indicate the narrator's inability to hear the name being supplied by the creature itself. In a manner reminiscent of the ellipsis encountered at the close of the entries for 10 July and 6 August, the final six instances, following the provision of the name 'Le Horla', suggest the narrator's unstated reflection upon its significance. Numerous critics have given their interpretation of the significance of the choice of 'horla' as the name for the creature troubling the narrator. Theodore Ziolkowski (1977, 1970) contends that it is 'presumably related to the French words *horrible, hors* [...] *hurler*' while Chambers (1980, 111) concentrates on the second of these suggestions because 'le "hors-là" — ce qui est extérieur — figure "l'autre" sous *toutes* ses formes' ['the "outside-there" — that which is exterior — represents "the other" in *all* its forms'] (original italics). It is significant that true resolution of this identification process is thwarted by the provision of a name which concretely means nothing but leaves the way open for multiple interpretations.

The sense of disintegration is at its most acute in the closing four paragraphs of this entry. The first of these, which considers the relative strength of the 'new being', is dominated by a sentence comprising ninety-three words, organized into weakly punctuated sub-clauses. It employs the device of multiple repetitive structures in consecutive clause groups to a more extreme degree than has been witnessed in any of the passages discussed previously:

> C'est que sa nature est plus parfaite, son corps plus fin et plus fini que le nôtre, que le nôtre si faible, si maladroitement conçu, encombré d'organes toujours

fatigués, toujours forcés comme des ressorts trop complexes, que le nôtre, qui vit comme une plante et comme une bête, en se nourrissant péniblement d'air, d'herbe et de viande, machine animale en proie aux maladies, aux déformations, aux putréfactions, poussive, mal réglée, naïve et bizarre, ingénieusement mal faite, œuvre grossière et délicate, ébauche d'être qui pourrait devenir intelligent et superbe. (*H* 934)

[It is that his/its nature is more perfect, his/its body is finer and more finished than our body, than our body which is so weak, so clumsily conceived, cluttered with organs which are always tired, always wound like overly complicated springs, than our body which lives like a plant and like an animal, barely feeding itself with air, grass, and meat, an animal machine prey to illness, deformity, putrefaction, labouring, badly tuned, naïve and bizarre, ingeniously poorly made, a crudely fashioned and delicate work of art, the draft of a being which could become intelligent and superb.]

The mixture of binary, ternary, and quaternary clause groups combined with the accumulation of imagery gives evocative expression to the narrator's desperation in the face of the relative weakness of man. This apprehension gives rise to an uncertainty which is betrayed by four interrogatives beginning 'pourquoi pas?' in the following two paragraphs. In the penultimate paragraph of the entry, the loss of control reaches its apogee as the narrator's thoughts become increasingly surreal. He imagines a giant butterfly, the size of one hundred universes, which flies from star to star and impassions the inhabitants of these other planets. The reader's impression that the narrator may now not even comprehend his own thoughts is fuelled by the repeated instances of ellipsis and exclamation marks. This passage is reminiscent of that encountered in *The Sylph* when Mikhail Platonovich describes his entry into the higher, poetic realm. The crucial difference between these two instances is that, in the Russian story, the reader is rescued from the effects of this incoherence by the voice of the publisher. In *Le Horla*, no such potential exists and the reader is left at the mercy of the disintegrating discourse of the diarist.

The penultimate and final paragraphs of the 19 August entry are separated by a break in the text formed by an entire line of elliptical points.[9] It is immediately followed by a question, 'Qu'ai-je donc?' ['What is wrong with me?'], the answer to which can be seen to reveal the potential significance of this interruption. The narrator alleges that his ailment is that: 'le Horla [...] me fait penser ces folies' ['the Horla [...] is making me think these mad thoughts'] (ibid.). In the light of this accusation, the break in the narrative can be seen to represent the boundary between the narrator's own thoughts and the preceding ones which he claims stem from the creature who possesses his soul. As such, the elliptical points give a more concrete textual form to the boundary between consciousnesses. The narrator's ability in these closing lines to qualify the preceding paragraphs as lacking in clarity and logic reveals that he has recaptured a measure of his rational powers. His ability now to read through his account with critical detachment supports his claim that responsibility for the obscure passages should lie with the Horla. The denouement of the story reveals, however, that the reclamation of rationality suggested here is only short-lived.

The first indication of this is the presence of a second entry dated 19 August. This is the first instance in *Le Horla* of two entries appearing with the same date and it intimates that the loss of verbal control is matched by a deterioration in structural rigour. Consideration of the time of action to which each entry makes reference provokes further confusion. In the first entry for 19 August, the diarist talks about the scientific journal that 'je viens de lire' ['I have just read'] (*H* 932). This implies that the passage of surreal reflection discussed above to which this reading gives rise occurs on the same day, the 19th. However, in the second of the 19 August entries, the narrator announces that the events to be recounted occurred when 'je me suis assis hier soir à ma table' ['I sat down yesterday evening at my table'] (*H* 935). The reference to 'yesterday' would therefore appear to locate these events as having happened on 18 August, that is, before those reported in the preceding entry. If this is indeed the case, the reader is faced with two questions. Firstly, if the actions involving the narrator's reflection took place on the 18th, why does the entry for that date make no mention of them? Secondly, why are they recorded in an entry subsequent to the one reporting events which actually took place at a later point in time? Whilst the answer to these questions naturally has to remain hypothetical, the need for the reader to pose them highlights how the notion of a diary as presenting a controlled and temporally ordered account of existence now finds itself under attack.

With its description of the temporary disappearance of the narrator's reflection, the second entry for 19 August brings the uncertainty prompted by the supernatural to its peak. This scene represents the culmination of the depiction in *Le Horla* of the supernatural as an element which disrupts normal rules of vision and visibility because the narrator alleges that it is the invisible creature which obfuscates his mirror image. The crucial role which this scene plays both in the development of the story and in Maupassant's depiction of madness explains the vast amount of critical attention which has been devoted to it. With reference to Maupassant's entire œuvre, Ponnau (1997, 304) observes:

> le motif du miroir acquiert [...] chez Maupassant une valeur obsessionnelle et cela dans la mesure même où loin de refléter le sujet placé devant lui, il occulte ses traits et, au sens fort du terme, l'éclipse.

> [the motif of the mirror acquires [...] in Maupassant an obsessional value and it does so to the extent that far from reflecting the subject placed in front of it, it obscures its traits and, in the extreme sense of the term, eclipses it.]

Michel Dentan (1976, 53) compares this mirror scene to the earlier hypnosis episode and argues that both should be seen as elements in the broader discussion of the status of writing and reality conducted by the author:

> Si l'on admet communément qu'un journal intime serait comme le 'miroir' ou la 'photographie' de celui qui l'écrit, ici au contraire, bien des signes (carton blanc, miroir vide, feuille blanche) semblent indirectement désigner l'écrit comme une opacité où se dérobe la réalité du moi écrivant: ils semblent en tout cas dire que cette réalité est en creux, qu'elle ne peut être perceptible que comme absence.

> [If we generally admit that a diary is the 'mirror' or the 'photograph' of the person who writes it, here on the contrary, numerous signs (the blank card, the empty mirror, the blank sheet of paper) seem to designate indirectly that which is written as an opaqueness in which the reality of the writing 'I' gives way: they certainly seem to be saying that this reality is hollow, and that it can only be perceived as an absence.]

During this mirror episode, the diarist acts in a manner which shows him employing the knowledge that he has acquired in the earlier page-turning incident. In a move which lends the discourse an unmistakably self-reflexive quality, he now attempts to entice the Horla into making an appearance by writing in his diary. When he is certain that the creature is reading over his shoulder, he abruptly stands up and turns round as if to confront his assailant. It is as he glances into the mirror at this point that he perceives the disappearance of his reflection:

> Eh bien?... on y voyait comme en plein jour, et je ne me vis pas dans ma glace!... Elle était vide, claire profonde, pleine de lumière! Mon image n'était pas dedans... et j'étais en face, moi! (*H* 935)

> [And so?... you could see into it as in full daylight, and I did not see myself in the mirror!... It was empty, profoundly clear and full of light! My image was not in it... and I was standing opposite it!]

The repeated ellipsis in these lines once again communicates the narrator's shock and apprehension at this irrational state of affairs. The syntactic devices employed in the description of the gradual reappearance of the narrator's reflection are strongly reminiscent of those highlighted in the discussion above of Spirite's first appearance in Guy de Malivert's mirror:

> Puis voilà que tout à coup je commençai à m'apercevoir dans une brume, au fond du miroir, dans une brume comme à travers une nappe d'eau; et il me semblait que cette eau glissait de gauche à droite, lentement, rendant plus précise mon image, de seconde en seconde. C'était comme la fin d'une eclipse. (*H* 936)

> [Then all of sudden I began to make myself out in a fog, deep in the mirror, in a fog as if through a layer of water; and it seemed to me that this water was gliding from left to right, slowly, making my image more and more precise with every passing second. It was like the end of an eclipse.]

As in Gautier's novella, Maupassant's diarist has recourse to repeated comparisons and to modal lexical verbs of perception. The sum effect of these devices is to obfuscate the discourse just as the image in the mirror is obscured.

The ambiguity generated during this scene is not simply the consequence of the terms the narrator uses to describe his perceptions, however. It stems equally from the manner in which he chooses to interpret what he sees. The contrast between his essentially rational approach during the experiments and his reactions in this scene is striking. According to how one chooses to interpret his behaviour, the narrator's response reveals either his new-found beliefs or his much-changed mental state. He describes the entity obscuring his reflection as lacking definite contours and resembling 'une sorte de transparence opaque' ['a sort of opaque transparency'] (*H* 936). Yet, he displays no awareness of the contradictions inherent in this oxymoron. Neither his ignorance of the true identity of the element which stands between him and the mirror nor his own explicit qualification of it as transparent prevents the narrator from concluding: 'Je l'avais vu!' ['I had seen him/it'] (ibid.). The confident tone of this declaration stands in defiance of the uncertainty which permeates almost every aspect of the preceding description. Furthermore, the irony of this statement cannot be overlooked. The narrator claims that his image is obscured by the invisible figure of the Horla. Yet, the defining characteristic of an invisible object is precisely its inability to obscure other elements. He also claims to have seen an invisible object. Therefore, whilst in his earlier experiments the narrator has invoked the rules of the rational to prove that he cannot have drunk the water, he now alleges the existence of a different set of rules in order to prove the existence of the Horla.

The ultimate threat to the coherence of the discourse, posed in the final diary entry, is the consequence of a partial but central information gap stemming from repeated ellipsis employed in preceding entries. From the moment in the account of 17 August when the Horla apparently knocks over furniture as it tries to escape the bedroom, the narrator increasingly talks about the potential of acting against it. Initially, however, the exact nature of the narrator's intentions remains unclear because they are frequently replaced by ellipsis: 'alors... alors... demain... ou après... [...] une heure viendra...' ['so... so... tomorrow... or afterwards... [...] an hour will come'] (*H* 932). Even when the narrator states and repeats his intention to kill the creature, he does not reveal any specific plan. The private nature of the narrator's communicative act in *Le Horla* means that the failure to provide this information is not a transgressive step. Whilst perhaps departing from the narrator's previous tendency to provide a level of informative detail which is unusual for a diary, the failure explicitly to note down his intentions is quite acceptable. Indeed, it might equally be inferred that the narrator's decision not to lay out his plan for killing the creature in his diary is motivated by a desire not to alert his victim to his intentions. Given the creature's apparent taste for reading his journal, any plan in writing would give the Horla advanced warning of his fate. Notwithstanding such theoretical admissibility, the absence of this crucial information renders the final entry more problematic for the reader.

The narrator's enigmatic claims in the opening lines of the entry for 10 September immediately create suspense: 'c'est fait... c'est fait... mais est-il mort?' ['it is done... it is done... but is he/it dead?'] (ibid.). In the first half of this entry, the information gap means that the air of assurance surrounding the narrator, communicated by the series of sixteen succinct verbal clauses to describe his measured activity, is not shared by the reader. Not until perhaps the twelfth or thirteenth of these clauses, when the narrator describes pouring the contents of his oil lamps over the carpet and furniture, does the reader realize that his intention is to kill the Horla by burning down his house. However, almost as soon as the reader is able to fill the first information gap regarding the plan, she is confronted by another which appears in the narrator's account of his observation from the garden of his house catching fire. This second gap cannot be justified by the lack of an audience for the narrator's speech act and, therefore, does constitute a more transgressive development. It consequently proves to be far more revealing of the narrator's mental state and to unsettle the reader to a greater degree. This gap is permitted to arise because of the symmetry which the narrator chooses to impose between the chronology of the action and that of his narration. He opts for a mode of 'sequentially ordered' temporal presentation (Bal 1997, 80) during the sixth paragraph of this entry in which the order of clauses in the 'siuzhet' exactly mirrors the order of events which constitute the 'fabula'. Having described with pleasure the sight of huge flames enveloping his house, the colours which these flames project into surrounding trees and the sound of windows shattering, he notes: 'Mais un cri, un cri horrible, suraigu, déchirant, un cri de femme passa dans la nuit, et deux mansardes s'ouvrirent! J'avais oublié mes domestiques!' ['But a cry, a horrible cry, very shrill, piercing, a woman's cry rang out in the night, and two attic windows opened! I had forgotten my servants!'] (*H* 937). The decision to delay his revelation of the servants' fate in the 'siuzhet' until the point which temporally corresponds to the discovery of this fact in the 'fabula' undeniably lends this account great dramatic impact. However, this retardation can also be considered to pose serious questions concerning the narrator's psychological state at this point. The narrator clearly announces that the events recounted in this entry have taken place on the previous day, 9 September. Therefore, the narrator's failure to reveal the presence of the servants at an earlier point of his account cannot be justified as the consequence of simultaneous narration. In fact, the posterior temporal stance displayed during this passage makes clear that, by the time the narrator begins his account of the fire, he is fully aware that he has burnt his servants to death. This temporal distance means that he could, therefore, provide the information at an earlier point. The decision not to do so and to preserve the exact sequential order of events gives the impression that the narrator has still not grasped the gravity of his actions. It is as if he has not assimilated the death of his servants into his recollection of the events and is as surprised by the discovery of this information in the telling as he was at the moment of action.

The closing four paragraphs of *Le Horla* see the narrator elaborate on the lack of conviction concerning the success of his attempt which has opened the final entry. Beginning with the interrogatives, 'mort? Peut-être?...' ['dead? Perhaps?...'] (*H* 938), the narrator gives voice to a sense of uncertainty which steadily grows into panic and desperation. These emotions lead to a loss of control, which is expressed by many of the techniques that have been discussed above. For instance, the first two of these paragraphs are dominated by six questions, each of which interrogate the possibility of visiting death upon a creature whose body is transparent. Repeated instances of ellipsis betray both the narrator's inability to provide definitive responses to his own questions and the sense of bewilderment which a potential answer in the negative would entail. This syntactic feature figures strongly in the final lines of the story as the narrator announces his belief that his attempt at murder has been unsuccessful: 'Non... non... sans aucun doute, sans aucun doute... il n'est pas mort... Alors... alors... il va donc falloir que je me tue, moi!...' ['No... no... without a doubt, without a doubt... he/it is not dead... So... so... I will therefore have to kill myself!...'] (ibid.). Amid the repetitions, incomplete sentences, and ellipses suggesting resignation and defeat, the conjunction 'donc' ['therefore'] draws particular attention to itself. It is a conjunction whose very nature suggests rational consequences, and yet it is employed at the close of a narrative which has depicted the apparent refutation of the most basic rational frameworks acknowledged by mankind. It effectively illustrates the drastic modifications which the narrator's sense of rationality has undergone since he sought medical advice for his sense of unease. Arguably, the ultimate lesson of this narrative is intended to highlight the impotence of rational thought, and yet the narrator's suggestion of suicide illustrates how his mental illness prevents him from grasping it. The defeat of rational thought and the narrative's final disintegration is illustrated by the fact that the close of the narrative takes the form of a fifth and final page break in the form of a whole line of elliptical points. Whilst the recurrence of this textual feature constructs a certain symmetry with the opening of the story, its unmistakable function is to deny closure to the end of the narrative. It ensures that the reader is left to ask a series of fundamental questions regarding the fate of both the narrator and the creature. By failing to provide a clear and concrete conclusion to the story, this break invites almost endless supposition as to what happens following this final entry. It has often been suggested that the break is proof of the end of the diary which, in itself, must signal the suicide of the narrator. It is surely the case though that to assign so confident a significance to an element of the text whose purpose is precisely to deny concrete interpretation is to diminish the impact of the narrative as a whole.

Part 3: Heterodiegetic Incoherence in *The Double*

Uncertainty is a central feature of *The Double* from the outset. However, the hesitation as a consequence of the apparently supernatural which is characteristic of the fantastic only begins to appear from the fifth chapter onwards. It is this chapter which contains the first allegation that Goliadkin is confronted by his double. Thereafter, challenges to the coherent quality of the discourse occur with increasing frequency, thereby hampering the reader's efforts to arrive at a definitive interpretation of events. As with *Le Horla*, the gradual disintegration of the discourse can be traced to three principal factors. Firstly, an examination of the fifth chapter will reveal how techniques employed in the novella's opening stages are now reinforced to suggest the narrator's unreliability. In the eight chapters that follow the first allegation of a doppelgänger, reader hesitation persists because no definitive information is provided either to confirm or to refute this irrational state of affairs. This absence is accounted for by two factors which constitute the second and third reasons for the disintegration of the discourse. On the one hand, the potential for validation from other characters in the fictional world, denied by the format of *Le Horla*, goes unexploited in *The Double* as both the voice and perspective of these figures are assigned an unconstructive role. Indeed, the occasionally destructive role played by these voices suggests that the entire fictional world is populated by characters of dubious reliability. More serious, though, is the manner in which the narrator fails to offer an additional perspective to that of Goliadkin. The narrator's non-fulfilment of conventional heterodiegetic responsibilities is achieved by techniques of confusion of voice through free indirect discourse and of almost complete alignment of visual perspective. These devices combine to leave the reader confronting a situation of acute disintegration of discursive significance.

Chapter 5 of *The Double* recounts a series of encounters between Goliadkin and a mysterious figure on the Fontanka embankment as the hero returns home just after midnight. In the build-up to the first appearance of this stranger, the reader becomes aware of the narrator's inconsistent exploitation of his heterodiegetic capabilities. For instance, at one moment, exhibiting his omniscience, he directly records Goliadkin's thoughts about the rising water level and the flood warning. However, in the very next sentence, both this ability and, more seriously, his most basic powers of observation are called into question as he reports, referring back to these thoughts: 'только что сказал или подумал это господин Голядкин, как увидел впереди себя идущего ему навстречу прохожего' ['no sooner had Mr Goliadkin said, or thought, this, than he saw a figure coming towards him'] (*D* 140). This sudden uncertainty is unexpected because, for a voice enjoying omniscience, possession of such basic knowledge should be unproblematic. The fact that this expression of fallibility occurs immediately prior to the revelation of the stranger's first appearance only lends it greater significance. Although the narrator's uncertainty specifically concerns the actions of the protagonist, it also influences the status granted to the subsequent clause. The reader is invited to ask why, if the narrator is unable to state with any conviction whether the protagonist speaks or thinks, his report of the presence of a passer-by should be considered reliable. Furthermore, when this breach in the narrator's abilities reappears in subsequent lines, it becomes impossible to dismiss as a momentary slip. For example, the narrator uses his omniscient access to present Goliadkin's reflections on the mysterious figure directly: 'этого запоздалого [...] может быть, и он то же самое, может быть, он-то тут и самое главное дело, и недаром идет' ['this passer-by is perhaps — he, himself, perhaps he is here and, what matters most, he is not walking for nothing'] (ibid.). Yet, the narrator then calls the very existence of these thoughts into doubt by remarking: 'может быть, впрочем, господин Голядкин и не подумал именно этого, а так только ощутил мгновенно что-то подобное и весьма неприятное' ['perhaps, indeed, Mr Goliadkin did not actually think this, but merely felt for a moment something resembling it and extremely unpleasant'] (ibid.). In the overall scale of this text, whether the protagonist thinks or speaks words may not be considered to be of crucial importance. However, the indication it gives of the problematization of the simplest acts of interpretation does not augur well for the reader's successful apprehension of subsequent, more disturbing events.

A far more significant information gap is created by the narrator's choice of focal point during the description of how Goliadkin and the mysterious figure walk past each other. The reader is keen to receive more details about the identity of this figure, and his approach towards Goliadkin would seem to offer the ideal opportunity to do so. However, this expectation remains unfulfilled because the moment when the figure walks closest to Goliadkin is simply not reported. The narrator describes the passer-by as being within a single yard of the protagonist but then, abruptly, his point of focalization shifts:

> Господин Голядкин тотчас, по всегдашнему обыкновению своему, поспешил принять вид совершенно особенный, — вид, ясно выражавший, что он, Голядкин, сам по себе, что он ничего, что дорога для всех довольно широкая и что ведь он, Голядкин, сам никого не затрагивает. Вдруг он остановился, как вкопанный, как будто молнией пораженный, и быстро потом обернулся назад, вслед прохожему, едва только его минувшему [...]. (ibid.)

> [Mr Goliadkin at once, in his usual way, hurriedly put on a very special air, an air clearly expressing that he, Goliadkin, went his own way, that he was all right, that the road was wide enough for everybody and that he, Goliadkin, would not interfere with anybody. Suddenly he stopped as if rooted to the spot, as if he had been struck by lightning, and then turned quickly round after the stranger, who had only that moment passed him [...].]

Instead of continuing to focus on the approach of the figure, the narrator turns his attention to Goliadkin's assumption of an 'air'. The description of this 'air' stands in place of the potentially more informative report of the stranger walking by. At the crucial moment, focalization shifts from an external point to an internal one; from giving a description of physical actions, the narrator switches to supplying in free indirect discourse the thoughts Goliadkin has about the attitude he needs to assume. By the time this switch is reversed, it is too late: the figure is now behind Goliakin and moving away from him so no full physical description can be given. The frustration occasioned to the reader by this period of seemingly misdirected focus is compounded by the report of the protagonist's reaction to the figure.

Although Goliadkin is confused by the figure's proximity, it appears to be a confusion based on a greater degree of information than has been supplied by the narrator to the reader. The protagonist asks himself: 'что, что это? [...] Да что ж это такое [...] что ж это я, с ума, что ли, в самом деле сошел?' ['What, what is this? [...] What on earth is [...] what is wrong with me, have I actually gone out of my mind?'] (*D* 141). With their tentative proposal of a rational explanation for events, these questions recall those posed frequently by protagonists of fantastic narratives in response to unusual events. However, a fundamental distinction exists between these other examples and the exploitation of this convention in *The Double*. In *Spirite*, for instance, the reader has been provided with a full description of the events which provoke Guy de Malivert's inquiry as to whether he is mad; the reader's uncertainty stems from the failure of the heterodiegetic voice to respond to it with additional commentary. Goliadkin's questions, however, are more disruptive because the event which prompts them has not even been described. The reader knows nothing about the identity of the passer-by which might prompt such anxious interrogation from Goliadkin. And the reader's inability to comprehend fully why Goliadkin needs to be asking these questions is the fault of the narrator. The shift in the point of focalization during the description of the figure passing by means that the reader can only surmise which aspect of this occurrence might give rise to the questions. The ambiguity they provoke is not, therefore, the result of the failure either by protagonist or by narrator to provide an adequate answer to them; it is the consequence of a lack of access to the reasons for which they might be asked. Denying the reader the information necessary to an understanding of Goliadkin's actions is a key technique exploited in *The Double* to give an accurate sense of his madness.

In the depiction of the subsequent appearances of the stranger in this fifth chapter, the narrator's unreliability is exacerbated by inconsistencies in the spatial unity of the fictional world. During their first encounter, Goliadkin and the mysterious figure are said to be walking in opposite directions. However, the reader is confused by the orientation of their second encounter when the narrator describes how: 'перед [Голядкиным] опять, шагах в двадцати от него, чернелся какой-то быстро приближавшийся к нему человечек' ['in front of [Goliadkin] again, about twenty steps away from him, was the small black figure of a man coming quickly towards him'] (ibid.). Unless the two are walking in a circle or have both turned around, it is difficult to see how they should still be walking towards each other when they meet for a second time. The spatial orientation of this scene is further complicated by the description of the men's third encounter:

Наконец, он увидел своего незнакомца на повороте в Итальянскую улицу.

Только теперь незнакомец уже шел не навстречу ему, а в ту же самую сторону, как и он, и тоже бежал, несколько шагов впереди. (D 142)

[Finally he saw his stranger at the corner of Italianskii Street. Only now the stranger was not coming towards him but going in the same direction as he was, and like him was also running, a few steps in front of him.]

How is it that these two men are now going the same way when, just previously, they have been heading in opposite directions? In the first chapter of this book, I have suggested that references to geographical entities argue for an equivalence between fictional and extrafictional worlds. Conventionally, this would be expected to extend to the laws of space and motion. However, this appears not to be the case here as references to actual streets and landmarks coexist alongside the depiction of an unacceptable physical state of affairs. The spatial incompatibility which prevails in this account provides an example of the 'malleability' of geography which creates 'an aura of the phantasmagorical' in Dostoevskii's fictional worlds (Roger Anderson 1986, 6). Whilst these rifts in spatial orientation may not be the specific responsibility of the narrator, they do nevertheless invite the reader to question his performance. At no point during the description of these encounters does the narrative voice comment upon their apparent inconsistency or provide justification for it. Whilst he may, quite legitimately, be unable to explain how these events come about, his failure even to comment upon their unusual nature creates the suspicion that he does not perceive them as transgressive. Consequently, questions arise concerning not simply the narrator's possession of authority but the extent to which he shares the reader's belief-system with regard to the rules of the rational world.

Given the mystery that surrounds this passer-by during these encounters, it might logically be expected that the provision of an identity for him would resolve a measure of the reader's uncertainty. However, in a manner which closely resembles the situation in *Le Horla*, this proves not to be the case. In actual fact, the naming of the character raises ambiguity to an acute level. The closing lines of the fifth chapter give a detailed depiction of the two men apparently in Goliadkin's room and eventually reveal the identity of the mysterious stranger:

Незнакомец сидел перед ним, тоже в шинели и в шляпе, на его же постели, слегка улыбаясь, и, прищурясь немного, дружески кивал ему головою. Господин Голядкин хотел закричать, но не мог, — протестовать каким-нибудь образом, но сил не хватило. Волосы встали на голове его дыбом, и он присел без чувств на месте от ужаса. Господин Голядкин совершенно узнал своего ночного приятеля. Ночной приятель его был не кто иной, как он сам, — сам господин Голядкин, другой господин Голядкин, но совершенно такой же, как и он сам, — одним словом, что называется, двойник его во всех отношениях... (D 143)

[The unknown man was sitting in front of him, also in a hat and an overcoat, on his own bed, slightly smiling and narrowing his eyes a little, he gave him a friendly nod. Mr Goliadkin wanted to cry out but could not, — to protest somehow, but he did not have the strength. His hair stood on end and he collapsed into a chair, insensible with horror. Mr Goliadkin completely recognized his nocturnal acquaintance. Mr Goliadkin's nocturnal acquaintance was none other than himself, — Mr Goliadkin himself, another Mr Goliadkin, but exactly the same as himself, — in short, what is called his double, in every respect...]

Doubles or doppelgängers should not exist in rationally ordered fictional worlds where human beings are original creations. If it could be definitively established that Goliadkin actually has such a double, hesitation could be resolved and Dostoevskii's novella would be classified as an example of the 'marvellous'. However, any such resolution is ruled out because of the difficulty encountered in identifying the voice which makes this irrational claim. The description of the stranger's dress, position, and actions as well as that of Goliadkin's horror and paralysis displays an appreciable degree of control, through both tone and measured construction. Despite shortcomings elsewhere in his performance, these discourse attributes are still indicative of the voice of the narrator. In the lines following the declaration that Goliadkin has recognized his companion, this sense of calm and control begins to evaporate. Specifically, the repetition of elements such as 'господин Голядкин' ['Mr Goliadkin'], 'сам' ['himself'], and 'ночной приятель' ['nocturnal acquaintance'] suggests the presence of a different voice. If the reader recalls the syntactic traits encountered during the protagonist's consultation with doctor Rutenshpits, she is likely to suspect that, in the crucial lines providing identification, the discourse bears traces of Goliadkin's voice. The absence of speech marks overtly signalling such a shift in voice means that these lines constitute an example of free indirect discourse. The reader confronts evidence of what Bal (1997, 50) labels 'interference between narrator's text and actor's text' where the interference is not overtly announced. The presence of free indirect discourse in the passage which alleges a supernatural state of affairs generates profound ambiguity primarily because 'it is not possible to decide whether the words [...] are the character's or the narrator's' (Chatman 1978, 202). This obfuscation of the source of information problematizes the question of how much authority to grant to the irrational claim. The possibility that the identification is provided by Goliadkin, and not by the narrator, undermines its reliability. The hero's tendency towards paranoiac allusion and incoherence, as well as his position on an inferior narrative level, is likely to discourage the reader from accepting the naming of the stranger as a statement of narrative fact.

Given the profoundly unreliable nature of this allegation of supernatural existence, one means of resolving hesitation would be for commentary or judgements to be provided by more reliable sources than the hero. However, despite the fact that the potential for introducing alternative experiencing personae into the narrative is ostensibly exploited, this proves to be ineffectual in resolving the ambiguity which lies at the heart of *The Double*. The visual perspective of these characters is entirely absent from the narrative as the reader is made to depend exclusively on Goliadkin's perception of events. Restricted and unreliable perspective is a recurrent feature of the novella, but a discussion of three particular scenes will provide ample illustration of its consequences.

In the novella's eighth chapter, an apparent confrontation between Goliadkin and his double over official papers is portrayed. Goliadkin is busying himself in response to a request to take documents to His Excellency when 'вдруг, и почти из-под руки Андрея Филипповича, стоявшего в то время в самых дверях, юркнул в комнату господин Голядкин-младший' ['suddenly, and almost under the nose of Andrei Filippovich, who was standing at that moment right in the doorway, Mr Goliadkin junior pranced into the room'] (*D* 164). The proximity of Andrei Filippovich, the office superior, to this seemingly supernatural appearance casts him in the role of potential witness, whose more objective testimony might aid interpretation. However, the possibility of receiving useful additional information is not fulfilled as the narrative focus remains trained on the double, neither recording the reactions of Andrei Filippovich from an external perspective (facial expressions or gestures), nor making a detour into his consciousness to report his thoughts. The narrator reports this character's repeated requests for the papers but these are never embellished with further details which might suggest that he experiences surprise or confusion at the presence of Goliadkin's doppelgänger. This lack of input from a more detached observer is frustrating on an initial level simply because it means that no new light is shed upon the question of the double's existence. In view of the narrator's earlier display of direct access into the mind of Goliadkin, however, the failure to enter the consciousness of Andrei Filippovich at this most opportune of moments makes it doubly so. It is not unreasonable to assume that the narrator's omniscience extends to more fictional characters than just the protagonist. Yet, the evidence presented during this scene suggests that this is not so. In fact, even the report that, when the double runs up to Andrei Filippovich, 'он не заметил ни одной из проделок его' ['he did not notice any of his manoeuvres'] (D 165), seems to be more an inference made from the protagonist's point of view than a statement informed by the narrator's omniscient privilege. This scene is representative of the narrator's performance throughout the novella. His possession of omniscience is never shown to extend beyond the mind of Goliadkin which results in the reader learning 'nothing at all about the inner life of any person except Goliadkin' (Terras 1969, 128). Cravens (2000, 63) explains how the actual narrative practice in *The Double* departs from initial expectations:

> At first glance, Dostoevsky's novel appears to be a standard third-person narrated novel: an external narrator relates the words, thoughts, and actions of the protagonist Yakov Petrovich Golyadkin. Upon closer examination, however, it becomes evident that the narrator narrates *only* Golyadkin's thoughts and actions; we learn the actions of other characters only when they appear in Golyadkin's vicinity, and we never have access to their thoughts. (original italics)

This restriction of narrator omniscience and alternative perspective leads to a situation in which the provision of information is at least as restricted as in the diary context of *Le Horla*.

The restricted access to the inner perspectives of characters other than Goliadkin does not lead to a concomitant suppression of alternative voices. Indeed, Goliadkin frequently converses with other members of the fictional world and their voices are regularly presented directly in the discourse. The paradox revealed by these passages of dialogue is that, far from clarifying the question of the double's existence, they actually serve to generate an even greater sense of confusion and ambiguity. The explanation for this failure is twofold: on the one hand, it stems from the unsettling lack of reliability displayed by Goliadkin's interlocutors and, on the other, from a further example of the narrator's refusal to contribute meaningfully to the construction of a coherent discourse.

Goliadkin's conversation with his colleague Setochkin in Chapter 6 initially appears to offer the reader some cause for optimism. Setochkin's comprehension of the reference Goliadkin makes to a new employee in the office at least confirms the existence of a second man. He even goes so far as to acknowledge that he shares the same name as Goliadkin. Nonetheless, the claim that this figure is a doppelgänger is effectively dismissed by his failure to acknowledge a resemblance between the two. It would seem only reasonable that the existence of two physically identical men who are not twins should be recognized by witnesses. Whilst Setochkin does concede that Goliadkin and the new employee share 'a family resemblance' (*D* 148), the clear distinction between this admission and the protagonist's much more strident claims challenge the doppelgänger interpretation. However, Setochkin's status as a reliable witness is undermined by the profound and unexpected shift in his opinions as the dialogue progresses. As if responding to pressure from Goliadkin, he subsequently admits that the two men could be mistaken for each other because: 'сходство в самом деле разительное [...] это даже чудесное сходство, фантастическое' ['the resemblance is indeed striking [...] it is even a miraculous, fantastic resemblance'] (*D* 149). As if this change of heart were not unsettling enough, Setochkin then goes much further when he implies that the new employee is in fact Goliadkin's double because the situation recalls that of his aunt who 'тоже перед смертию себя вдвойне видела...' ['also just before her death saw her double...'] (ibid.). Is the reader to understand that Setochkin now believes that the other Goliadkin is indeed the protagonist's double? It is almost impossible to say. What is clear is that Setochkin's contradictory claims must cast his entire testimony into doubt. As such, both his initial claim that Goliadkin and the new employee share nothing more than a passing resemblance as well as his later claim that the figure is the hero's double become equally incredible. Fantastic narratives are built upon the balance struck between contradictory claims or interpretations. The fundamental and profoundly unsettling distinction presented by *The Double* is that both claim and counterclaim are voiced by a single character with almost no time lapse between them.

As with the threats to spatial unity discussed above, responsibility for the unnervingly contradictory opinions expressed by Setochkin cannot be laid at the narrator's door. Nevertheless, this figure does have some part to play in the reader's growing sense of bewilderment during this scene. The conversation between Goliadkin and his colleague is presented as an extended passage of direct dialogue. During this dialogue, the narrator provides only peremptory tags for the different parts of the speech, allowing them to stand relatively independently. The consequence of this more mimetic method of presentation is that it drastically reduces the opportunities available to the narrator for supplying enlightening interpretation of its content. The reader consequently receives no help in constructing the true significance of Setochkin's words from the voice which is still considered to be the most authoritative. The combination of Setochkin's unreliability and the narrator's silence serves to render the ambiguity which already surrounds the existence of the double even more profound.

In Chapter 9 of *The Double*, this impression of the absence of any reliable or coherent voices in the discourse is clearly reinforced. The chapter describes the attempts Goliadkin makes to send a series of letters to his double. In terms of the potential it offers for substantiation of the existence of the doppelgänger, this episode is granted a status similar to that of the scene with Setochkin discussed above. If a letter can be written and successfully delivered to the other Goliadkin, the reader may well be persuaded to believe in his presence. The most significant passage in this episode is the scene between Goliadkin and Petrushka following the composition and apparent dispatch of the first of four letters in which the hero complains about the double's treatment of him. In this episode, Petrushka is cast in the role of potential witness. The letter is presently directly in the narrative but is interrupted on two occasions to allow Goliadkin's thoughts about the appropriateness of its tone to be recorded. When satisfied, the protagonist summons Petrushka and asks him to enquire after the other Goliadkin's address with Vakhrameev at the office and then to deliver the letter. Acute doubts regarding the successful execution of, and more fundamentally the possibility of executing, this task are raised in the dialogue between Goliadkin and his servant when the latter has supposedly returned from delivering the letter.

The difficulties for both reader and protagonist begin when Petrushka denies all knowledge of a letter: 'никому я не отдавал никакого письма; и не было у меня никакого письма… вот как!' ['I didn't give no letter to nobody. I never even had no letter… that's the truth'] (*D* 178). In the face of Goliadkin's protests, Petrushka not only persists in this denial but goes as far as to disavow the existence of anyone called Vakhrameev. However, just like Setochkin before him, Petrushka proves incapable of remaining consistent in his account as he subsequently begins to deny his own claims. He now admits to having gone to the office, 'право слово, вот был же' ['to tell the truth, I was there'] (*D* 179), and to having been given the address for the other Goliadkin by Vakhrameev. The dialogue then becomes almost farcical as Petrushka lapses into contradictory statements in consecutive declarations, first denying and then confirming the existence of a letter: '"Какое письмо? и не было никакого письма, и не видал я никакого письма." […] "Отдал его, отдал письмо"' ['"What letter? There wasn't no letter, and I never seen no letter!" […] "I handed it over, I gave the letter to him"'] (*D* 180). The reader is completely at a loss to decide whether Petrushka has been able to deliver the letter or not. Charles Passage (1954, 31) is just one of a number of critics to comment on the significance of this episode:

> Here Dostoevskii does not quite play fair with the reader. In each of several details, he is evasive when we would like to know precisely what happens. […] The question arises as to whether there were even any letters except as Mr Goliadkin composed them, both originals and replies. Quite possibly, he maintained both parts of the correspondence himself. Or still more probably, there is simply no rational explanation.

Passage arguably underplays the impact of these exchanges upon the reading experience. Such a contradiction-ridden account of events would be unsettling in any narrative. However, in the context of the fantastic, such inconsistency becomes far more significant because it complicates the reader's ability to make any judgement regarding the actual state of affairs in the fictional world. The hesitation provoked by this dialogue is sustained because the voice of the narrator is again almost entirely absent during it. The core of the dispute over the letter takes the form of twenty-five statements: thirteen from Goliadkin, twelve from Petrushka. Of these, only three of Goliadkin's declarations are accompanied by any input from the heterodiegetic voice;

the remainder stand unattributed. On the rare occasions when he does intervene, the narrator contents himself with descriptions of how the protagonist speaks. The narrator's tags fail to provide any useful clues as to the actual situation and are another indication of his inability to access the minds of other fictional characters. Compounding as it does the questionable reliability of the two participants and the contradictory nature of the claims both between and within the individual speech acts, this narrator silence ensures that the reader is left with an acute sense of uncertainty. Although doubts regarding Goliadkin's sanity are not raised as explicitly in Dostoevskii's novella as they are in *Le Horla*, these narrative techniques inscribe them on a discourse level in much the same way as syntax does in Maupassant's story. The restricted access to alternative perspectives imbues the narrative with a sense of claustrophobia, as if the reader were locked inside the mind of the protagonist. The revelation of widespread unreliability amongst members of the fictional world suggests that questionable reason is not confined to the character of Goliadkin alone; the apparent breakdown in rational thought processes comes to seem universal and inescapable.

In the scene with Setochkin, it is the narrator's failure to record this character's thoughts which undermines interpretation. In the dialogue with Petrushka, it is his refusal to provide commentary which allows confusion to reign. Elsewhere in *The Double*, the absence of the narrator's voice or visual perspective as an independent source of information causes reader uncertainty. To a considerable degree, the incoherence which establishes itself as a feature of the novella is the result of free indirect discourse in which the narrator's voice appears to merge with that of the protagonist. The potential for creating ambiguity by means of the interference between voices has been noted in Chapter 1 above. The exploitation of free indirect discourse in Dostoevskii's novella develops this potential to a strikingly extreme degree. Indeed, whilst only particular instances of this device can be highlighted here, it actually represents an ever-present feature of *The Double*. The resulting sense of a disintegration in coherent discourse is compounded by gaps which arise when the protagonist's perspective is compromised by a loss of consciousness or sight. Such instances illustrate the almost indivisible alignment of the narrator's point of view with that of Goliadkin in a visual reflection of the effects produced by free indirect discourse.

During the description of Goliadkin's arrival in the office in Chapter 10, the reader is told that he is received coldly by his co-workers. The hero's sense of foreboding as to the reasons for this reception is apparently confirmed as the entry of another figure is reported:

В кучке молодых окружавших его сослуживцев вдруг, и, словно нарочно, в самую тоскливую минуту для господина Голядкина, появился господин Голядкин-младший, веселый по-всегдашнему, с улыбочкой по-всегдашнему, вертлявый тоже по-всегдашнему, одним словом: шалун, прыгун, лизун, хохотун, легок на язычок и на ножку, как и всегда, как прежде, точно так, как и вчера, например, в одну весьма неприятную минутку для господина Голядкина-старшего. (D 194)

[In the group of young colleagues surrounding him, suddenly and, as if on purpose, at the most discouraging moment for Mr Goliadkin, Mr Goliadkin junior appeared, as cheerful as always, wearing his little smile as always, and as restless as always, mischievous, jumping about, fawning, guffawing, light of tongue and fleet of foot, as he always was, precisely as he had been on the previous day, for example, at a very unpleasant moment for Mr Goliadkin senior.]

Is it the case that this description establishes definitively that Goliadkin is pursued by his double? Arguably not. In an echo of the account of the figure's presence in Goliadkin's bedroom in Chapter 5, a number of the syntactic traits in this report suggest that it is not informed by the voice of the heterodiegetic narrator alone. For instance, the repetition of particles such as 'as always' and 'at a [...] moment' creates a hesitant style of speech more typical of Goliadkin. The five participles listed in immediate succession betray an anxious emotional state which seems inappropriate for the narrator. The use of the diminutive form of 'smile' ['улыбочка'] is also more indicative of Goliadkin's personalized speech style. Arguably the clearest signal that this description is not guided by the narrator's perspective is the temporal deictic marker, 'вчера' [distorted by translation but literally, 'yesterday'], which cannot be reconciled with this voice's stance. The narrator's posterior temporality implies that he does not enjoy the contemporaneity with the action in the fictional world which would justify a reference to 'yesterday'. The acceptable temporal deictic marker for this voice would be 'в предыдущий день' ['the previous day'] or 'за день до этого' ['a day before this']. The use of 'yesterday' therefore signals the presence of the voice of a character situated in the present moment of the action — Goliadkin.

Confirmation that it is the voice of the protagonist which interferes with the narrator's discourse during this description is provided by the negative subjectivity which colours the references to Goliadkin junior. Indicators of the personal language situation of the protagonist are discernible in the passage quoted above, but make themselves felt more strongly in the description of the alleged handshake between the two men:

> Но каково же было изумление, исступление и бешенство, каков же был ужас и стыд господина Голядкина-старшего, когда неприятель и смертельный враг его, неблагородный господин Голядкин-младший, заметив ошибку преследуемого, невинного и вероломно обманутого им человека, без всякого стыда, без чувств, без сострадания и совести, вдруг с нестерпимым нахальством и с грубостию вырвал свою руку из руки господина Голядкина-старшего [...]. (D 195)

> [But what was the consternation, outrage, and fury, what was the shame and horror of Mr Goliadkin senior, when his adversary and deadly enemy, the ignoble Mr Goliadkin junior, having realized the mistake of the persecuted and innocent man he had perfidiously betrayed, without shame, without feeling, without compassion or conscience, suddenly snatched his hand away from Mr Goliadkin senior with unbearable effrontery and discourtesy [...].]

This passage is replete with nouns, adjectives, and adverbial expressions which cast Goliadkin senior in a positive light whilst betraying a violently negative attitude towards Goliadkin junior. The particular judgmental bias of this description unmistakably indicates how the voice and opinions of the fictional protagonist have infiltrated the narrator's discourse. The presence of free indirect discourse creates ambiguity because, as noted above, the obscured source of information raises questions of reliability. However, its presence also poses interpretative problems which go substantially beyond a more conventional degree of ambiguity. The interference of voices suggests that the narrator relinquishes the position of detached observation typical of heterodiegetic voices and places himself 'directly into the experiential field of the character' (Roy Pascal 1977, 9). This alignment of voices deprives the narrator of any perceptible role in guaranteeing the coherent quality of the discourse. During this passage of free indirect discourse, the voice of Goliadkin seems to dominate and, although the past tense indicates that the heterodiegetic narrator is not entirely absent, this voice makes no constructive contribution to interpretation. This lack of mediation leaves the partial, subjective, and paranoiac description of events provided by Goliadkin's voice as the reader's sole source of information. The narrator is powerless to counteract the increasing sense of diminished control as the protagonist's voice comes to the fore.

The failure of this narrator as a detached commentator upon the voice of the protagonist extends to his duties regarding visual perspective. In the twelfth chapter of *The Double*, Goliadkin is described visiting His Excellency in order to solicit his favour and protection. The reader's ability to gain a coherent picture of events occurring during this episode is threatened by Goliadkin's sudden loss of sight:

> Когда наш герой вошел, то почувствовал, что как будто ослеп, ибо решительно ничего не видал... Мелькнули, впрочем, две-три фигуры в глазах: 'Ну, да это гости', — мелькнуло у господина Голядкина в голове. Наконец наш герой стал ясно отличать звезду на черном фраке его превосходительства, потом, сохраняя постепенность, перешел и к черному фраку, наконец получил способность польного созерцания... (*D* 215)

> [When our hero entered, he felt as though he had gone blind, because he could see absolutely nothing... Then two or three figures flashed before his eyes; the thought 'So these are guests' — flitted into his mind. Finally our hero began to distinguish clearly the star on His Excellency's black coat and then gradually the black coat and at last he regained the power of full vision...]

In heterodiegetic narratives, it is conventional to expect that restrictions in the protagonist's consciousness will be supplemented by information from the narrative voice. This convention operates in *Spirite* when Guy de Malivert's avowed lack of consciousness during the period when he writes to Mme d'Ymbercourt does not prevent the composition of the letter being narrated. However, when Goliadkin loses the power of sight here, no alternative perspective steps in to fill the void. The elliptical points at the end of the first sentence above effectively signal that, for the unspecified period of time when Goliadkin is 'blind', the narrative provides no information. This ellipsis reveals the position of dependence upon Goliadkin's perspective into which the reader is forced; if the protagonist experiences nothing, the reader will be informed of nothing. Exaggerating the syntactic obfuscation which mirrors the obscuring of the narrator's reflection in *Le Horla*, the protagonist's blindness in *The Double* is given textual expression by means of a temporary blank in the discourse. Only when Goliadkin begins to recover his sight do piecemeal descriptions and hypotheses start to fill this blank. Just as in Maupassant's story, the presence of blanks implies the failure of rational discourse to make sense of experience.

The ambiguity created in this scene by the faltering visual perspective of the protagonist is rendered more acute by the reappearance of a familiar motif: the mirror. This motif has first played a significant role during the scene in the restaurant narrated in Chapter 9 when Goliadkin is asked to pay for eleven patties when he claims only to have eaten one. Goliadkin's confusion regarding the consumption of patties is resolved when he notices that: 'в дверях, которые, между прочим, герой наш принимал доселе за зеркало, стоял один человечек, — стоял он, стоял сам господин Голядкин' ['in the doorway, which, by the way, our hero had until then taken for a mirror, stood a little man, — he was standing, Mr Goliadkin himself was standing'] (*D* 174). In the later scene at His Excellency's, Goliadkin turns away from one seemingly familiar figure who makes him uneasy only to be confronted by another 'strange guest':

> В дверях, которые герой наш принимал доселе за зеркало, как некогда тоже случилось с ним, появился *он*, — известно кто, весьма короткий знакомый и друг господина Голядкина. Господин Голядкин-младший действительно находился до сих пор в другой маленькой комнатке [...]. (*D* 216; original italics)

> [In a doorway which our hero had until then taken for a mirror, as had also happened before, *he* appeared, — and it is known who, the very close acquaintance and friend of Mr Goliadkin. Mr Goliadkin junior had in fact until that moment been in another small room [...].]

Just as in the earlier restaurant scene, Goliadkin's confusion of a mirror and a doorway is reported in a quite offhand manner, as if the information were inconsequential. Yet, the revelation of this confusion obliges the reader to admit another potential explanation for the existence of Goliadkin junior. Alongside the existing possible interpretations of the figure as a colleague onto whom Goliadkin projects a similarity, a figment of his deluded reason or an actual doppelgänger, the reader is now invited to consider the possibility that he is no more than Goliadkin's reflection. Even though this description reports that Goliadkin resolves his mirror/doorway confusion, the simple fact that such an approximation is posited suffices to ensure that the reader's uncertainty is not similarly silenced.[10] In a narrative which is typified by the provision of incomplete and obscured information, the presence of the merest hint of an alternative interpretation is sufficient to exacerbate existing ambiguity. Whilst the nature of the roles assigned to the mirror in *Le Horla* and *The Double* may be distinct, a broad similarity can be observed in the consequences they produce. In Maupassant's story, the temporary disappearance of the narrator's image and its replacement with the form of the Horla arguably ushers in the period of the greatest loss of discursive control. If this scene is considered to be the catalyst for the narrator's ultimate decision that the only way to defeat the Horla is to kill himself, its contribution to disintegration of both discourse and self is of paramount importance. In *The Double*, the final chapter of the novella, which describes the consequences of the double's appearance at His Excellency's, portrays a similar decisive shift towards disintegration. The account of Goliadkin secreting himself in the woodpile outside the house before being invited back in, only to find himself carted off to the insane asylum by Rutenshpits, is dominated by faltering visual perspective and increasing physical and emotional disorientation. The exploitation of free indirect discourse is now exaggerated to the point where it assumes the appearance of stream of consciousness as the voice of the narrator disappears almost completely. The mirror scenes in both *Le Horla* and *The Double* can therefore be considered to signify the moment of final victory of the apparently irrational assailants over their human hosts, expressed on a textual level by the overwhelming force of discursive disintegration.

Neither in *Le Horla* nor in *The Double* does the depiction of the protagonist as possibly insane enable the reader to resolve her interpretative hesitation. The presence of discursive disintegration in both 'du dedans' and 'du dehors' accounts of madness insists upon the failure of the written word to rationalize alienated experience. Theoretically, a reader might expect a homodiegetic narrative of madness to differ markedly from a heterodiegetic account. And broadly speaking, *Le Horla* exploits the potential of syntax predominantly while *The Double* favours the manipulation of an array of narrative techniques. However, in practice, these two works have far more in common than not in terms of how they achieve the disintegration of coherent discourse. Both Maupassant and Dostoevskii employ the stock devices of the fantastic in a more exaggerated or problematized form than the first four texts I have discussed. The reader's experience of proximity to mental breakdown in both works is the consequence of the presence (actual or created) of a single, unreliable narrative voice. The switch to a diary format for the second version of *Le Horla* imposes an isolated voice whose descent into madness or confrontation with the supernatural cannot be confirmed by any other witness. The fact that Dostoevskii's novella exploits techniques to circumvent so completely the supposedly protective framework of heterodiegesis means that it represents the more transgressive depiction of incoherent experience. The profound confusion caused to Goliadkin by the appearance of his double apparently succeeds in contaminating all those around him, including the heterodiegetic narrator. This narrative voice seems to evaporate as an independent presence in the face of Goliadkin's alienation, leaving the reader with no filter between herself and the increasingly incoherent fictional world. Therefore, in both *The Double* and *Le Horla*, narrative and syntactic techniques are exploited to ensure that the disintegration of fictional self is reflected in the disintegration of rational discourse. The reader is left to confront alone a profound sense of bewilderment and hesitation.

Notes to Chapter 3

1. Some debate surrounds the number and identity of the various versions of this story. André Targe (1975, 446–59) considers there to be three versions: the first *Le Horla* of 1886, the second of the same title in 1887, and the third, *Le voyage du Horla*, published in July 1887. Neil Cornwell (1990, 100) acknowledges only the first two versions of the story and believes the germ of the idea to have first appeared in *Lettre d'un fou* (1885). However, Jacques Finné (1980, 74) considers the original version of the story to be *Un fou?* (1884). For my purposes, I will consider the 1886 version to be the first and the 1887 version to be the second.

2. Although Dostoevskii made attempts at revision immediately after publication, and then again in 1847, 1859, between 1861–65, and finally in 1866, when a reworked version appeared in the third edition of his collected works, he never considered the project satisfactorily completed. For a

detailed discussion of the alterations made between the 1846 and 1866 versions of the novel, see David Gasperetti (1989, 217–18) and John Jones (1983, 55–67). For the purposes of the present discussion, I will refer to the 1866 version of the novel which is the one more widely read.

3. References to *Le Horla* are taken from *Contes et nouvelles*, Paris: Gallimard, 1979.

4. Matthew MacNamara (1986, 159) believes that binary, ternary, and accumulative verbal sentence structures such as those highlighted here are typical of Maupassant. He attributes a lesser impact to the latter technique than is proposed in this chapter, although he clearly signals the impression of a search for satisfactory terms on the part of the speaker:

After the point at which […] the narrator disposes of his syntactical nucleus, he is free on several occasions to stop accumulating further details. As he repeatedly declines to avail himself of this grammatical freedom the notations added do more than represent certain motifs; they also reproduce the temporal and qualitative progression of his search for the expression that will ultimately satisfy him. The successive discretionary elements can be read as afterthoughts, statements complementary to, and suggested by those which have just been written.

5. References to *The Double* are taken from *Polnoe sobranie sochinenii v tridtsati tomakh*, vol. I, Leningrad: Nauka, 1972.

6. The provision of physical proof suggesting that events cannot be dismissed as an hallucination or dream is a crucial ingredient in texts of the fantastic. Consider, for example, the ring found in the bridal suite by the narrator in *La Vénus d'Ille*, the green figurine left upon the narrator's table in Gautier's *Le Pied de momie* (1840), or the silver key to his dead wife's tomb which the comte d'Athol finds on the bedroom floor in Villiers de l'Isle-Adam's *Véra* (1874).

7. The French subject and object pronouns, 'il' and 'le', allow for an ambiguity not permitted in English. A translation of these by 'he' and 'him' would suggest a degree of humanization not clearly indicated in the original; hence my decision to use both 'he' and 'it' to denote the creature.

8. The significance of the invisible creature's reading of a book during this scene has been noted by critics (see Ross Chambers 1980, 112; Radu Turcanu 1998, 393). Shoshana Felman (1978, 66) draws a link between the experience of madness and the act of reading:

Toute lecture, dit Nerval, est une sorte de folie, puisqu'elle repose sur une illusion et nous pousse à nous identifier avec des héros imaginaires. La folie n'est rien d'autre qu'une lecture vertigineuse: le fou est celui qui est pris dans le vertige de sa propre lecture. La démence est, avant tout, folie du livre, le délire, une aventure du texte.

[Every act of reading, says Nerval, is a type of madness, given that it relies on an illusion and prompts us to identify ourselves with imaginary heroes. Madness is nothing other than vertiginous reading: the madman is the one who gets caught up in the vertigo of his own reading. Insanity is, first and foremost, the madness of the book; delirium is an adventure of the text.]

This motif is exploited more forcefully in the scene to be discussed below of the narrator's enticement of the Horla by feigning reading.

9. This is the third of five instances of this textual feature. The first is located at the opening of the narrative before the first diary entry and is not consistently reproduced in the various reprints of the story. The second appears in the entry for 16 July following the account of the consequences of the hypnosis which doctor Parent performs on the narrator's cousin, Mme Sablé, in Paris. In this instance, the page break could simply represent a temporal shift as the lines following it bring the reader forward to the present moment of the diary composition and away from the moment of the action. However, it could also express the narrator's stupefaction at what he has witnessed. Arguably, both of these possibilities are developed by this third appearance of the feature which appears to mark a shift between consciousnesses. The fourth instance, located between the entries for 21 August and 10 September, indicates both a geographical shift from the house to the Hotel Continental in Rouen and a temporal break given that, at twenty days, this is the second longest interval between entries. The fifth instance is found at the end of the story and will be discussed later in this part.

10. The approximation drawn here between the doorway and the mirror represents another popular motif of the fantastic, linked to the ambiguity of human existence and the perception of reality. In *Spirite*, the first description of the baron de Féroë is given as he stands in a doorway. This physical location is symbolic of the role which this character plays in the fictional world. He is illustrated as

straddling the boundary between the natural world and the supernatural one and it is he who alerts Guy de Malivert to the proximity of the spiritual realm (*S* 231). Whilst the interference between rational and spiritual worlds illustrated in *Spirite* and *The Double* may be quite distinct, the motif of the doorway is exploited to similar ends. In Dostoevskii's novella, the fact that confusion arises because the figure of the double is in a doorway taken to be a mirror indicates the ambiguous existence he has in the fictional world. Whilst not a spirit in the sense of those encountered in Gautier's novella, Goliadkin junior does occupy a questionable position in terms of his adherence to either the natural or the supernatural world.

CHAPTER 4

Narrative Play and Generic Disruption: Hesitation and Self-Consciousness

Introduction

The first and second rules which Todorov says govern the fantastic focus upon the obligations of the text and the characteristics of hesitation. The third brings the role of the reader very much to the fore as it is claimed that this figure must adopt a certain attitude to the text and that, crucially, 'il refusera aussi bien l'interprétation allégorique que l'interprétation "poétique"' ['he will equally refuse the allegorical and the "poetic" interpretation'] (F 38). Todorov justifies this need for a rejection of allegory by explaining the problems which this literary mode poses to the fantastic:

> Premièrement, l'allégorie implique l'existence d'au moins deux sens pour les mêmes mots; on nous dit parfois que le sens premier doit disparaître, d'autres fois que les deux doivent être présents ensemble. Deuxièmement, ce double sens est indiqué dans l'œuvre de manière *explicite*: il ne relève pas de l'interprétation (arbitraire ou non) d'un lecteur quelconque. [...] Si ce que nous lisons décrit un événement surnaturel, et qu'il faille pourtant prendre les mots non au sens littéral mais dans un autre sens qui ne renvoie à rien de surnaturel, il n'y a plus de lieu pour le fantastique. (F 68–69; original italics)

> [Firstly, allegory implies the existence of at least two meanings for the same words; we are sometimes told that the primary sense must disappear, at other times that both meanings must be present together. Secondly, this dual sense is indicated in the text *explicitly*: it does not fall to the interpretation (arbitrary or not) of a given reader. [...] If what we read describes a supernatural event, but it is nevertheless necessary to take the words not in their literal sense but in another sense which is entirely unrelated to the supernatural, there is then no more room for the fantastic.]

What is striking in these lines is the similarity between Todorov's characterization of allegory and popular concepts of irony. Jonathan Culler's (1974, 187) proposition that 'an ironic statement has a literal meaning, but that meaning is only semblance and the true proposition is hidden and must be reconstructed' reveals in part why allegory and irony can be considered to be related phenomena. Moreover, the inclusion of Nikolai Gogol's *Hoc* (*The Nose*) in Todorov's survey of allegory demonstrates how certain works can span both allegorical and ironic modes and how the two categories can become conflated. This final chapter exploits this similarity in order to examine how successfully the fantastic operates in playful, self-conscious, or ironic texts.

The incompatibility which is alleged between allegory and the fantastic prompts a question which this chapter endeavours to answer. To what extent is the experience of hesitation necessary to the fantastic problematized in works which treat the conventions of the genre ironically?

The dismissal of allegory in the fantastic cannot simply be extended unquestioningly to irony. Notable distinctions exist between the two modes, which means that the potential for an 'ironic fantastic' might well remain realizable. Unlike allegory, which typically constructs '[un] double sens', irony enjoys a signifying potential which reaches beyond just a second plane of meaning. Lilian Furst (1984, 12) underlines this distinction when she contends:

> [the effect of irony] is prismatic: through hints and suggestions it arouses in the reader an inkling of latent layers of signification. [...] It says not so much the *opposite* to what is meant as something *other than* is stated. There is a crucial difference between 'opposite' and 'other than': 'opposite' is limited and limiting, [...] while the modification into 'other than' opens up that latitude, that spiritual freedom of movement in which irony thrives. (original italics)

Irony's construction of a prism of alternative meanings may crucially allow it to escape the particular obstacle encountered by allegory: the fact that its non-literal meaning is not related to the supernatural. Although irony may subvert a first layer of signification, by proposing multiple alternative meanings it sustains the possibility that one of these may still involve the supernatural. Narrative play, an ironic attitude, and the concomitant recycling of conventions in certain texts can all lead to a removal of semantic security, which does not occur in allegory. This theoretically preserves the potential for hesitation. The semantic multiplicity in irony raises the spectre, effectively denied by allegory's simple duality, of a more profoundly unsettling discursive experience for the reader.

Before this discussion begins, it is useful to reflect briefly upon the characteristics of the reader to which this chapter makes reference. The irony and playfulness deployed by the works to be examined here is aimed, quite specifically, at the conventions of the fantastic. However, while in allegory the alternative meaning is indicated 'explicitly', in irony the additional layers of signification are 'latent'. Consequently, a discussion of texts which are acutely aware of their generic lineage demands that the existence of an equally knowledgeable reader be posited. As Linda Hutcheon (1988, 127) points out, the success of play with an intertext 'demands of the reader not only the recognition of textualised traces of the literary and historical past but also the awareness of what has been done — through irony — to those traces'. Throughout *Introduction à la littérature fantastique*, Todorov makes reference to a 'lecteur implicite'. This is the image or function of the reader as projected by the literary text. However, my analysis of the recycling of conventions envisages a less neutrally functional concept of the reader. In the reference it makes to real rather than abstract emotions experienced in response to narrative play, my discussion envisages a figure which corresponds most closely to Stanley Fish's concept of the 'informed reader'. Fish (1980, 87) characterizes this figure as 'neither an abstraction, nor an actual living reader, but a hybrid — a real reader (me) who does everything within his power to make himself informed'.[1] Whilst reluctant to add yet another term to an already extensive list, the paramount importance I attach to the generic competence of this figure in what follows leads me to refer to her as an 'initiated reader'.

This chapter examines the compatibility of irony and the fantastic in the context of Théophile Gautier's *Onuphrius, ou les vexations d'un admirateur d'Hoffmann* and Nikolai Gogol's *The Nose*. A first version of Gautier's story was published in *La France Littéraire* in August 1832 under the intriguing title *Onuphrius Wphly*. In October of the same year, a second version appeared in *Le Cabinet de lecture* with the slightly modified title, *L'Homme vexé, Onuphrius Wphly*. The present discussion refers to the third and final version of the story (henceforth called simply *Onuphrius*), which was published in the journal *Jeunes-France* in 1833. The eponymous hero of Gautier's story is a young painter and poet of singular appearance whom many people take to be mad. The story recounts a series of events which he believes involve a supernatural agent: his portrait of his girlfriend, Jacintha, has a moustache painted on it; his elbow is nudged and he smudges his work; his paints explode and his brushes go hard inexplicably; when playing draughts his pieces are moved by an unknown finger wearing a large ruby ring. Onuphrius becomes convinced that the figure responsible is none other than the devil; and he is increasingly affected as these interventions become more and more outlandish. The devil apparently climbs out of a mirror to remove part of Onuphrius's brain, thereby allowing his thoughts to float freely away; he then appears at a party, and as the hero is about to recite his own work, he fills his mouth with the poetry of other writers in gelatinous form. The sight of Jacintha leaving the party with the devil is the last straw for Onuphrius. He contracts a fever and, although he recovers physically, mentally he is lost and sinks into madness.

Nikolai Gogol (1809–52) is often referred to as the father of the Russian short story. Whilst Pushkin came to prose relatively late in his career, Gogol, despite also writing a number of plays, made his most significant contributions in prose. In spite of being viewed in some circles as one of the first exponents of Russian realism, Gogol's stories were imbued with a sense of the otherworldly from the very beginning of his career. His two earliest collections, *Evenings on a Farm near Dikanka* (1831–32) and *Mirgorod* (1835), are set in his native Ukraine and are steeped in the folk belief in witches, monsters, and elemental spirits. The shift to St Petersburg in his mature work sees a new focus upon the plight of the so-called 'маленький человек' ['little man'], but the presence of the devil as an agent subverting reality is always discernible. *The Nose*, like *Onuphrius*, appeared in two early incarnations before the publication of its third and definitive version. The first version was reputedly turned down by the *Moscow Observer* in February 1835 for being too 'trivial' and 'filthy'. It was then rescued thanks to publication in Pushkin's newly founded journal, *The Contemporary*, in September 1836. The final 1842 version, referred to here, appeared in the edition of Gogol's collected prose published in that year. The story begins with a barber, Ivan Iakovlevich, finding a nose in his loaf of bread one morning. He recognizes the nose as belonging to one of his clients, Major Kovalev, who in turn awakens to find a flat space where his nose used to be. As Ivan Iakovlevich attempts to get rid of the nose, Kovalev tries to retrieve his lost organ by visiting a newspaper office, the police, and, finally, a doctor. Meanwhile, the nose appears around St Petersburg riding in a carriage and dressed in the uniform of a state councillor. Some days later the nose is returned by the police as it tries to escape to Riga in a stagecoach before it eventually reattaches itself inexplicably to Kovalev's face. One of the final scenes in the story sees Ivan Iakovlevich holding Kovalev gently by the nose as he shaves his chin.

Whilst these brief summaries indicate the presence of events which may seem typical of the fantastic, the problems that playfulness and irony pose to their categorization are suggested by the numerous contradictory critical responses each has provoked. For example, Michel Crouzet (1992, 22) characterizes *Onuphrius* as 'un conte fantastique qui prend le fantastique comme objet, qui est écrit contre et pour le fantastique' ['a fantastic story which takes the fantastic as its object, which is written both against and for the fantastic'] and whose satirical edge means that 'sa présence parmi les récits fantastiques est peut-être discutable' ['its presence among fantastic narratives is perhaps debatable']. Pierre-Georges Castex (1951, 222) opts to distance the story from the genre when he maintains that it 'ne peut pas passer pour un vrai conte fantastique [parce que] Gautier ne nous donne jamais à croire que son héros soit réellement victime d'interventions malignes' ['cannot pass for a true fantastic story [because] Gautier never has us believe that his hero is really the victim of diabolic interventions']. However, Peter Whyte (1984, 3) strongly disagrees with this point of view and is firmly convinced that Gautier's story is 'un conte fantastique proprement dit' ['a fantastic story in the true sense']. Gogol's *The Nose* seems to have elicited almost as many characterizations as there are critics who have commented upon it. The story's interrogation of its generic predecessors is indicated by Charles Passage's (1963, 164) suggestion that 'without an understanding of Hoffmann its *pointe* is bound to be missed'. Generic or modal categorizations of *The Nose* range from absurd (Richard Peace), to surrealist (Simon Karlinsky), to nonsense (Gary Morson), to uncanny (Donald Fanger), to marvellous (Neil Cornwell), to fantastic (James Woodward, Ann Shukman) without forgetting sexual fantasy, social satire, and naturalism.[2] The sheer variety of opinions indicates how narrative play and irony lead these works to occupy an ambiguous generic position. However, what I would like to argue below is that the interrogation of conventions enacted by each story achieves a positive extension, rather than a destruction, of the accepted boundaries of the fantastic.

Part 1: Early Departures from Generic Conventions

I argued in Chapter 1 that the creation of a verisimilar fictional world is a crucial component in fantastic narratives. Factors such as geographical and temporal references, reasonable and largely sympathetic protagonists, and the reliable and authoritative performance of the narrator all help to persuade the reader of an equivalence between the fictional and the extrafictional world. *Onuphrius* and *The Nose* both announce their unconventional status by disrupting the usual exploitation of these factors. In fact, even those elements which appear to retain most conformity to generic norms, namely the titles of the two works, are not without hints at their playful, intertextual nature.

The reader's experience of a fictional text begins even before the first word of the narrative as it is moulded by features which Genette (1997, 3) labels 'paratexts'. Examples of such elements include the name of the author, the design of the cover, the title of the work, its preface, dedication, or epigraph. Among these, obviously, it is titles, subtitles, and epigraphs which are most frequently used to reveal information about the genre, mode, or contents of a work. The title of Gogol's story comprises a single word and stands entirely alone, unelaborated by any other informative paratext. Despite referring to a recognizable human organ, its consequent relatively enigmatic status aligns it with the fantastic and such previously discussed examples as *Spirite* and *Le Horla*. It also clearly associates itself with the numerous works whose titles reveal the genre's predilection for isolated or detached body parts: Philarète Chasles's *L'Œil sans paupière* (1832), Gérard de Nerval's *La Main enchantée* (1832), Théophile Gautier's *Le Pied de momie* (1840), and Guy de Maupassant's *La Main* (1884), for instance. The title's indication of a self-consciously playful attitude can be traced to the fact that 'нос' ['nose'] is a reversal of 'сон' ['dream'], one of the rational explanations frequently employed to resolve hesitation in the fantastic. Indeed, dreaming is one of the theories initially considered by Kovalev to explain the disappearance of his nose. The knowledge that, in the original manuscript version of the story, all the unusual events were to have been given such an oneiric resolution only strengthens the suggestion that Gogol's title ironically interrogates the fantastic. While Gogol hints at the significance of his title only obliquely, Gautier is far more explicit in indicating the relationship between his story and the literary tradition. Whilst the main title, 'Onuphrius', may offer few clues, the subtitle, 'ou les vexations d'un admirateur d'Hoffmann', overtly announces a dialogue between this work and that of one of the leading figures in the fantastic canon. In so doing, it creates a set of expectations for the initiated reader which moves beyond the suspense conventionally aroused by an enigmatic title. The initiated reader is asked to bring to bear on Gautier's story not only her knowledge of Hoffmann, but also her appreciation of the genre to which this author made such a notable contribution. The characterization of Onuphrius as an admirer of the German author allows the initiated reader to form an impression of the hero before she gets to the first narrative clause. Similarly, the use of the negatively tinted 'vexations' rather than the more neutral 'adventures', for instance, invites the reader to imagine that the story may not be a straightforward imitation of, or homage to, Hoffmann.

In their various ways, both *The Nose* and *Onuphrius* depart from generic convention by building fictional worlds in which verisimilitude is threatened. This threat is not immediately apparent in *The Nose* as it initially appropriates techniques commonly associated with realist fiction. Anticipating the quality of information provided in the opening lines of *The Double*, Gogol's heterodiegetic narrator locates the action of the fictional world quite specifically in both time and space. The reader is informed that the opening scene occurs on 25 March in a flat on Voznesenskii Prospekt in St Petersburg. Indeed, this is just the first in a series of references to actual geographical places which are encountered throughout *The Nose* as the characters are depicted on Isakievskii bridge, by the river Neva, on Nevskii Prospekt, or at Kazan cathedral. Nor does the narrator delay in identifying the fictional protagonists of the first two parts of the story: Ivan Iakovlevich is a 'цирюльник' ['barber'], while Kovalev is a 'коллежский асессор' ['Collegiate Assessor']. Such details not only allow the reader to form an impression of the characters' relative status but suggest that the narrator is reasonably well-informed and willing to share his knowledge. In contrast, markedly fewer efforts are made in *Onuphrius* to persuade the reader of the existence of a verisimilar story world. The action is not definitively located as the only references are to geographically non-specific features such as 'le cadran de Saint-Paul' ['the clock of Saint Paul'] (*O* 31).[3] Although in the opening pages, the question of the time of day is a significant issue between Onuphrius and Jacintha, this is not accompanied by any indication of the day, month, or year when the action takes place. Furthermore, the narrative voice proves to be less helpful than its counterpart in *The Nose* in terms of its provision of straightforward information. Whereas basic details of identity are supplied immediately in Gogol's story, the first character to appear in the fictional world of *Onuphrius* remains effectively anonymous for the opening thirty lines: the figure waiting for the hero to return is simply referred to as 'elle' or 'la jeune fille', before eventually being named as Jacintha.

The construction of a mimetic fictional world has also been seen to depend on the actions or reactions of the characters which inhabit it. It is the norm in the fantastic for characters to react to an apparently supernatural event in a manner which reveals that it departs markedly from the usual state of affairs. In *The Nose*, the two main protagonists again appear, at least initially, to honour this model by registering shock or surprise in response to the irrational. For instance, upon finding a detached nose in the middle of his loaf of bread, Ivan Iakovlevich's face is etched with an expression of 'ужас' ['horror'] and he is subsequently described as being: 'ни жив ни мертв' ['neither alive nor dead'] (*N* 45).[4] Whilst Ivan Iakovlevich does not look for a rational explanation for this unusual occurrence as many of his generic counterparts would, this is justified by his inability to provide any type of interpretation: 'черт его знает как это сделалось' ['the Devil knows how it happened'] (ibid.). When, in Part 2 of the story, Kovalev awakens to discover that instead of a nose he has a smooth, flat space in the middle of his face, he is reported to experience 'great astonishment' (*N* 47). His immediate reaction is more generically conventional than Iakovlevich's because he does attempt to establish whether he is the victim of an unfortunate illusion:

> Ковалев велел подать воды и протер полотенцем глаза: точно, нет носа! Он начал щупать рукою, чтобы узнать: не спит ли он? кажется, не спит. Коллежский асессор Ковалев вскочил с кровати, встряхнулся: нет носа!... (*N* 48)

> [Kovalev asked for some water and rubbed his eyes with a towel: it was true, there was no nose! He began to pinch himself, to find out whether he was asleep; it seemed he was not. Collegiate Assessor Kovalev jumped out of bed, and shook himself: no nose!...]

This failure to discover a rational explanation prompts Kovalev to enact a series of less conventional responses to the supernatural which will be discussed below. The suspicion that the value-system operating in Gogol's fictional world may not equate to that in the actual world is first aroused by the report that Ivan Iakovlevich's horror at finding the nose 'был ничто против негодования, которое овладело его супругою' ['was nothing compared to the indignation which seized his wife'] (*N* 45). Praskov'ia Osipovna is neither shocked nor frightened by the discovery of the nose but instead explodes with anger, accusing her husband of being a 'villain' for having 'cut it off' and threatening to drag him to the police. She seems not in the least concerned by the irrational nature of the event and prefers to devote her efforts to upbraiding her husband than to working out how such a thing could have happened. Gradually, her generically less conventional response seems to influence

Ivan Iakovlevich himself whose reaction now suggests that a different reality may exist in the fictional world of *The Nose*. His horror appears to stem less from the discovery of the nose *per se* than from the fact, firstly, that he has recognized it and, secondly, that 'хлеб — дело печеное, а нос совсем не то' ['bread is something you bake while a nose is completely different'] (ibid.). Such unconventional reactions are shown to be widespread when, during Kovalev's visit to the newspaper office, the clerk, having admitted that the noseless face is 'чрезвычайно странно' ['extraordinarily strange'] (*N* 57), shows no further interest and seeks no additional explanation. Even the doctor whom Kovalev consults, typically cast as the voice of reason in the fantastic, fails to register the surprise which might confirm the rational as the dominant force in the fictional world. He acts as if Kovalev's missing nose is the most run-of-the-mill ailment, asking how long ago the 'misfortune' occurred before launching straight into an examination (*N* 63).

The departure from generic conventions in terms of reactions to the supernatural is arguably more marked in *Onuphrius*. Typically, the fictional protagonist in the fantastic has been seen to be a reasonable, relatively unexceptional man who displays no undue predisposition to a belief in the supernatural. Gautier's protagonist breaks this mould. At an early stage of the narrative, Onuphrius reacts to the realization that it is almost midday, and not ten o'clock as he had believed, by attributing this misapprehension to the intervention of irrational forces. He refuses to countenance the possibility that the discrepancy in time is the result of an unfortunate but entirely rational mistake. He prefers to make a more unusual accusation: 'il faut que quelque diablotin se soit amusé à pousser ces aiguilles; c'est bien dix heures que j'ai vu!' ['it must be that some imp has amused himself by moving the hands; I definitely saw ten o'clock'] (*O* 26). Brief as it is, this allegation alerts the initiated reader to the fact that Onuphrius displays an uncustomary willingness to see supernatural forces at work in his world. Therefore, while the reader in Gogol is disturbed by a seeming reluctance to acknowledge the supernatural as supernatural, in *Onuphrius* she is put on her guard by the fictional protagonist's readiness to see the supernatural in what could be entirely natural, everyday situations. The presentation of this type of response clearly offers a challenge, if not to the rules of the fantastic, at least to the conventions which usually operate within it.

The non-conformity of these fictional protagonists as regards their reliability also extends to their physical appearance and personality. Compared with the relatively unremarkable protagonists in *Spirite*, *The Queen of Spades*, *La Vénus d'Ille*, and *The Sylph*, Onuphrius would have far greater difficulty blending into the crowd. The defining trait of his physiognomy is a dissonance which, as well as creating a less than positive overall impression, acts as an implicit warning to the reader. His appearance combines elements of: young ('quelque chose d'enfantin' ['something childlike']) and old ('un front de vieillard' ['the forehead of an old man']); pale ('ses traits blêmes et fatigués' ['his pale and tired features']) and colourful ('deux lèvres d'un rose assez vif' ['two lips of a quite bright pink']); and sad ('tout le haut de la tête était grave et réfléchi' ['all the upper part of his head was serious and thoughtful']) and happy ('un sourire jeune' ['a young smile']) (*O* 28). To a reader initiated in the fantastic, such contradictions suggest that Onuphrius straddles the boundary between worlds, belonging fully neither to the natural nor to the supernatural realm.[5] His position on this threshold is underlined by the presence of a generically key adjective in the narrator's summary of his physiognomy: 'ainsi fait, Onuphrius ne pouvait manquer d'avoir l'air assez *singulier*' ['made in this way, Onuphrius could not but have a *singular* appearance'] (ibid.; my italics). This singularity extends to the way he walks:

> ses mouvements étaient heurtés, saccadés; ses gestes anguleux, comme s'ils eussent été produits par des ressorts d'acier; sa démarche incertaine, entrecoupée d'élans subits, de zigzags, ou suspendue tout à coup [...]. (ibid.)

> [his movements were halting, spasmodic; his gestures were angular, as if they had been produced by steel springs; his gait was uncertain, punctuated by sudden accelerations, zigzags, or complete standstills [...].]

The lack of conventional human fluidity in these movements encourages the impression that, in line with the intertextual reference in the subtitle, Onuphrius is closer in nature to an automaton than to a man.[6] Although such characteristics are commonly found in the fantastic, they are not usually displayed by the central protagonist. By assigning attributes commonly associated with harbingers of the supernatural to its main hero, *Onuphrius* recycles a generic convention to original effect. The depiction of a hero and focalizing persona who appears to be less firmly rooted in the natural world than is usual clearly problematizes the experience of hesitation by suggesting his less than reliable status.

This is also the picture drawn of the two main protagonists in *The Nose*, albeit in what appear to be less generically conscious terms. Neither figure is given the positive, or at the very least neutral, character traits that the initiated reader would expect to find. Ivan Iakovlevich is initially described by his wife as not only 'мошенник' ['a rogue'], but 'пьяница' ['a drunk'], 'пачкун' ['a good-for-nothing'], as well as being 'бревно глупое' ['a blockhead'] (*N* 45). Any protests that this characterization displays the bias of a dissatisfied spouse are effectively silenced by the narrator's own declaration that Ivan Iakovlevich is indeed 'пьяница страшный' ['a terrible drunk'] (*N* 46). Whilst Kovalev might be expected to be a more respectable man given his superior professional status, some of his character traits suggest a portentous unwillingness to accept the realities of life. In particular, he is shown to be arrogant and overly concerned with his rank and standing in society. For instance, he prefers to use the military equivalent of his civil title, calling himself not a Collegiate Assessor but 'Major'. Despite his relatively mediocre position, he conducts himself as if he were a figure of great reputation, telling tradeswomen: 'ты приходи ко мне на дом; квартира моя в Садовой; спроси только: здесь ли живет майор Ковалев?' ['come to my place: my apartment is on on Sadovaia Street; you just need to ask: does Major Kovalev live here?'] (*N* 48). Consequently, the perspectives of both Gogol's protagonists will be granted a lesser authority by the initiated reader not simply because they do not possess the hierarchical superiority of the heterodiegetic voice but because they display personality traits which undermine their potential reliability.

The exercise of narrative and generic play in *Onuphrius* and *The Nose* can be traced as much to each narrator's manner of telling his tale as to the personality of the characters or the organization of plot components. The narrators of both stories are heterodiegetic, enjoy omniscient privilege, and occupy a posterior temporal stance. These characteristics are established more gradually in *Onuphrius* where the narrator initially relies on supposition and only subsequently reveals direct access to the mind of the protagonist. However, both narrators display a trait which is far less frequently encountered in the genre of the fantastic: self-consciousness. The two stories provide persuasive illustration of Lanser's (1981, 176) contention that the presence of a heterodiegetic voice need not preclude the use of the first-person pronoun, that 'third-person' narrators can still be 'I's. To a greater degree than in any of the heterodiegetic narratives discussed previously, the narrators of *Onuphrius* and *The Nose* display an awareness of themselves as storytellers, of their role in the discursive situation, and of the presence of a reader. Such self-consciousness and overtness is an important prerequisite for the manipulation of both generic conventions and the initiated reader. This can be seen to be a two-step process. The first stage depends upon the argument which states that 'narrators capable of saying 'I' [...] are also able to make evaluative commentary about textual events and characters' (Lanser 1981, 183). Secondly, this ability to indulge in self-reflexive commentary opens the door to knowing narrative play because 'irony involves the attribution of an evaluative, even judgmental attitude' (Hutcheon 1994, 37).

From an early stage, the narrator in *Onuphrius* proves to be willing to volunteer personal opinions concerning the protagonist. For instance, reflecting upon Onuphrius's reaction to the series of misfortunes which befall him as he tries to paint Jacintha's portrait, the narrator remarks: 's'il eût été seul, je crois qu'en dépit du premier commandement, il aurait attesté le nom du Seigneur plus d'une fois' ['if he had been alone, I believe that in spite of the first commandment, he would have taken the Lord's name in vain more than once'] (*O* 26). The readiness of this narrator to figure overtly in the discourse by means of the first-person pronoun is evident once again when he describes Onuphrius's emotional state before he became acquainted with Jacintha: 'il était si malheureux, que je ne souhaiterais pas d'autre supplice à mon plus fier ennemi' ['he was so unhappy that I would not have wished any more suffering on my worst enemy'] (*O* 30). In the first two parts of *The Nose*, the narrator makes fewer subjective pronouncements than the voice in Gautier. However, he is still keen to offer opinions on the action, although their contribution to reader knowledge is debatable. Describing the cool reception Kovalev receives on his visit to the superintendent of police, the narrator states: 'не знаю, хотя бы он даже принес ему в то время несколько фунтов чаю или сукна, он бы не был принят слишком радушно' ['I do not know whether, even if he had brought with him a few pounds of tea or some cloth, he would have been received particularly joyfully'] (*N* 58). Such commentary draws attention to the narrator and his discursive act. Although he is not a member of the story world, by volunteering opinions so explicitly, he attributes to himself a more visible role as an actor in the narrative. The impact upon hesitation of this tendency towards greater visibility will be discussed below.

These two narrators are also particularly keen to demonstrate an awareness of the communicative act in which they are engaged. Such consciousness has been shown above to be an indicator of competence but, in the narratives under discussion here, it is employed far more ostentatiously and to different effect. The narrator in *The Nose* is eager to persuade the reader that he is conscious of his informative responsibilities: 'необходимо сказать что-нибудь о Ковалеве, чтобы читатель мог видеть, какого рода был этот коллежский асессор' ['it is necessary to say something about Kovalev, so that the reader can see what sort of man this collegiate assessor was'] (*N* 48). He even goes so far as to shoulder the blame when such biographical information is delayed: 'но я несколько виноват, что до сих пор не сказал ничего об Иване Яковлевиче' ['but I am somewhat at fault for, thus far, having said nothing about Ivan Iakovlevich'] (*N* 46). Such self-consciousness is typical of the narrators in Gogol's Petersburg stories; they frequently make themselves visible and their attitude to their discursive obligations is often ironic. The narrator in *Onuphrius* shows similar tendencies as he explicitly announces the delayed provision of information about the hero: 'avant d'aller plus loin, quelques mots sur Onuphrius' ['before going any further, a few words about Onuphrius'] (*O* 28). He also seeks to reassure the reader by overtly noting a transition in this passage of background details: 'Onuphrius, comme je l'ai déjà dit, était peintre, il était de plus poète' ['Onuphrius, as I have already said, was a painter, he was also a poet'] (*O* 29). Such indications of self-consciousness constitute the first step these two texts make towards a diversion of attention away from the action of the story world to the action or status of the discourse. This type of diversion is potentially transgressive in the fantastic in view of Todorov's insistence that the reader's hesitation should focus on the status of events rather than on the status of the discourse.

Finally, both *Onuphrius* and *The Nose* appear keen to draw the reader into assuming a more active role in the construction of the discourse and, in so doing, to assign to her a particular profile or status. Having acknowledged his responsibility in providing orienting information, the narrator in *The Nose* then calls upon the reader to employ these details correctly: 'читатель теперь может судить сам, какого было положение этого майора, когда он увидел вместо довольно недурного и умеренного носа преглупое, ровное и гладкое место' ['the reader can now judge for himself what sort of situation this Major found himself in when instead of a not unattractive and reasonably proportioned nose, he saw a ridiculous, even, and smooth space'] (*N* 49). Such comments cast the reader in the role of a competent addressee, capable of reconstructing the sense of the narrative. This acknowledgement of reader competence is also clearly perceptible in *Onuphrius* where a feeling of narrator-reader parity is seemingly encouraged. During his description of Onuphrius's bizarre physical appearance, the narrator compliments the reader's interpretative abilities by conceding: 'je n'ai pas besoin de vous le dire, Onuphrius était Jeune-France et romantique forcené' ['I do not need to tell you that Onuphrius was a Jeune-France and a fanatical romantic'] (*O* 28). This attempt to encourage the reader to participate actively in the narrative takes a more playful turn as the narrator states: 'il avait peur. De quoi? Je vous le donne à deviner en cent' ['he was afraid. Of what? I'll give you a hundred guesses'] (*O* 30–31). Departures from the generic norm call out to the initiated reader to be recognized. The nature of these overt addresses helps to construct an image of the reader as a broadly competent figure. They effectively encourage the reader to believe that a possession of competence will permit her to enjoy an accessible and rewarding narrative experience. However, as the subsequent two parts of this chapter will show, this expectation is undermined by the development of the stories, most notably in the case of *The Nose*.

Part 2: Ironic Exploitation of Generic Models

Basic plot features such as the appearance of the devil or the loss of a nose and its reincarnation in full dress uniform are sufficient to align *Onuphrius* and *The Nose*, however provisionally, with the genre of the fantastic. Such elements call out, in particular, to what Hutcheon (1994, 5) labels a 'discursive community' whose members are those readers who are conversant in the genre and who share similar assumptions regarding the rules and conventions which operate within it. Such communities are also an indispensable precursor to the functioning of irony as Hutcheon (1994, 18) makes clear:

> if you understand that irony can exist (that saying one thing and meaning something else is not necessarily a lie) and if you understand how it works, you already belong to one community: the one based on the knowledge of the possibility and nature of irony. It is less that irony creates communities, then, than discursive communities make irony possible in the first place.

The Nose and *Onuphrius* depend upon their discursive communities recognizing how the fantastic functions conventionally in order to realize when its standard models are being redeployed ironically. Both the practice and perception of irony reveal the non-hermetic, intertextual nature of each literary narrative and the dynamic properties of the concept of literary genre. Irony demands recognition of the fact that 'literary structure does not simply *exist* but is generated in relation to *another* structure. [...] [it exists] as an *intersection of textual surfaces* rather than a *point*' (Kristeva 1982, 65; original italics). H. R. Jauss's (1982, 23) theory of an aesthetic of reception depends upon the twin ideas of dynamism and intertextuality:

> A literary work, even when it appears to be new, does not present itself as something absolutely new in an informational vacuum, but predisposes its audience to a very specific kind of reception by announcements, overt and covert signals, familiar characteristics, or implicit allusions. It awakens memories of that which was already read, [...] and with its beginning arouses expectations for the 'middle and end', which can then be maintained intact or altered, reoriented, or even fulfilled ironically in the course of the reading according to specific rules of the genre or type of text. [...] A corresponding process of the continuous establishing and altering of horizons also determines the relationship of the individual text to the succession of texts that forms the genre. The new text evokes for the reader (listener) the horizon of expectations and rules familiar from earlier texts, which are then varied, corrected, altered, or even just reproduced.

The experience of reading *Onuphrius* and *The Nose* represents an enactment of Jauss's theory of the 'horizon of expectations' in both an intratextual and an intertextual, generic sense. The ironic fulfilment of these expectations is both verbal and situational and manifests itself both covertly and overtly. The irony directed at generic conventions threatens the normal practice of provoking hesitation in two ways. Firstly, departures from the generic model take the form of a trivialization or undermining of the supernatural. Secondly, the ironic exploitation of intertexts leads each narrative to draw a greater degree of attention than is the norm to the performance of the discourse. As a consequence, the status of fictional events becomes of only secondary importance, a situation unlikely to encourage the reader to hesitate in the generically conventional sense.

A discussion of storytelling techniques in each work provides the best way to begin to consider how generic conventions are ironized. The aspects of narrator performance in *The Nose* discussed in the first part of this chapter might encourage the belief that this voice possesses a conventional level of competence. However, from the very earliest stages, Gogol's narrator fails to present his tale with the expected level of skill in any consistent manner. The particular idiosyncrasies of this performance are suggestive of characteristics commonly associated with the 'skaz' narrative voice. This concept in Russian fiction was first proposed by Boris Eikhenbaum in an article of 1919 discussing Gogol's *The Overcoat*. He defined 'skaz' as a narrative style which imitates oral or colloquial speech in a written form. Lubomir Doležel's later definition of it (1980, 22) as 'a narrative where all the norms and rules of the narrative act are made a target of irony' reveals why its exploitation in *The Nose* might complicate the provocation of hesitation. 'Skaz' narration can be embodied by a variety of features such as superfluous words, puns, and stylized speech. From this last category, I will concentrate on the tendency Gogol's narrator shows towards digression and excessive detail.

For all its 'straightforward, official-sounding account of events' (Maguire 1994, 190), the opening sentence of *The Nose* grabs the reader's attention with its announcement that a 'необыкновенно странное происшествие' ['unusually strange occurrence'] (*N* 44) has taken place. Rather than immediately identifying this event as the reader desires, however, the narrator digresses and instead reports how Ivan Iakovlevich was woken up by the smell of hot bread, hardly a 'strange occurrence'. The reader is further frustrated by the additional details of dubious relevance provided in parenthesis in the second sentence. Having given the name, patronymic, and profession for Ivan Iakovlevich, the narrator goes on: 'фамилия его утрачена, и даже на вывеске его — где изображен господин с намыленною щекою и надписью: 'и кровь отворяют' — не выставлено ничего более' ['his surname has been lost, and even on his shop sign, which depicts a gentleman with a well-soaped cheek and has the inscription: "Blood-letting also performed", nothing else is displayed'] (ibid.). Leaving aside the absurdity of a man's surname having been lost, this interjection serves no informative purpose for a reader who is eager to be told more about the strange event announced in the previous sentence. Indeed, the reader is made to endure further description of domestic banality before the discovery of the nose in the loaf of bread is finally reported. It might be argued that this early example of retardation of information serves the generically conventional purpose of generating suspense. However, the nature of the details provided to achieve this delay arguably mocks the 'epistemic hunger' of the initiated reader (Popkin 1993, 148). In *The Double*, the reader's hunger to discover the identity of the passer-by is thwarted because the narrator's focus is directed internally rather than externally at the crucial moment. In *The Nose*, however, this frustration is more unsettling, but also more amusing, because the narrator's focus is misdirected to apparently irrelevant and absurd details.

The provision of the details regarding Ivan Iakovlevich's shop sign actually proves to be emblematic of the performance of the narrator throughout Gogol's story. He repeatedly reports unnecessary details which distract attention from what might tentatively be considered to be the main plot line: Kovalev's efforts to retrieve his nose.[7] For instance, in the description of Kovalev's visit to the newspaper office, the narrator provides a seemingly endless list of details about the other clients and the advertisements they wish to post:

> В одной значилось, что отпускается в услужение кучер трезвого поведения; в другой — малоподержанная коляска, вывезенная в 1814 году из Парижа; там отпускалась дворовая девка девятнадцати лет, упражнявшаяся в прачечном деле, годная и для других работ; прочные дрожки без одной рессоры; молодая горячая лошадь в серых яблоках, семнадцати лет от роду; новые, полученные из Лондона, семена репы и редиса; дача со всеми угодьями; двумя стойлами для лошадей и местом, на котором можно развести превосходный березовый или еловый сад; там же находился вызов желающих купить старые подошвы, с приглашением явиться к переторжке каждый день от восьми до трех часов утра. (N 54–55)

> [One sought employment for a coachman of sober habits; another advertised a barely used calash, imported in 1814 from Paris; elsewhere a position was sought for a nineteen-year-old serf-girl, who had trained as a laundress, but was suitable for other work; a sturdy droshky, missing one spring; a spirited young horse with grey dappled markings, only seventeen years of age; new turnip and radish seeds imported from London; a country cottage with all amenities; stabling for two horses and land on which to plant an excellent birch or fir grove; another notice invited all those anxious to purchase old boot soles to visit the auction rooms any day, between 8 and 3 a.m.]

In giving such an exaggeratedly detailed account, of which there are numerous other examples in *The Nose*, the narrator appears to be playing at being an informative voice. It is as if he feels the need to account for every element which comes into range, displaying what Popkin labels (1993, 164) a 'diachronic urge'. However, whilst he may model himself on a competent, informative voice, Gogol's narrator succeeds only in frustrating the reader because not one of the plethora of details he supplies bears any relevance to the main point of interest. The reader is keen for information which might help to resolve the mystery of Kovalev's nose and would expect a reliable narrator to share this desire; the tendency to provide irrelevant details at frequent and inappropriate junctures can therefore only create a distance between narrator and reader.

This impression of distance is reinforced by the narrator's seeming inability to remain focused on the main plot line. Faltering reliability has been seen to be a stock technique for provoking hesitation in the fantastic. However, *The Nose* redeploys this device in original form by having it stem, at least in part, from the inclusion of ironic digressions. For instance, when describing Kovalev's visit to the police commissioner, the narrator records at great length the objects cluttering the house as if as evidence of the many bribes he has taken. And before any details of the doctor's advice to Kovalev about his detached nose are given, the narrator reveals that this character eats fresh apples every day and cleans his teeth for forty-five minutes with five different types of brush. This tendency towards easy distraction is not peculiar to the narrator; it is shared by other characters, particularly Kovalev. During his pursuit of the nose into Kazan cathedral, the protagonist gets sidetracked by the sight of a beautiful girl and is on the point of addressing her when he remembers his missing organ.[8] Conventionally, such an apparently irrational event as the loss of a nose would be expected to hold centre stage because of the doubts it provokes about the rules governing the world. In Gogol's story, however, the gravity of the event is called into question because it cannot even command the unwavering attention of the narrator or protagonist. And if the figure charged with recounting these events appears less than fully absorbed in their ramifications, it is unlikely that the reader will feel encouraged to make the emotional or intellectual investment necessary to hesitation. Moreover, these digressions severely threaten the sense of there being an ascending plot line in *The Nose*. In his third property of the fantastic, Todorov claims that the fantastic is a genre which emphasizes particularly strongly the convention of reading from left to right. He relates this to Peter Penzoldt's (1952, 16) contention that fantastic narratives build steadily to a climax which is most commonly the apparition of the supernatural. The form which narrative unreliability takes in Gogol's story, and the overall performance of this narrator, clearly constitutes a rebuttal of this convention. Not only do his digressions undermine any sense of the fictional events building to a climax, but his tendency to become distracted from the main story line suggests that events might not even be worthy of being brought to such a peak.

The narrator in *Onuphrius* does not share the 'skaz' attributes of his Gogolian counterpart. Nevertheless, the manner in which this voice describes apparently supernatural events still frequently problematizes the reader's perception of them and, in particular, the question of whether or not they should be considered ambiguous. Conventionally, heterodiegetic narratives use switches in point of view to circumvent the obstacles which an elevated degree of authority poses to the presence of uncertainty. The confusion of point of view which can result from such switches is a potent tool in the provocation of hesitation. In *Onuphrius*, this technique is reconfigured so that the alleged presence of a supernatural event, rather than its status, is called into question. For example, this is how one of Onuphrius's mishaps with Jacintha's portrait is depicted:

> Il était presque fini, il n'y avait plus que deux ou trois dernières touches à poser, et la signature à mettre, quand une petite peluche, qui dansait avec ses frères les atomes dans un beau rayon jaune, par une fantaisie inexplicable, quitta tout à coup sa lumineuse salle de bal, se dirigea en se dandinant vers la toile d'Onuphrius, et vint s'abattre sur un rehaut qu'il venait de poser. (O 32)

> [It was almost finished; there were only two or three last touches to make and the signature to add, when a little bit of fluff which was dancing in a beautiful yellow ray with its brothers the atoms, by some inexplicable fantasy, left its luminous ballroom, meandered its way towards Onuphrius's canvas, and came to rest on a highlight he had just added.]

In attributing an active will to a little piece of fluff, this description challenges the laws of the rational world. The use of the proximal deictic verb 'venir' suggests that the perspective informing this report belongs to the fictional protagonist and not the narrator. Given Onuphrius's tendency towards credulity, the reliability of this account is therefore undermined. However, the effect created by a generically standard description of a supernatural occurrence from an unreliable perspective appears not to suffice in this story; it has to be embellished. The movement of the piece of fluff is described in such overly poeticized and exaggerated terms that its status is threatened further. This overstatement is suggestive of an ironic perspective which can only belong to the heterodiegetic narrator. Hutcheon (1994, 156) names exaggeration and its opposite, understatement, as the second of five categories of signals of irony. The other four are changes of register, contradiction, simplification, and repetition. It is as if this embellished terminology is designed to highlight the incongruity of assigning active force to a piece of fluff. In so doing, it reminds the reader that what is being narrated is actually no more than fluff falling on a painting, hardly proof of a disruption of rational laws. Therefore, the confusion of the perspective of the protagonist with the voice of the narrator in this instance is manipulated in such a way as to challenge the creation of ambiguity. The initiated reader is informed implicitly through the use of key exaggeration that the narrator does not concur with the protagonist's supernatural interpretation. This departs markedly from the silence of the heterodiegetic voice which conventionally follows such interpretations and which has been seen to sustain ambiguity in other works.

A similar distancing of the perspectives of narrator and protagonist is achieved by the ironic exploitation of another poetic device during the description of Onuphrius's visit to M. de ★★★. When the designated hour of his meeting with Jacintha arrives and he is still on the road, Onuphrius apparently perceives an animation of the surrounding buildings:

> Les clochers s'inclinaient sur le chemin creux pour le regarder passer, ils le montraient au doigt, lui faisaient la nique et lui tendaient par dérision leurs cadrans dont les aiguilles étaient perpendiculaires. Les cloches lui tiraient la langue et lui faisaient la grimace, sonnant toujours les six coups maudits. (O 33–34)

> [The church towers bent over the hollow road to watch him pass, they pointed at him, thumbed their noses at him, and mockingly stretched out their faces on which the hands were perpendicular. The bells stuck their tongues out at him and pulled faces, all the while sounding the six cursed strokes.]

It is not difficult for the reader to imagine that the protagonist believes that the buildings really do become animate and rebuke him for being late. However, just as the description of the piece of fluff is undermined by poetic exaggeration, so this allegation is questioned by the use of clichéd anthropomorphism. Anthropomorphism is frequently employed in literary texts which in no way depict challenges to the rational fabric of the fictional world to amplify the description of emotional states by projecting them onto inanimate elements. Yet the use of such a device in a genre which frequently blurs the distinction between animate and inanimate, and the decision to do so in such a stereotypical manner, seems ironically inappropriate. The reliability of this description is also undermined by the presence of ironic exaggeration. The clocktowers do not simply sound six o'clock but: 'c'était un tutti de cloches, un concerto de timbres flûtés, ronflants, glapissants, criards, un carillon à vous fendre la tête' ['it was a tutti of bells, a concerto of flute-like tones, roaring, squealing, piercing, a chiming to make your head split'] (O 33). These two devices combine to indicate the unreliability of the protagonist's perspective to such an extent that the reader is unlikely to hesitate in response to these descriptions.

Chapter 2 above has shown how conventional fantastic texts often present multiple voices offering different, frequently contradictory, interpretations of the same event. Moreover, in heterodiegetic narratives, occasional cracks are permitted to appear in the narrator's skill and access to information which facilitate ambiguity. *Onuphrius* presents a manipulation of narrative voice which recycles these two models in an extreme and acutely disruptive fashion. In so doing, it succeeds in ironizing not only the conventions of the fantastic but also those of the narrative act in a wider sense. Despite a slower revelation of stance than in *The Nose*, the attitude and performance of Gautier's narrator still convinces the reader of his heterodiegetic authority. However, this assessment is abruptly challenged by the manner in which the narrator introduces the account of Onuphrius's dream, midway through the story:

> Il fit une multitude de rêves incohérents, monstrueux, qui ne contribuèrent pas peu à déranger sa raison déjà ébranlée. En voici un qui l'avait frappé et qu'il m'a raconté plusieurs fois depuis. (O 36)

> [He had a multitude of incoherent, monstrous dreams which made no little contribution to the derangement of his already disturbed mind. Here is one which struck him and which he has recounted to me on several occasions since.]

Whilst the first sentence is entirely consistent with heterodiegetic authority, the second signals a fundamental modification of the narrator's relationship to his speech act and to the story world. Both this introduction and the description of how he subsequently disturbs Onuphrius's dream, 'il en était là de son rêve lorsque j'entrai dans l'atelier' ['he was at this point of his dream when I entered the studio'] (O 43), see the narrator leave his external reporting position, walk directly into the fictional world, and apparently assume homodiegetic authority. Such a shift confuses the reader and poses unsettling questions regarding the narrator's performance up until this point. Having established his omniscient privilege early on, the narrator repeatedly exploits it to tell the reader of the protagonist's unvoiced thoughts and emotions: 'il eut un instant la pensée d'escalader les bords du ravin' ['at one moment he had the idea of climbing the sides of the ravine'], 'il se persuada que ce n'était que l'ombre' ['he persuaded himself that it was nothing but the shadow'] (O 33, 34). However, the revelation that he exists on the same fictional plane as Onuphrius revokes the heterodiegetic status which confers omniscient privilege. If the narrator is a homodiegetic figure, he possesses no more access to the minds of characters than any other ordinary mortal, and so the validity of all prior statements betraying omniscience must be called into doubt. For as long as the illusion of heterodiegesis was maintained, such statements were accepted at face value; the shift to homodiegesis means that they now undermine the decorum of the text. The disruption caused by this sudden reconfiguration is exacerbated by the fact that, following this revelation, the narrator fails to modify his earlier behaviour in any perceptible way. He persists in providing descriptions which the reader now recognizes must be beyond his powers of perception: 'Onuphrius commençait à se sentir mal' ['Onuphrius began to feel unwell'], 'Onuphrius, craignant que le dandy ne lui jouât quelque tour, changea le fauteuil de place' ['Onuphrius, fearing that the dandy was playing a trick on him, moved the armchair'] (O 44, 48). The lack of any justification for this privileged access to information must now render such descriptions unreliable but in a manner which departs markedly and ironically from normal practice in the fantastic.

The performance of the narrator in *Onuphrius* implies that he endeavours to inhabit the boundary between homodiegesis and heterodiegesis, displaying traits typical of both. The difficulty Whyte (1984, 5) has in categorizing the narrative mode of the story (he labels it both homodiegetic and extradiegetic) would seem to confirm this. His behaviour corresponds to the second method of destroying reliability posited by Doležel (1980, 22) according to which the narrator 'takes an ironic attitude towards his authentication authority and thus turns the narrating act into a not binding game'. Not only do the shifts between heterodiegesis and homodiegesis mock the technique of switching voices typical of the fantastic, they also problematize the reader's perception of the boundaries between herself, the narrator, and the fictional world. In so doing, *Onuphrius* recalls the closing pages of Hoffmann's *The Golden Pot*, where the narrator abruptly modifies his position from outside the boundaries of the fictional world to within its confines. In the German story, the consequence of the positional shift is to blur the boundary between fiction and extrafictional reality. This brings the reader into far closer proximity to the apparently supernatural realm and denies her the possibility of dismissing the irrational as without consequence upon her extratextual existence.[9] The ambivalent position which the narrator in *Onuphrius* occupies is similarly destabilizing. On a primary level, it undermines his reliability as a storyteller by blurring the question of his access to information. However, it also interrogates the conventional model of narrative transmission. His position astride the boundary between homodiegesis and heterodiegesis signals the narrator's willingness to disrupt not only the conventions of the genre of the fantastic, but, in a wider sense, the customary practices of storytelling. Lanser (1981, 160) acknowledges that a narrative voice need not be either first- or third-person but can be more or less heterodiegetic or homodiegetic. However, according to accepted narrative models, no narrator can be both. The relatively early revelation of this threshold position threatens hesitation because it represents a further step in diverting attention away from events and towards the narrative performance. The initiated reader expects to be confronted with reports whose reliability is dubious; she is far less prepared, however, for this unreliability to stem from the idiosyncratic nature of the principal narrative voice.

The subtitle of *Onuphrius* indicates one of Gautier's favoured methods for ironizing the supernatural in this story: the use of explicit intertextual reference. The main body of the narrative is replete with such references which are more or less author-specific. For instance, while Hoffmann remains by far the dominant figure, the reader also encounters mention of Jean Paul, Bodin, Delrio, Bekker and Berbiguier de Terre-Neuve-du-Thym, amongst others.[10] The appearance of such names can be seen to recycle ironically the convention of claiming mimetic status by making reference to actual historical figures. *Onuphrius* announces its ludic nature by choosing to mention only those historical figures which form the work's literary reality rather than its mimetic reality. The summary of Onuphrius's preferred reading matter makes clear the common thread which runs through these various intertextual nods: 'il ne lisait que des légendes merveilleuses et d'anciens romans de chevalerie, des poésies mystiques, des traités de cabale, des ballades allemandes, des livres de sorcellerie et de démonographie' ['he read only marvellous legends and ancient novels of chivalry, mystical poetry, cabbalistic treatises, German ballads, and books on sorcery and demonography'] (O 29). As with the mention of Hoffmann in the title, such references encourage the reader to expect that this narrative will bear some resemblance to those modes in which the supernatural or otherworldly plays a central role. However, the development of Gautier's story ironically undermines these expectations because it is precisely intertextual reference which complicates the status of the supernatural.

The extensive use of explicit intertextual reference during the description of Onuphrius's personality indicates that he is more than simply 'un admirateur d'Hoffmann'. He seems rather to be a product of the genre which this author initiated. Like the implicit intertextual references employed during the earlier depiction of his physical appearance, these explicit examples undermine his reliability as an experiencing persona. The narrator describes how Onuphrius's reading, and very specifically the influence of Hoffmann, affects his beliefs:

> Quand il était seul dans son grand atelier, il voyait tourner autour de lui une ronde fantastique, le conseiller Tusmann, le docteur Tabraccio, le digne Peregrinus Tyss, Crespel avec son violon et sa fille Antonia, l'inconnue de la maison déserte et toute la famille étrange du château Bohême; c'était un sabbat complet, et il ne se fût pas fait prier pour avoir peur de son chat comme d'un autre Mürr. (O 31)

> [When he was alone in his large studio, he saw circling around him in a fantastic dance councillor Tusmann, doctor Tabraccio, the dignified Peregrinus Tyss, Crespel with his violin and his daughter Antonia, the unknown woman from the deserted house and the whole strange family from Castle Bohemia; it was a complete sabbath and he would not have needed persuading to be afraid of his cat as if it were another Mürr.]

All of the figures whom Onuphrius believes he sees are characters from the fiction of Hoffmann who are somehow connected with the otherworldly. As such, the convention of hesitation is placed squarely before the initiated reader. Yet, because the cast of the vision consists exclusively of intertextual, fictional characters, the reader will not experience the generically conventional ambiguity. One of the characteristic features of the fantastic is the depiction of confrontations between its heroes and unusual, often rationally impossible creatures. However, the act of casting fictional characters in this role ensures that the reader will not grant this scene the degree of credence necessary for hesitation. As inhabitants not simply of *another* world but of another *fictional* world, Onuphrius's visitors do not enjoy the same potential as Spirite, Mikhail Platonovich's sylph, or Goliadkin's double. The shift in rational laws needed to permit the appearance of these three beings would still not justify the intervention of Hoffmann's fictional creations. This being the case, the initiated reader has no choice but to dismiss Onuphrius's vision as illusory and to regard him as a protagonist whose perceptions are not to be trusted.

This assessment of Onuphrius is underlined by the report of his reflections upon the misadventures which befall him as he paints Jacintha's portrait. The protagonist's strategy for trying to account for the various unusual occurrences is as follows:

> Il se rappela toutes les histoires d'obsession, depuis le possédé de la Bible jusqu'aux
> religieuses de Loudun; tous les livres de sorcellerie qu'il avait lus: Bodin, Delrio,
> Le Loyer, Bordelon, le *Monde invisible* de Bekker, l'*Infernalia*, les *Farfadets* de M. de
> Berbiguier de Terre-Neuve-du-Thym, le *Grand et le Petit Albert*, et tout ce qui lui
> parut obscur devint clair comme le jour [...]. (*O* 32)

> [He recalled all the stories of obsession from the possessed of the Bible to Loudun's
> nuns; all the sorcery books he had read: Bodin, Delrio, Le Loyer, Bordelon, *The
> Invisible World* by Bekker, *Infernalia*, *Sprites*, by M. de Bergiguier de Terre-Neuve-
> du-Thym, *Albert the Great and the Small*, and everything which seemed vague to
> him became as clear as day [...].]

What apparently becomes clear to Onuphrius following this consideration is that the
devil is responsible for his misfortunes. However, his interpretation is undermined
because it is based solely on intertextual reference. Any ambiguity which might be
raised by the spectre of the supernatural is effectively dispelled because the protagonist
insists on interpreting events in the real world according to his experience of literary,
non-actual sources. He makes accusations based less upon the facts observable in
reality than upon literary experience. This is, in fact, characteristic of the atmosphere
which prevails throughout Gautier's story where the fictional world appears to be
governed more by intertextuality than by extratextual reality. In fact, the narrator
confirms this when he summarizes the consequences of a literary diet upon
Onuphrius's perception of reality:

> avec cela il se faisait, au milieu du monde réel bourdonnant autour de lui, un
> monde d'extase et de vision où il était donné à bien peu d'entrer. Du détail le plus
> commun et le plus positif, par l'habitude qu'il avait de chercher le côté surnaturel,
> il savait faire jaillir quelque chose de fantastique et d'inattendu. [...] les yeux de
> son âme et de son corps avaient la faculté de déranger les lignes les plus droites et
> de rendre compliquées les choses les plus simples [...]. (*O* 29)

> [with this he created, in the middle of the real world buzzing around him, a
> world of ecstasy and of visions which very few are permitted to enter. Thanks
> to his habit of always looking for the supernatural, he knew how to conjure up
> something fantastic and unexpected from the most banal and positive detail. [...]
> the eyes of his soul and of his body were capable of distorting the straightest of
> lines and of complicating the simplest of things [...].]

The horizon of expectations created by these intertextual references is consistently
subverted by their ironic deployment. In one sense, it is possible to perceive
similarities in the questionable reliability established for Onuphrius and that which
bedevils the protagonists of *Le Horla* and *The Double*: Ponnau's characterization
(1997, 34) of Gautier's hero as suffering from 'une monomanie fantastique' makes this
clear. However, the crucial distinction is that, in *Onuphrius*, the 'monomania' which
conventionally triggers uncertainty is precisely what makes ambiguity unlikely. The
explicit intertextual references are the discursive incarnation of the protagonist's ability
to distort the most straightforward phenomena into examples of the supernatural.
And such distortion puts the reader on her guard.

Reflecting the effect created by the narrator's digressions in *The Nose*, Gautier's
story further complicates the process of reader hesitation by depicting the supernatural
more light-heartedly than is usual. For instance, the allegation that an invisible figure

interferes just as Onuphrius prepares to add the all-important touch to his portrait is generically conventional; the form which this supposed intervention takes is not:

> un coup violent dans le coude fit dévier sa main, porter le point blanc dans les sourcils, et traîner le parement de son habit sur la joue encore fraîche qu'il venait de terminer. (O 27)

> [a violent nudge of his elbow moved his hand, put the white spot in her eyebrows, and dragged the facing of his tunic across the cheek which he had just finished and which was still wet.]

Despite being qualified as 'catastrophic', this mishap does not sit convincingly alongside events such as the dead countess's wink, the statue's murder of Alphonse, or the disappearance of the water in *Le Horla* in terms of seriousness. Rather than betraying the intervention of a malefic creature from a supernatural realm, this and the discovery of the moustache, the exploding paints, and the stiffened brushes are closer in nature to the harmless and juvenile pranks schoolchildren play in art class. Castex (1951, 221) acknowledges this when he characterizes the supernatural incidents in Gautier's story as 'quelques mésaventures anodines dont la vie ordinaire fournit maint exemple' ['some trivial misadventures of which everyday life provides ample examples']. Such incidents are more likely to provoke mirth than fear in the mind of the reader. The irony intended by this more frivolous tone is unmistakable in Onuphrius's supposition as to why the devil should have chosen him as a victim:

> il se rappela qu'il avait fait, il n'y a pas bien longtemps, un tableau de saint Dunstan tenant le diable par le nez avec des pincettes rouges; il ne douta pas que ce ne fût pour avoir été représenté par lui dans une position aussi humiliante que le diable lui faisait ces petites niches. (O 32)

> [he recalled that, not so very long ago, he had painted a picture of Saint Dunstan holding the devil by the nose with a pair of red tongs; he was convinced that it was for representing him in such a humiliating position that the devil was playing these tricks on him.]

Such a frivolous motivation is scarcely in line with the conventional fantastic. As a provocation of supernatural powers, this portrait is hardly in the same league as Germann frightening the countess to death or Alphonse symbolically placing a ring on the Venus's finger. It also reinforces the impression of *Onuphrius* as a self-reflexive narrative in which all elements are somehow related to artistic pursuits. The sustained lack of seriousness in the nature of apparently irrational events suggests that the fantastic is here being made the target of 'ludic irony' (Hutcheon 1994, 49). Such irony teases the reader gently and implies a measure of the comic tone experienced in Gautier's story.

In *The Nose*, characters have been seen to be unwilling to register surprise or shock at the intervention of the otherworldly. This gradually develops into a more widespread atmosphere of incongruity in which generically appropriate reactions or opinions are almost entirely absent. For example, Kovalev's initial reaction to the loss of his nose meets the reader's expectations. However, his subsequent use of unsuitable descriptions or comparisons of his predicament is unsettling. When set against Alphonse's exclamation, 'I am bewitched', on seeing the Venus's bent finger or Mikhail Platonovich's claim that seeing the sylph means that he is the 'witness of a great mystery', Kovalev's casting of his noseless situation as 'неприлично' ['improper'] seems ironically understated, even inappropriate. The loss of a nose may be many things, but 'improper' is unlikely to be the reader's first thought. This tendency is more obvious in Kovalev's emotional outburst following his unsuccessful trips to the newspaper office and the police commissioner. Whilst the narrator describes him as losing heart and falling into despair, the protagonist's choice of comparative terms suggests that he is more concerned by the manner of his loss than the loss itself:

> Будь я без руки или без ноги — все бы это лучше; будь я без ушей — скверно, однако ж все сноснее; но без носа человек — черт знает что: птица не птица, гражданин не гражданин, — просто возьми да и вышвырни за окошко! И пусть бы уже на войне отрубили или на дуэли, или я сам был причиною; но ведь пропал ни за что ни про что, пропал даром, ни за грош!... (*N* 59)

> [If only I was without an arm or a leg — it would have been far better; or without my ears — that would have been bad, although still more bearable; but without his nose a man — the devil knows what he is: neither man nor beast, — just take him and throw him out of the window! At least if it had been cut off in the war or in a duel, or if I had lost it through some fault of my own; but it disappeared without rhyme or reason, just like that!...]

The impression created by this lament is compounded by the incongruously banal appropriation of the loss of a nose to that of 'пуговица, серебряная ложка, часы или что-нибудь подобное' ['a button, a silver spoon, a watch, or something similar'] (*N* 60). Ambiguity is frequently provoked in the fantastic by the struggle to find terms which can approximate supernatural events to a recognizable, rational state of affairs. The terms of Kovalev's comparison, however, appropriating the loss of a body part to that of an everyday, metallic object, must be considered to mock all of these conventional syntactic endeavours.

Kovalev is far from being alone in his incongruous reactions to the seemingly otherworldly. Having been shown that Kovalev has no nose, the clerk in the newspaper office initially expresses sympathy for his plight. However, repeated reports from the narrator of how this clerk takes snuff and wipes his own nose while talking to Kovalev suggest that all is not as it should be. These descriptions culminate in an offer from the clerk which, in its inappropriate thoughtlessness, makes a mockery of his earlier sympathizing: 'не угодно ли вам понюхать табачку? это разбивает головные боли и печальные расположения; даже в отношении к геморроидам это хорошо' ['would you care for a pinch of snuff? It cures headaches and melancholic states; it is even good in respect of haemorrhoids'] (*N* 57). The reader is confronted by layers of irony here stemming from the obviously illogical offering of snuff to a man who has no nose, to the more grotesque suggestion that Kovalev should partake because it will help his piles. The lack of sympathy in the clerk's snuff-offering is matched by the physical brutality subsequently visited upon Kovalev by the doctor. It is arguably this scene in *The Nose* above all others which signals a disruption of the fantastic by the introduction of the grotesque. When the doctor is summoned to help Kovalev following the return of his nose, he acts in a way which coincides neither with the initiated reader's generic expectations, nor with the general standards of medical practice:

он поднял майора Ковалева за подбородок и дал ему большим пальцем щелчка в то самое место, где прежде был нос, так что майор должен был откинуть свою голову назад с такою силою, что ударился затылком в стену. Медик сказал, что это ничего [...] и в заключение дал опять ему большим пальцем щелчка, так что майор Ковалев дернул головою, как конь, которому смотрят в зубы. (*N* 63)

[he lifted Major Kovalev's head by the chin and flicked his thumb so hard against the place where there had previously been a nose that the Major had to pull his head away with such force that he hit the back of it against the wall. The doctor said this was nothing [...] and in conclusion gave him another flick with his thumb, so that Major Kovalev tossed his head like a horse having its teeth examined.]

The grotesque parodies the fantastic by complicating with humour any sympathy which the reader might be tempted to feel for Kovalev's predicament.[11] The comic implications of the grotesque are even more obvious in the description of the protagonist desperately attempting to reaffix his nose:

Он поднес его ко рту, нагрел его слегка своим дыханием и опять поднес к гладкому месту, находившемуся между двух щек; но нос никаким образом не держался.
    'Ну! ну же! полезай, дурак!' говорил он ему. Но нос был как деревянный и падал на стол с таким странным звуком, как будто бы пробка. (*N* 63)

[He lifted it to his mouth, warmed it slightly with his breath and once again placed it on the smooth space between his two cheeks; but the nose absolutely would not stay in place.
    'Now! Now then! Stay put, you fool!' he said to it. But the nose was like wood and fell onto the table with a strange noise, as if it were a cork.]

As if the depiction of a man attempting to stick his nose back onto his face were not sufficiently ridiculous, Gogol goes one step further by having Kovalev try to improve his chances of success by making the nose tacky. The futility of the attempt is further underlined by the grotesque description of the non-adhesive nose falling onto the table like something wooden. The exaggeration in these scenes problematizes the likelihood of reader hesitation in a similar way to the light-hearted nature of the supernatural in *Onuphrius*. The supernatural is vulgarized and any tendency towards ambiguity is overtaken by a sense of the comic.

Hutcheon (1994, 15) argues that irony always has an 'edge' and, as such, it must always have a 'target'. Whilst the examples of an ironic attitude towards the supernatural featured above may jeopardize her experience of hesitation, they do not direct their 'edge' at the reader. Indeed, membership of the discursive community of the fantastic enables the initiated reader to interpret, and even collude in, the irony which is targeted at the conventions of the genre. This collusion is proved by the fact that, for the most part, the reader finds this irony humorous and light-hearted. However, in *The Nose*, this is not always the case. There are moments in Gogol's story when the initiated reader finds herself in irony's sights. What I would like to suggest here is that, while the reader's initiation into the genre has previously allowed her to appreciate the playfully non-conformist attitude of the story, it is now precisely this factor which makes her the target of irony. Knowledge of *The Nose*'s implied intertexts conditions the initiated reader to experience certain sensations in response to the narrative; these are then, in turn, ironized. More specifically, the reader's sense of surprise or frustration in the face of particular episodes betrays her belief in the existence of what I would like to call a 'hierarchy of rationality'. Belief in such a system is acquired through initiation into the fantastic. What is mocked in *The Nose* is the expectation that any such hierarchy should operate in a genre which is defined, in part, by the presence of the irrational.

The first initiated-reader reaction to be targeted by irony is the surprise provoked by what Karlinsky (1976, 126) labels the Gogolian 'course of action' that Kovalev undertakes in order to retrieve his nose. The author-specific label Karlinsky uses to characterize the decisions to visit the police commissioner and the newspaper office before eventually summoning a doctor implies that he does not find these actions entirely customary. Part of the surprise is generated by the failure of either narrator or protagonist to justify them. For instance, Kovalev's choice of a first visit to the police commissioner is simply announced but not explained while the trip to the newspaper office is undertaken just as he is on the point of heading off to the police station. Such sudden, unjustified decisions help to explain the belief that *The Nose* mocks 'a serious attitude towards plot and [...] ordinary assumptions about intentionality' (Fanger 1979, 122). However, this is not the only explanation for the reader's surprise. More significantly, Karlinsky's label implies that Kovalev's actions could have taken a different, non-Gogolian form. Put simply, the initiated reader is likely to consider that Kovalev's decisions could have been more reasonable. While this response may, in part, be the consequence of an extra-literary hypothesis, it is primarily conditioned by the reader's experience of the fantastic. For the initiated reader, Kovalev's behaviour does not tally with that displayed by the protagonists in more conventional works. For instance, Maupassant's diarist's first reaction on discovering the disappearance of water from his bedside is to conduct a series of amateur but persuasive experiments. In *The Sylph*, the publisher responds to Mikhail Platonovich's irrational claims by enlisting the help of a medical expert. In fact, this latter example, in particular, helps to highlight the seeming unacceptability of Kovalev's actions: recourse to a doctor is only the final step taken by Gogol's protagonist when generic expectations dictate that it should be amongst the first. Experience of texts such as these conditions the reader to believe in a hierarchy of rationality according to which an immediate call to a doctor is an acceptable response to the loss of a nose but a trip to the police is not. By subverting this conventional framework, *The Nose* exposes the existence of such a belief-system only to reveal its absurdity when applied to the supernatural. The reader is forced to confront the fact that, when dealing with the sudden and inexplicable loss of a nose, no action can be considered to be appropriate or reasonable. The irony present in this series of events effectively 'forces [the reader] to move through stages of self-consciousness, stepping back continually to judge [his] prior judgements without ever finding firm ground' (Culler 1974, 185).

The efforts to apply this rational framework to *The Nose* are further ironized by the frustration which generic experience prompts. Although irony means that the reader's initial horizon of expectations is not fulfilled, the eventual recovery of the nose offers some hope of a satisfactory denouement. The reader still hopes that the nose will go back to its rightful place and that the story will have a 'happy ending'.

Such an optimistic outlook is proof of the reader's reluctance, despite a weight of clues to the contrary, to relinquish belief in conventional story-telling techniques. However, at least temporarily, these hopes are thwarted by the doctor's refusal even to attempt to reaffix Kovalev's nose:

> 'Нет, нельзя. Вы уж лучше так оставайтесь, потому что можно сделать еще хуже. Оно, конечно, приставить можно; я бы, пожалуй, вам сейчас приставил его; но я вас уверяю, что это для вас хуже. [...] Предоставьте лучше действию самой натуры. Мойте чаще холодною водою [...].' (*N* 63–64)

> ['No, impossible. You would do better to leave it as it is because you might make it worse. It could of course be stuck on; I could do it right now; but I assure you that it would be worse for you. [...] Better to let nature take its course. Wash often with cold water [...].']

Generic knowledge allows the reader to expect that consultation with a doctor might facilitate some sort of satisfactory resolution. Such figures are regularly called upon in the fantastic to decipher the true status of events or, at the very least, to endeavour to put right the unfavourable consequences to which such events give rise. The doctor's reaction in *The Nose*, therefore, is frustrating. However, the frustrated reader is the ironized reader because, whilst it might defy the generic model, the doctor's refusal actually represents a quite reasonable response to the situation. Irony forces the reader to adopt a critical distance from his judgements and to realize that the belief that a doctor should endeavour to reaffix Kovalev's severed nose is quite ridiculous. Whilst it may be admissible to feel frustration at the doctor's unsatisfactory justification for his refusal, it is quite unacceptable to object to the refusal in itself. Exposure to the fantastic teaches the reader a rational logic; Gogol's story signals its unconventional nature by ridiculing the reader who tries to apply it here. It obliges the initiated reader to recognize that the normal correlations, associations, and interpretations she has learned in reading the genre prove to be inoperative in this text.

In a more restricted, though textually more explicit, sense, the reader of *The Nose* is also made the target of irony because of the presence of metatextual commentary. The potential for an exploitation of such commentary has been created by the narrator's earlier display of self-consciousness; this lends the narrative the reflexivity necessary to metatextuality. The closing passages of the second part of *The Nose* feature several lines which, while ostensibly related to events in the story world, can also be considered to pass comment upon the discourse which comprises these events. Two such instances occur during the narrator's report of the reaction of Petersburg residents to rumours of the nose's perambulations along Nevskii Prospekt in the guise of a state councillor. For example, an old colonel, exasperated by his failure to catch sight of the nose in the shop window where he had expected to find it, is reported to exclaim: 'как можно этакими глупыми и неправдоподобными слухами смущать народ?' ['how can people be troubled by such stupid and improbable rumours?'] (*N* 67). Similarly, the narrator goes on to record the displeasure caused to a group of 'worthy and well-intentioned persons' by these same rumours: 'один господин говорил с негодованием, что он не понимает, как в нынешний просвещенный век могут распространяться нелепые выдумки' ['one gentleman announced with annoyance that he did not understand how in the present enlightened age such ridiculous fictions could spread'] (ibid.). These statements can be considered to stand, quite acceptably, as nothing more than commentary by fictional characters upon a state of affairs in their world; in fact, they represent the type of generically conventional response to the supernatural which is so rarely encountered in *The Nose*. However, perhaps precisely because of their distinction from what has become the norm for this particular text, the initiated reader is likely to see in them a metatextual potential. These fictional characters pass comment upon the credulity of people confronted by stories regarding the wanderings of a nose; the discourse which the reader is engaged in recounts the story of the detachment of a nose. The symmetry between the story-world event and the reader's activity suggests that the fictional comments might reach out beyond the parameters of the story world to comment upon the nature of the discourse which creates it. According to this metatextual interpretation, the reader is cast in the role of the person 'troubled by such stupid and improbable rumours', the extrafictional voice is the figure who 'spreads' them and *The Nose* itself becomes the 'ridiculous fiction'. As such, the old colonel's criticism serves obliquely to ironize the reader by suggesting that her willingness to grant any degree of credulity to Gogol's story world is misplaced. By agreeing to believe in the events depicted by the narrator in *The Nose*, the reader is characterized as no better than the misguided fictional characters who believe in the presence of the nose on Nevskii Prospekt. Echoing the attention which the 'skaz' approach to storytelling draws to the performance of the narrator, this ironic metatextual commentary brings both narrator and reader into centre stage. In so doing, it redirects the focus away from fictional events and towards the status of the discourse. Foreshadowing the effect achieved by the self-conscious declarations encountered in the closing passages of *The Nose* and *Onuphrius*, this shift leads to a type of hesitation which would appear to be incompatible with Todorov's theory of the genre.

Part 3: Problematizing the Status of the Discourse

The ironic games played by *Onuphrius* and *The Nose* reach a peak in their closing passages as the structures which underpin the discourse as a whole are undermined. In *The Nose*, the targeting of the initiated reader achieved by this removal of discursive security builds upon ironic strategies the story has already been seen to deploy. In *Onuphrius*, this is more of a departure because, prior to the closing paragraphs, the initiated reader has generally been cast as a positive colluder in the irony. In both works, the ground for the ultimate problematization of the status of the discourse is laid by having the narrator move towards a more visible position at the forefront of the communicative act. In *Onuphrius*, this move is signalled when the narrator ceases to record the stages in the protagonist's slide towards insanity and reflects instead upon the nature of, and reasons for, his condition:

> Sorti de l'arche du réel, il s'était lancé dans les profondeurs nébuleuses de la fantaisie et de la métaphysique; mais il n'avait pu revenir avec le rameau d'olive; il n'avait pas rencontré la terre sèche où poser le pied [...]. (O 51)

[Having left the ark of reality, he had cast himself into the obscure depths of fantasy and metaphysics; but he had found himself unable to return with the olive branch; he had not reached dry land on which he could set foot [...].]

The hyperbolic use of religious imagery in this description offers proof that the ironic distance established earlier between narrator and protagonist is maintained. In *The Nose*, the narrator signals his more overt presence by pronouncing the type of aphoristic statement in which he has indulged on a couple of previous instances: 'чепуха совершенная делается на свете. Иногда вовсе нет никакого правдоподобия' ['the most absurd things do happen in life. Sometimes they lack all verisimilitude'] (*N* 67).[12] This comment provides pre-emptive judgement upon the account of how Kovalev awakens one morning to find his nose suddenly back in its rightful place. In the opinion it offers upon the nature and, most importantly, the credibility of story-world events, it anticipates those judgements the narrator will make in the closing two paragraphs of the story.

The penultimate paragraph of *The Nose* sees the narrator refining this more general declaration to acknowledge specifically the unusual nature of the story he has just recounted. In the opening lines, he makes implicit claims for the referential status of the 'fabula' but also aligns himself with the reader by recognizing its improbability: 'вот какая история случилась в северной столице нашего обширного государства! Теперь только, по соображении всего, видим, что в ней есть много неправдоподобного' ['and this story happened in the northern capital of our vast country! Only now, when we ponder it all, do we see that it contains much that is highly improbable'] (*N* 70). These remarks encourage the reader because, by conceding the slippery nature of events in the fictional world for the first time, they extend the possibility that the narrator might now assume a more reliable attitude. The epistemically hungry reader will hope that this recognition of implausibility represents the first step towards the narrator indicating how the events should be interpreted. The embedded heterodiegetic voice in Pétrus Borel's *Gottfried Wolfgang* (1833) makes a similar concession at the close of the story and offers a model of resolution which Gogol's narrator could follow:

L'invraisemblance de cette aventure, dont quelques détails ont dû choquer, sans doute, l'esprit rigoureux de certains lecteurs, s'expliquera d'une manière toute naturelle, lorsque nous aurons dit que Gottfried Wolfgang, [...] mourut pensionnaire dans une maison de fous. (1973, 152)

[The implausibility of this adventure, of which a number of details must undoubtedly have shocked the rigorous nature of certain readers, will be explained entirely naturally when we say that Gottfried Wolfgang [...] died in a lunatic asylum.]

Borel's narrator effectively instructs the reader to resolve interpretative hesitation by assigning the story of a student's encounter with an executed woman to the category of the uncanny. The reader need not be concerned by the apparent threat which the fictional events offer to the rational world because they are no more than the imaginary product of a madman's vision.[13] The narrator's ironic failure to fulfil these expectations in *The Nose* is announced by the exclamation mark which closes the first sentence quoted above. The debunking of the conventional model and of the reader's hopes is enacted as the narrator proceeds to enumerate the queries which the narrative throws up for him. He does no more than casually acknowledge that the disappearance of the nose is 'сверхъестественное' ['supernatural'], choosing instead to give greater emphasis to the implausibility of an incident which, for the initiated reader, is far less important: 'как Ковалев не смекнул, что нельзя чрез газетную экспедицию объявлять о носе?' ['how could Kovalev not realize that it is not done to advertise about a nose through a newspaper office?'] (*N* 70). The promise briefly held out by the narrator's admission of confusion is, thus, ironically swept aside as he focuses his attention upon an inappropriate example from the array of unusual fictional events. The ironic intention behind this display of self-consciousness is reinforced as the narrator entirely unnecessarily argues that his objection to the advertisement is not because he is 'tight-fisted'. He goes still further in undermining his own objection when he mimics Kovalev's tendency towards incongruous reaction as he describes events as 'неприлично, неловко, нехорошо' ['improper, inconvenient, incorrect'] (ibid.). Such remarks indicate the distance between the value-judgements of the narrator and those of the initiated reader; and it is this discrepancy which allows the latter to infer the presence of irony. This ironic response to expectations warns the reader that the narrator is likely to prove an unreliable, incompetent judge of his own discursive act, who will continue to depart from the conventional models of both the fantastic and the storytelling act.

In *Onuphrius*, the narrator's acknowledgement of the problematic nature of events initially appears to be more conventional and to follow the example of *Gottfried Wolfgang*. The narrator addresses the reader directly to admit that the conclusion, which describes how Jacintha quickly forgets the stricken Onuphrius, might seem incompatible with what has gone before: 'n'est-ce pas, lecteur, que cette fin est bien commune pour une histoire extraordinaire?' ['is it not the case, reader, that this ending is rather banal for an extraordinary story?'] (*O* 52). By means of such a remark, the narrator appears to pre-empt the response of an initiated reader who may be dissatisfied with this denouement. However, Gautier's narrator departs from the more conventional model offered by Borel when he brushes aside the reader's concerns to state: 'Prenez-la ou laissez-la, je me couperais la gorge plutôt que de mentir d'une syllabe' ['Take it or leave it, I would cut my throat sooner than lie in a single syllable'] (ibid.). Ostensibly, this ultimatum is still aimed at persuading the reader of the veracity of the conclusion of the story. Nevertheless, owing to the coincidence of gender between the nouns 'la fin' and 'l'histoire', it is not unreasonable to interpret it more widely as applying to the narrative as a whole. The persuasive power of this claim is undermined, however, because the initiated reader suspects that it simply serves as further evidence of the narrator's playful attitude.

The narrator of *Onuphrius* uses this statement to play games with the conventions of claiming referentiality. Although works in the fantastic typically argue for their status as credible, 'real' accounts, this is most often done in an oblique or covert manner by voices other than that of the principal narrator. The decision by Gautier's narrator to raise this question so explicitly represents a further instance of the ironic exploitation of intertextual reference. The exponent of the fantastic who most frequently makes overt claims for the veracity of his discourse is Hoffmann. In *The Golden Pot* (1814), for example, the heterodiegetic narrator is keen to persuade the reader that, despite its many strange events, his story has actually taken place:

> [...] in the night watches in which I am recording his extraordinary story, I have still to recount many peculiar events, which, like a ghostly apparition, turned the everyday lives of ordinary people topsy-turvy, and I fear that you may end up believing neither in Anselmus nor in Archivist Lindhorst; you may even have some unjustified doubts about Sub-Rector Paulmann and Registry Heerbrand, although the latter two worthy gentlemen, at least, are still walking the streets of Dresden. (1992, 20)

The overt claim made for the truth-value of the discourse in *Onuphrius*, intended to recall those encountered in Hoffmann, undermines itself in two ways, however. Firstly, the terms the narrator employs to insist that he has told honestly of actual events are ironically exaggerated in an echo of the style confronted during earlier descriptions of apparent supernatural intervention. The narrator adapts the Hoffmann intertext to an extreme point and his suggestion that he would die rather than lie sits uncomfortably with the type of light-hearted narrative which has gone before. Secondly, this parodic claim closes a narrative which has made notably fewer efforts than its generic counterparts to earn referential status through actual discursive practice. The referential context of *Onuphrius* at every turn is the literary and not the mimetic or the actual after which texts in this genre conventionally strive. The protagonist is a creation of the genre, his belief-system is informed by the fantastic, and his encounters with apparently supernatural forces are all literary or artistic in nature. This final claim for truth and reliability is ironic because, by being at such odds with the narrative's own previous practice, it cannot but strike the reader as an empty, literary posture.

After having admitted that he finds his own story implausible, the narrator in *The Nose* also appears to make efforts to pre-empt the critical reaction which it might arouse. He repeats that he is unable to understand how Kovalev's nose found its way into Ivan Iakovlevich's loaf of bread and goes on to protest:

> Но что страннее, что непонятнее всего, — это то, как авторы могут брать подобные сюжеты. Признаюсь, это уж совсем непостижимо, это точно... нет, нет, совсем не понимаю. Во-первых, пользы отечеству решительно никакой; во-вторых... но и во-вторых тоже нет пользы. Просто я не знаю, что это... (*N* 70)

> [But what is stranger still, and hardest of all to understand, — is how authors can choose such subjects. I recognize that this is quite incomprehensible, it is just... no, no, I simply do not understand. Firstly there is absolutely no benefit to the fatherland; secondly... no, and secondly there's no benefit either. I simply do not know what this is...]

To contemporary readers of Gogol's story, these protestations would have recalled the views expressed by critics who insisted that literature should be useful or beneficial to society and mankind above all else. Indeed, as a consequence of this resemblance, certain more recent commentators choose to take this protest at face value, as an anticipation of these critics' reservations:

> Mindful of how irritating *The Nose* was sure to prove for such a mentality, Gogol incorporated into his story's penultimate paragraph a prepackaged response from this particular critical camp. [...] This little disclaimer served to forestall the expected kind of criticism — a clever stratagem that produced exactly the results Gogol intended. (Karlinsky 1976, 129)

However, the self-conscious irony in which the narrator's protests are steeped must lead to the suspicion that Gogol is not being 'mindful' here in any conventional sense. It is extremely difficult to believe, as Karlinsky does, that these lines serve as straightforward a purpose as attempting to silence a group of unfavourably disposed critics although, admittedly, this might have proved to be one of its consequences. The stability of these lines is undermined, on the one hand, by multiple markers of irony. The narrator's apparent exasperation at the uselessness of his story is overstated with the repetition of ellipsis and of his contentions 'нет' ['no'] and 'во-вторых' ['secondly']. Such markers perform the same function as the exclamation mark highlighted above. Furthermore, this repetition betrays his struggle to find any more than one reason to protest against the story's subject matter. He implicitly ridicules his own complaints by making the same point twice. As a consequence of his exaggeratedly hesitant terms, the narrator's contention that stories should serve a constructive purpose is ironically mocked. For the initiated reader, this protest poses additional problems. The self-consciousness of the narrative voice gives the reader the unmistakable 'sense of the fictional world as an authorial construct set up against a background of literary tradition and convention' (Alter 1975, xi). These lines represent the apogee of the tendency highlighted earlier whereby attention is devoted to the status and performance of the discourse rather than to the nature of fictional events. The narrator's expression of feigned dissatisfaction destroys any tacit assumption of the referential status of the story world presented in *The Nose*. By making clear the artifice of the story world created by the narrative act, Gogol's narrator places *The Nose* on the very boundaries of the genre of the fantastic. This revelation of reflexivity does not, however, resolve reader hesitation. Rather, it provides the strongest possible motivation for it to be redirected towards the status of the narrative act.

Before the narrator in *Onuphrius* plays with the conventions of referentiality in the final lines of the story, he provides a summary of events in an alternative form. Following his reflection upon the nature of Onuphrius's alienation, the narrator temporarily renounces his verbal tools when he reproduces a statistical table in the text. The statistics, which he claims were published the previous year by one doctor Esquirol, provide an overview of causes of male and female madness divided up according to categories of: 'love, religious devotion, politics or loss of fortune' (*O* 51). This statistical table must be seen to undermine the narrative act ironically. A first level of irony can be detected in the fact that this table simply reproduces popular stereotypes of gender and madness: women are more likely to go mad because of love, men because of politics. By simply re-expressing widely held, unscientific clichés, the statistics ironically thwart the expectation of deeper scientific insight which they have encouraged. Furthermore, *Onuphrius* ironically recycles the convention in the fantastic of employing science to support interpretative claims because the statistical table proves to be fallible and uninformative. The reliability of the information contained in the table is undermined because it is unable to account for all cases of madness. Alongside the four categories accounting for 190 patients is one case which is simply labelled: 'pour cause inconnue' ['for unknown cause']. Despite the fact that this is a single exception, it is sufficient to prove the inefficacy of the attempt to impose a scientific framework upon madness. The crucial importance of this failure is underlined by the narrator's revelation that: 'celui-là, c'est notre pauvre ami' ['that one is our poor friend'] (ibid.).

It is arguably the revelation that this one outstanding, unresolvable case concerns Onuphrius which constructs the most powerful irony in this closing passage. The fact that the narrator reproduces Esquirol's table and that it mentions the protagonist suggests that he feels it necessary to give Onuphrius's fate alternative expression. The inclusion of the table invites the reader to infer that the narrator believes that his verbal narrative has not accounted satisfactorily for the case of his hero. If it had done, there would be no need for the table. Consequently, the status of the discourse is undermined by the fact that, following all his efforts to describe Onuphrius's adventures and afflictions in poetic terms, the narrator turns his back on these tools and takes refuge in mathematical discourse. In so doing, he covertly suggests that figures might succeed where language and poetic discourse have failed. The ultimate irony presented by this table, however, is that, either as a clarification of, or wholesale replacement for, the narrative which has preceded it, it fails utterly. By classifying Onuphrius as 'cause inconnue', the reader is denied any additional information which might shed more light on events in the story. Onuphrius is simply the odd one out, the case which cannot be accounted for, and so the narrator's decision to favour statistics over poetic description is lampooned. In a more implicit manner than that exploited in *The Nose*, the initiated reader is forced to turn his attention to the status of the discourse rather than to the fictional events. He is effectively asked to hesitate over the efficacy of poetic discourse to depict human experience satisfactorily. The reader becomes less concerned about whether Onuphrius actually encounters a devil in a velvet suit and more preoccupied with the question of whether narrative discourse is the most appropriate vehicle for reporting any such meeting.

Such a reorientation of reader hesitation is also effected by the final lines in *The Nose*. In the very last paragraph of the story, the narrator's ironic posturing peaks in a way which ensures that the most acute ambiguity concerns the status of the discourse. Having apparently dismissed, through reflexivity, all claims that the narrative might have had to referentiality, the narrator now performs a complete about-face. Persisting in his show of feigned exasperation, he now claims:

> А, однако же, при всем этом, хотя, конечно, можно допустить и то, и другое, и третье, может даже... ну да и где же не бывает несообразностей?... А все, однако же, как поразмыслишь, во всем этом, право, есть что-то. Кто что ни говори, а подобные происшествия бывают на свете, — редко, но бывают. (*N* 70)

> [But all the same, all things considered, although, of course, it is possible to concede this, that and another thing, and maybe even... yes, well, where does incongruity not exist?... And everything, however, when you think it over, in all of this, there is something. Whatever you might say, such things do happen in the world — rarely, but they do happen.]

Previous concerns that events recounted in the narrative are 'improbable' are seemingly dismissed as the narrator now admits that occurrences such as the loss of a nose and its reappearance in full dress uniform can, and even more crucially, do sometimes occur. Despite all the rebuttals which she has come up against in *The Nose*, the initiated reader still bears witness to man's need to 'impose significance on the empirical reality around him' (Brooke-Rose 1981, 4). The narrator's reflections on reality suggest that the perspicacious initiated reader might be able to find a deep significance in his discourse, if only she were to make sufficient effort. However, at the same time, these closing paragraphs parody the idea of sense-making in much the same way as the implicit mocking of this reader's hierarchy of rationality discussed earlier has done. In virtually the same breath as he holds out the hope that significance might exist, the narrator ridicules the reader's beliefs and ironizes the idea that meaning necessarily has to exist. The narrator appears implicitly to say: 'I do not know what to make of this narrative, so what hope is there for you, the reader?' and in so doing makes the reader a victim of his discourse. As Peace (1981, 132) contends: 'The absurdity of the story is thrown back at the reader as something which defeats even the author himself, and he, disclaiming his story in this fashion, is in effect perpetrating a joke against the reader'. While the narrator in *Onuphrius* claims that he would rather slit his throat than tell a lie, the heterodiegetic voice in *The Nose* states first that the events recounted are fictional and too implausible to have existed anyway, before apparently changing his mind and claiming that they are possible and could, consequently, have existed. By means of such manoeuvres, the validity of the narrator's discourse is undermined because 'the same authority which has asserted fictional facts, fictional existence, raises doubts about these facts, about their existence' (Doležel 1980, 22). Is the reader now to believe that, because the events exist, she ought to try to decipher their true nature? Or does she not need to do so because, being so bizarre, they should be dismissed as sheer impossibility? The initiated reader of the fantastic is well versed in the slippery status of fictional events. She has ample experience of the questionable reliability of voices in the discourse making apparently irrational claims. However, her generic competence has not taught her to expect that the narrative voice will change the status of fictional events from one moment to the next so self-consciously and playfully. By means of his discursive games and ironic attitude, the narrator in *The Nose* places the story world on the cusp of fictional existence and non-existence. Consequently, not only do the fictional events depicted challenge the laws of the rational, but the fictional discourse also interrogates the laws of literary convention. The initiated reader effectively loses sight of the fictional events behind the mass of verbal and narrative games which are played. The centre of gravity for the initiated reader's hesitation is thus shifted from the fictional events to the narrative performance, a situation which poses difficulties for the generic categorization of Gogol's story.

The Formalists advocated the idea that literary evolution is driven forward by the practice of parody which renews canonical convention. *Onuphrius* and *The Nose* bear witness to a very similar procedure of challenging and extending the generic model of the fantastic by means of a ludic, ironic attitude. The ironic attitude displayed by both the extrafictional voice and the narrator, in conjunction with an initiated reader, opens up the parameters of the fantastic. It underlines the notion of genre as being in a state of dynamic flow where new forms are eternally sought. In these two stories, early differentiation from the standard practice of the fantastic alerts the initiated reader to the fact that a less mimetic fictional world is being created. This differentiation is then quickly developed into a more concerted process of ironically recycling conventions. Eventually, the initiated reader becomes a target of this process. Whilst the self-reflexive and playful performance of the narrative voices manifests itself in a variety of different ways in the two works, its primary consequence is to shift hesitation away from fictional events and towards the status of the discourse. Indeed, in its most extreme incarnation, the narrative irony interrogates not only the conventions of the fantastic but those of literary discourse as a whole. For Todorov, such redirection of ambiguity away from the nature of events to that of the text destroys the fantastic.

However, I believe it is possible to consider the result of such ironic interrogation of conventions more positively. Both *Onuphrius* and *The Nose* occupy a position on the cusp of the genre. They are not examples of the practice of the 'fantastique-pur'. However, the twin elements of the supernatural and hesitation do still coexist, albeit in a modified configuration. By putting Todorov's objection regarding the focus of hesitation to one side, both of these works should still be considered to belong to the genre of the fantastic. The originality they generate by exploiting the established conventions of the genre advocates an extension of the Todorovian notion of the fantastic. Furthermore, it provides a paradigm for the future development of the genre. The reflexivity exhibited by both works, which sees *Onuphrius* offering an experience of the fantastic almost entirely determined by reference to other fantastic intertexts and where *The Nose* argues for the futility of imposing signifying structures upon fictional discourse, indicates how the genre will develop in the modernist period. By regenerating the model of the fantastic proposed by Hoffmann, these two works open the door to such twentieth-century examples as Franz Kafka's *Metamorphosis* (1912) or Mervyn Peake's *Gormenghast* (1950).

Notes to Chapter 4

1. Alternative notions of this figure include the 'implied reader' (Booth, Iser), the 'model reader' (Eco), the 'super-reader' (Riffaterre), the 'narratee' (Prince), the 'ideal reader' (Culler), and the 'literent' (Holland).

2. Peace (1981, 132) claims that 'absurdity is everywhere in this story'. Karlinsky (1976, 123) sees *The Nose* as 'the most authentically surrealistic of Gogol's works'. Morson (1992, 226) believes that the story 'stands as Gogol's purest, and perhaps most profound, piece of nonsense'. Fanger (1979, 240) contends that unlike *Viy*, *The Nose* remains 'entirely in the realm of the uncanny'. Cornwell (1990, 234) ventures that 'the independence of the nose in Gogol's story, would surely not be "believable" to any reader, other than on a fairy-tale or marvellous level'. Woodward (1982, 63) sees the story as an example of the fantastic/absurd where the former is used to indulge in social criticism while Shukman (1989, 66) characterizes it as 'a unique and dazzling example of the fantastic'. Robert Maguire (1974, 26) summarizes another raft of classifications of the story:

   At various times the story has been read as a mere joke; as a parody on Romanticism; as an imitation of the large European literature of 'nosology' [...]; as a commentary on philistine philosophy; as a deliberate exercise in nonsense [...].

3. References to *Onuphrius, ou les vexations d'un admirateur d'Hoffmann* are taken from *L'Œuvre fantastique: Nouvelles*, Paris: Bordas, 1992. It might be argued that the description of Onuphrius's soul flying over the Louvre and the Porte Saint-Martin later in the story locates the fictional world in Paris. However, it is indicative of the playful nature of this narrative voice that these isolated geographical references are provided during the account of the protagonist's dream, thereby designating the location of unconscious activity but not of conscious, actual action. Any assumption that the hero's waking existence is spent in the same city must remain just that: unconfirmed supposition.

4. References to *Nos* are taken from N. V. Gogol, *Sobranie sochinenii v shesti tomakh*, vol. 3, Moscow: Khudozhestvennaia literatura, 1959.

5. In *Spirite*, the use of such epistemological paradox in the description of the figure in the mirror reveals the contradiction commonly encountered in the depiction of personae associated with the supernatural. This generic convention is also persuasively illustrated by the description of the mysterious female figure whom the protagonist of Pétrus Borel's *Gottfried Wolfgang* encounters at the foot of the guillotine:

> La figure de l'inconnue, quoique couverte en ce moment d'une pâleur mortelle, et portant l'empreinte profonde du désespoir, était d'une beauté ravissante. [...] Son teint, d'une blancheur éblouissante, était comme relevé par une profusion de cheveux noirs comme du jais, qui flottaient négligemment sur l'ivoire de ses épaules. Ses yeux étaient grands et pleins d'éclats; mais on remarquait dans leur expression quelque chose de hagard. (1973, 150–51)

> [The face of the unknown woman, although shrouded at that moment in a mortal paleness and carrying the profound imprint of despair, was of a ravishing beauty. [...] Her complexion, of a dazzling whiteness, was accentuated by a profusion of jet black hair which barely floated on her ivory shoulders. Her eyes were large and full of sparks; but in their expression, something wild was discernible.]

The terms of this description pre-empt the revelation that the woman has actually been executed prior to her encounter with the protagonist. Borel's heroine also speaks with a voice which 'impressionna singulièrement' (ibid.). Examples of this adjective or adverb have also been noted in *Spirite* and *La Vénus d'Ille*.

6. Hoffmann's *The Sandman* sees the hero, Nathaniel, fall in love with Olympia, who turns out to be nothing more than a mechanical doll created by Coppelius.

7. Suggesting that such a main plot line exists in *The Nose* is somewhat presumptuous given the manner in which the story consistently debunks conventions of story-telling. For instance, it proves to be far more difficult to provide a plot summary for *The Nose* than for any of the other works discussed in this book. Indeed, the tendency towards excessive detail and digression, highlighted only briefly here, results in a situation in which Gogol's story becomes all 'siuzhet' and no 'fabula'.

8. In a similar fashion, but with an arguably stronger comic edge, the policeman who eventually returns Kovalev's nose shows limited interest in the fact of his discovery, preferring to discuss his mother-in-law's short-sightedness and his family's living arrangements.

9. The narrative voice in *The Golden Pot* mirrors that in *Onuphrius* by means of its heterodiegetic status, omniscient privilege, self-consciousness, and the use of direct address to the reader. This latter technique, in particular, persuades the reader that the narrator occupies a position similar to her own, outside the story world. Consequently, when the fictional world is shown to be governed by rules which permit the supernatural, the reader has no reason to consider that this depiction has any ramifications for her extratextual world. However, during the Twelfth Vigil, the narrator describes how he receives a letter from one of the fictional characters containing directions which, when followed, lead him to experience a vision of the protagonist's fate. The report of the receipt of this letter performs the same function as the narrator's entry into Onuphrius's studio in Gautier's story: it shifts the boundary between the fictional and extrafictional worlds. If the narrator can interact with fictional characters, he must inhabit their world. The sense of intimacy which the narrator has established with the reader consequently suggests that the latter must also exist in far closer proximity to the fictional world than previously thought. The reader's dismissal of the threat of the supernatural is thus invalidated.

10. Crouzet (1992, 240) explains the significance of these particular authors: Bodin is the author of *De la démonomanie* (1580), Delrio was a Dutch Jesuit who wrote *Disquisitionum magicum libri sex* in the sixteenth century, the Dutch theologian Bekker published *Le Monde enchanté* in 1691, while

Berbiguier de Terre-Neuve-du-Thym was a contemporary of Gautier, whose work recounts his incessant persecution by demons. Further to these, we also find reference to Le Loyer (who wrote *Discours et histoires des spectres, visions et apparitions des esprits* in 1605), Bordelon (who published a denunciation of the devil with an unfeasibly long title in 1710) and to *Infernalia: ou anecdotes, petits romans, nouvelles et contes sur les revenants, les spectres, les démons, et les vampires* which Nodier published in 1822. Jean Paul's *Traumdichtungen* (*Dreams*), published over a number of years at the end of the eighteenth and the beginning of the nineteenth centuries, expresses his metaphysical thought.

11. The ironic impact of an introduction of the grotesque can also be perceived in the depiction of the wedding-night scene in Rabou's *Le Ministère public*. The more conventional horror of the discovery of a severed head in the nuptial bed is undermined by the description of Desalleux's attempts to kill this head with the aid of an iron poker (1963, 115):

A chaque fois que la barre de fer se levait, la tête faisait adroitement un saut de côté et laissait frapper l'arme à vide. Cela dura quelques minutes jusqu'à ce que, s'élançant par un bond prodigieux par-dessus l'épaule de son adversaire, elle disparut derrière lui [...].

[Every time the iron bar was raised, the head adroitly moved to one side, leaving the bar to strike nothing but air. This lasted for several minutes until, making a prodigious leap over its adversary's shoulder, the head disappeared behind him [...].]

12. One particularly notable earlier example of this type of statement is to be found when the police officer unexpectedly returns the missing nose. The narrator begins by describing Kovalev's pleasure but then breaks off to note:

Но на свете нет ничего долговременного; а потому и радость в следующую минуту за первою уже не так жива; в третью минуту она становится еще слабее и наконец незаметно сливается с обыкновенным положением души, как на воде круг, рожденный падением камешка, наконец сливается с гладкою поверхностью. (*N* 62)

[But nothing lasts long in this world, and that is why in the second minute our joy is never as vivid as in the first; by the third minute it becomes even weaker and eventually merges with the usual state of our soul, just as a ripple created by a stone falling on water eventually merges with the smooth surface.]

13. It is difficult to overlook the resemblance between the closing lines of Borel's story and the conclusion of Pushkin's *The Queen of Spades*. The interpretative resolution provided in Borel's story is not, however, mirrored by Pushkin's narrator, who draws no such explicit explanatory link between events and Germann's madness. Consequently, in *The Queen of Spades*, the reader is left to ask whether the apparently irrational fictional events are the (imaginary) product of the protagonist's insanity or its (real) trigger.

CONCLUSION

Over thirty years since *Introduction à la littérature fantastique* broke new ground, efforts to understand the fantastic and its related modes in greater depth continue apace. The recent monographs by Nicholas Royle and Dorothea E. von Mucke bear witness to the potential for analysis offered by the genre. The present work identifies itself very strongly with the critical legacy of Tzvetan Todorov. Underpinning this study throughout has been the acceptance of his proposal that the fantastic depends for its existence upon the coexistence of the supernatural and hesitation. The fantastic thrives when ambiguity regarding which of a natural or supernatural interpretation for fictional events should be accepted as reliable and ultimately convincing persists. However, my interest in the genre is fired by the inadequacy I perceive in the efforts of Todorov and his various successors to account for how this hesitation is provoked. Although *Introduction à la littérature fantastique* rightly argues that uncertainty can be felt by fictional protagonist and reader alike, it is a desire to understand the reactions of the latter which has informed this investigation. It is not enough to state simply that a reader's inability to impose one interpretation at the expense of another stems from the nature of fictional events. Whether a reader is consciously aware of it or not, she is affected not by the events directly but by the particular combination of techniques used to depict them. After all, in the context of the literary narrative, events have no existence outside their linguistic representation; fictional events are discourse events. Therefore, the desire to account cogently for reader hesitation has necessitated a focus upon the various devices employed in story construction and, most importantly, narration. This is the most significant contribution offered to the field of studies of the fantastic by the present work.

The critical method invoked to describe these devices in as clear a manner as possible can also be seen to build upon Todorov's approach. The structuralist approach of *Introduction à la littérature fantastique* allowed the literary text to take centre stage whilst various extratextual issues such as genre history and author biography were largely ignored. Narratology builds upon the foundations established by structuralism but seeks to give greater prominence than its predecessor to the addresser figure in Jakobson's model of communication. The two most important incarnations of this figure in narratology are the narrator, who imparts the discourse to the reader, and the extrafictional voice, which is responsible more broadly for the organization of the discourse, including the characteristics of the narrator. It is these two personae who participate in the representation of fictional events; it is to these two, therefore, that the various syntactic and narrative devices encountered in a literary text should be attributed. Narratology can consequently make strong claims to be the most informative theoretical framework through which to investigate how such devices contribute to the experience of hesitation. The models proposed by Genette and Lanser, amongst others, have allowed a more complete picture to be drawn of how a fictional world is made to appear stable and of how a reader's access to information is controlled. Key issues in narratology such as the profile of a narrative voice, the interrelationship between different voices, and the exploitation of point of view have proved to be of fundamental importance in the pursuit of hesitation in the fantastic. However, it has not been my intention to assess the devices contributing to uncertainty in an abstract manner; my interest consistently lies in the action or effect of a technique. This approach is suggested by Todorov's definition of the 'pure fantastic' as an evanescent genre which ceases to exist at the moment that ambiguity is resolved. The reader's reaction to, and interpretation of, fictional events is therefore of paramount importance. And this is where narratology falls a little short. It has difficulty accounting for the impact upon the reader of the devices functioning within the text. Therefore, particularly in Chapters 3 and 4 above, I have supplemented this critical methodology with reference to Jauss's theory of the aesthetics of reception and Hutcheon's notion of discursive communities. It is hoped that such an approach has allowed a comprehensive account of hesitation to be given; not only the manner in which it is produced, but also the way in which it is received.

The belief that the roots of hesitation lie in the narrative and syntactic devices employed within literary discourse has imposed upon this book a practice of close textual analysis. Because the existence of hesitation can be influenced by individual words or clauses, analysis has had to be focused at a point of maximal proximity to the text. Nor is this close textual reading restricted to those passages where the supernatural is described. While the description of the apparently irrational event may represent the epicentre from which a substantial degree of the text's ambiguity emanates, an accurate appreciation of its functioning and impact can only be achieved through consideration of the wider context. Neither descriptions, nor the techniques employed within descriptions, function in isolation; they are necessarily conditioned by those which surround them. One consequence of this approach is that it has permitted the discussion of only eight primary texts. However, I believe that the insights provided by these readings have the potential for a far wider application than simply to the works discussed. The stock of narrative and syntactic devices which have been shown to contribute to reader hesitation will prove to be equally pertinent to other texts belonging to the fantastic. The key to this wider applicability is the discussion, most notably in Chapters 1 and 2, of hesitation in different diegetic contexts. Chapter 1 offers a model of the devices used to create ambiguity in heterodiegetic texts, while Chapter 2 undertakes the same task by looking at homodiegetic texts. Although the manner in which devices are combined in any given text may be unique, the techniques themselves are more universal. Therefore, rather than searching for a work which closely resembles *The Queen of Spades* in order to find the same techniques in action, the reader can be confident of the likelihood that any heterodiegetic narrative in the fantastic will reveal a functional coincidence.

This book has adopted a broadly dualistic approach to theoretical thinking about the fantastic. On the one hand, I have used my reading of the chosen primary texts to test pre-existing claims for the genre, particularly those proposed by Todorov. Chapter

1 has engaged with the broadly held view that heterodiegesis is an unsuitable vehicle for the fantastic. Its illustration of how *Spirite* and *The Queen of Spades* convince the reader of the mimetic status of the fictional world and of the reliability of the narrative voice initially makes such a claim appear valid. However, by revealing how switches in point of view, in particular, can be employed to sidestep these apparent obstacles to ambiguous interpretation, the marginalizing of heterodiegesis in the fantastic has been shown to be untenable. Chapter 2 is prompted by the desire to look beyond the claim, which Todorov readily admits is naïve and simplistic, that homodiegesis is the ideal mode for the fantastic because of the sympathy it encourages between narrator and reader. The discussion of personality has insisted upon the contribution made to hesitation by the discrepancy between the narrator's beliefs and the nature of the irrational event. Chapter 3 has advocated a revision of the reductive role assigned to the concept of madness by Todorov and argues that texts do exist in which the coexistence of insanity and the supernatural is exploited to elicit an even more acute degree of uncertainty. The final chapter addresses Todorov's claims regarding the attitude which a reader must adopt towards the literary text in order for hesitation to be possible. Pursuing the similarities which exist between his characterization of allegory and popular concepts of irony, I have examined the potential for the fantastic to exist in narratives which present playful and self-conscious narrative voices.

However, the aim of this book has not been simply to test out existing theory. It has also endeavoured to propose a number of more original ideas about how literary narratives provoke hesitation. Throughout the four chapters of this study, the issue of the relative authority and reliability of voice claiming the existence of the supernatural has been seen to lie at the very heart of the genre. The practice of the fantastic has been seen to be a game in ensuring that information is not provided from a single source which enjoys sufficient reliability for its account to be trusted fully. Such a situation would see the fantastic resolved into one of the neighbouring genres where ambiguity ceases to exist. In the case of heterodiegetic narratives, switches in point of view from the authoritative perspective of the narrator to the more fallible viewpoint of a fictional character achieve this effect. In both *Spirite* and *The Queen of Spades*, this technique is occasionally developed to more transgressive effect when the heterodiegetic voice is shown to be something less than completely reliable. The device of having different voices lobby for conflicting interpretations of events has, in fact, been shown to be a generic stock-in-trade. *The Sylph* and *La Vénus d'Ille* in Chapter 2 have illustrated how, in the homodiegetic context, it is the presence of a multiplicity of narrative voices which prevents the reader from arriving at a single interpretation of events. In Odoevskii's story, in particular, the impossibility of establishing a hierarchy of authority between these various voices guarantees that the reader will be unable to decide unambiguously whether or not the supernatural actually existed. In Dostoevskii's *The Double*, the reader's confusion, and the impression of the disintegrating sanity of Goliadkin, is the consequence of the indivisibility of the voices of narrator and protagonist. Free indirect discourse has thereby been demonstrated to be a potent tool in the provocation of interpretative ambiguity. It creates a sense of an isolated perspective informing the narrative which is encountered, albeit under different narrative conditions, in Maupassant's *Le Horla*. The examination in parallel of these two works has illustrated how faltering coherence, as an expression of compromised sanity, can be achieved equally effectively in homodiegetic and heterodiegetic texts. What all of the primary texts discussed in this book have proved is the need for the exponents of the fantastic to keep the reader asking not simply 'is this event supernatural or not?', but 'who sees this event?', 'who is telling me about this event?', and, most importantly, 'can I trust this voice?'.

This book is intended to function not only as an examination of the theory of the fantastic, but also as an illustration of the genre in practice. Equally, the discussion has endeavoured to be of interest as much for what it has to say about the fantastic as about the individual works which have served as its basis. Arguably with the exception of Odoevskii's *The Sylph*, the stories and novellas selected for a reading of the genre had already received a significant amount of critical attention. Nevertheless, I believe that this study has succeeded in making fresh observations and encouraging critical appreciation of all of them. The specific focus on the question of interpretative ambiguity has meant that hitherto neglected and, in some cases, negatively judged aspects have been reassessed. For instance, the analysis of reader hesitation in *The Double* has promoted the view that the performance of the narrative voice is not regrettably destructive, but rather is a powerful tool in the illustration of mental instability. Similarly, reading Gogol's *The Nose* as an example of the fantastic has uncovered how skilfully the story calls upon the initiated reader's knowledge of the genre, only to make her the target of irony.

Arguably the most significant factor contributing to a renewed appreciation of the eight primary texts discussed is the comparative approach employed throughout this book. The examination of how hesitation is provoked in Odoevskii's *The Sylph* has, it is hoped, been enriched by the reading in parallel of Mérimée's *La Vénus d'Ille*. Equally, an understanding of the impact of switches in point of view in *The Queen of Spades* is deepened by the illustration of how this same device is deployed in *Spirite*. Most important, however, is the fact that this comparative approach gives greater weight to the claims that the techniques highlighted form the fundamental, discursive basis of the fantastic. Not only that, but, by demonstrating how similarities of practice exist at a deeper level than the thematic or symbolic, the argument that the fantastic is a genre which straddles national and linguistic boundaries becomes more persuasive. On the strength of narrative and syntactic factors alone, therefore, it is possible to argue that the fantastic enjoyed a pan-European existence during the nineteenth century.

When work on this project began, it was not my intention to propose an extension to the generic scope of *Introduction à la littérature fantastique*. Satisfaction with Todorov's contention that the defining elements of the fantastic are the supernatural and hesitation informed the decision not to examine examples of related genres such as magical realism, science fiction, or fairy tales. However, the process of analysing techniques used to prompt reader uncertainty has led me to recognize that Todorov's definition of the genre is restricted in one important sense. This has made itself felt particularly forcefully during the discussion in Chapter 4 of the impact on the fantastic of playful or ironic narrative attitudes. Arguably, however, this chapter only makes more obvious a realization which has been imposing itself over the course of the preceding chapters. That is, the recognition as untenable of Todorov's declaration that the fantastic is threatened if reader hesitation is directed at the discourse. The starting point for this investigation of how hesitation is provoked is the conviction that the depiction of fictional events exerts a greater influence upon interpretation than the events *per se*. It has proved that the techniques operating in the discourse to control the reader's perception play the most significant role in determining a work's adherence to the genre of the fantastic. Whilst on one level, therefore, hesitation may concern the status of fictional events, on a more fundamental level, uncertainty unavoidably focuses upon the status of the discourse which gives these events their existence. If the discursive techniques used to depict events are considered to play the pivotal role, it becomes unacceptable to contend that, in the fantastic, hesitation cannot, or should not, be directed at the status of the discourse. The most notable consequence of this discovery is that it imposes a reconsideration of the manner in which Todorov's definition of the fantastic would exclude ludic, self-reflexive narratives. The realization that, in actuality, the fantastic always and necessarily directs hesitation at the status of the discourse means that self-conscious and self-reflexive texts which play with their own status must henceforth be considered to be compatible with the genre of the fantastic. Provided that they continue to confront the reader with the basic natural/supernatural dilemma, ludic and ironic texts represent an acceptable subcategory within the fantastic. Todorov's formulations of the fantastic should consequently be extended to include this group of texts.

BIBLIOGRAPHY

Primary Texts

Texts used as basis of discussion

DOSTOEVSKII, F. M. (1866), *Dvoinik,* in *Polnoe sobranie sochinenii v tridtsati tomakh,* vol. 1, Leningrad: Nauka, 1972

GAUTIER, T. (1833), *Onuphrius, ou les vexations d'un admirateur d'Hoffmann,* in *L'œuvre fantastique: Nouvelles,* Paris: Bordas, 1992

—— (1865), *Spirite,* in *L'Œuvre fantastique: Romans,* Paris: Bordas, 1992

GOGOL, N.V.(1836), *Nos,* in *Sobranie sochinenii v shesti tomakh,* vol. 3, Moscow: Khudozhestvennaia literatura, 1959

MAUPASSANT, G. DE (1887), *Le Horla,* in *Contes et nouvelles,* Paris: Gallimard, 1979

MÉRIMÉE, P. (1837), *La Vénus d'Ille,* in *Romans et nouvelles,* Paris: Gallimard, 1951

ODOEVSKII,V. F.(1837), *Sil'fida,* in *Sochineniia v dvukh tomakh,* vol. 2, Moscow: Khudozhestvennaia literatura, 1981

PUSHKIN, A. S. (1834), *Pikovaia dama,* in *Polnoe sobranie sochinenii v desiati tomakh,* vol. 6, Moscow: Akademiia Nauk, 1957

Texts used for subsidiary reference

BOREL, P. (1833), *Gottfried Wolfgang,* in *La France fantastique de Balzac à Louys,* ed. by J.-B. Baronian,Verviers: Gérard, 1973

CAZOTTE, J. (1772), *Le Diable amoureux,* Paris: Gallimard, 1981

CHASLES, P. (1832), *L'Œil sans paupière,* Collection électronique de la Bibliothèque municipale de Lisieux, 1997

GAUTIER, T. (1831), *La Cafetière,* in *L'Œuvre fantastique,* 2 vols, ed. by Crouzet, Paris: Bordas, 1992, pp. 11–18

—— (1834), *Omphale,* in *L'Œuvre fantastique,* 2 vols, ed. by Crouzet, Paris: Bordas, 1992, pp. 58–66

—— (1836), *La Morte amoureuse,* in *L'Œuvre fantastique,* 2 vols, ed. by Crouzet, Paris: Bordas, 1992, pp. 75–102

—— (1840),*Le Pied de momie,* in *L'Œuvre fantastique,* 2 vols, ed. by Crouzet, Paris: Bordas, 1992, pp. 139–150

HOFFMANN, E. T. A. (1814), *The Golden Pot,* in *The Golden Pot and Other Tales,* trans. by Ritchie Robertson, Oxford: World's Classics, 1992

HUGO, A. (1833), *L'Heure de la mort,* in *Anthologie du conte fantastique français,* ed. by P.-G. Castex, Paris: José Corti, 1963

NERVAL, G. DE (1832), *La Main enchantée,* in *Œuvres complètes,* ed. by J. Guillaume & C. Pichois, 3 vols, Paris: Gallimard, 1984–93

—— (1855), *Aurélia ou Le rêve et la vie,* in *Œuvres complètes,* ed. by J. Guillaume & C. Pichois, 3 vols, Paris: Gallimard, 1984–93

NODIER, C. (1806), *Une Heure ou La Vision,* in *Contes,* ed. by P.-G. Castex, Paris: Garnier, 1961

—— (1837), *Inès de Las Sierras,* in *Contes,* ed. by P.-G. Castex, Paris: Garnier, 1961

ODOEVSKII, V. (1840), *Kosmorama*, in *Sochineniia v dvukh tomakh*, vol. 2, Moscow: Khudozhe-strennaia literature, 1981

—— (1841), *Salamandra*, in *Sochineniia v dvukh tomakh*, vol. 2, Moscow: Khudozhestrennaia literature, 1981

POTOCKI, J. (1803–15), *The Manuscript Found in Saragossa*, trans. by Ian Maclean, London: Penguin, 1996

RABOU, C. (1832), *Le Ministère public*, in *Anthologie du conte fantastique français*, ed. by P.-G. Castex, Paris: José Corti, 1963

VILLIERS DE L'ISLE-ADAM (1874), *Véra*, in *Anthologie du conte fantastique français*, ed. by P.-G. Castex, Paris: José Corti, 1963

Secondary Literature

ALTER, R. (1975), *Partial Magic: The Novel as a Self-Conscious Genre*, Berkeley: University of California Press

ANDERSON, R. B. (1972), 'Dostoevsky's Hero in *The Double*: A Reexamination of the Divided Self', *Symposium*, 26, 101–13

—— (1986), *Dostoevsky: Myths of Duality*, Gainesville: University of Florida Press

APTER, T. E. (1982), *Fantasy Literature: An Approach to Reality*, London: Macmillan

ARMITT, L. (1996), *Theorising the Fantastic*, London: Edward Arnold

AUERBACH, E. (1953), *Mimesis: the Representation of Reality in Western Literature*, Princeton: Princeton University Press

BAKHTIN, M. (1981), *The Dialogic Imagination: Four Essays*, trans. by C. Emerson & M. Holquist, Austin: University of Texas Press

—— (1984), *Problems of Dostoevsky's Poetics*, trans. by C. Emerson, Manchester: Manchester University Press

BAL, M. (1997), *Narratology*, trans. by C. van Boheemen, 2nd edn, Toronto: University of Toronto Press; orig. pub. 1985

BANCQUART, M.-C. (1976), *Maupassant: conteur fantastique*, Paris: Minard

BARONIAN, J.-B. (1978), *Panorama de la littérature fantastique de langue française*, Paris: Stock

BARTHES, R. (1968), 'L'effet de réel', *Communications*, 11: 84–89

—— (1970), *S/Z*, Paris: Seuil

—— (1973), *Le plaisir du texte*, Paris: Seuil

BÉGUIN, A. (1946), *L'âme romantique et le rêve*, Paris: José Corti

BELLEMIN-NOËL, J. (1971), 'Des formes fantastiques aux thèmes fantasmiques', *Littérature*, 2: 103–18

—— (1972), 'Notes sur le fantastique (textes de Théophile Gautier),', *Littérature*, 8: 3–23

—— (1973), 'Fantasque Onuphrius', *Romantisme*, 6: 38–48

BESSIÈRE, I. (1974), *Le Récit fantastique: la poétique de l'incertain*, Paris: Larousse

BONHEIM, H. (1990), *Literary Systematics*, Cambridge: Brewer

BONNEFIS, P. (1981), *Comme Maupassant*, Lille: Presses universitaires de Lille

BOOTH, W. (1971), *The Rhetoric of Fiction*, 2nd edn, Chicago: University of Chicago Press

—— (1974), *A Rhetoric of Irony*, Chicago: University of Chicago Press

—— (1979), *Critical Understanding: The Powers and Limits of Pluralism*, Chicago: University of Chicago Press

BOWMAN, F. P. (1960), 'Narrator and Myth in Mérimée's *La Vénus d'Ille*', *French Review*, 33: 475–82

BRIGGS, A. D. P. (1983), *Alexander Pushkin: A Critical Study*, London: Croom Helm

BROOKE-ROSE, C. (1981), *A Rhetoric of the Unreal: Studies in Narrative and Structure, especially of the Fantastic*, Cambridge: Cambridge University Press

BROOKS, P. (1984), *Reading for the Plot: Design and Intention in Narrative*, New York: Knopf

CAILLOIS, R. (1965), 'Au cœur du fantastique', in his *Cohérences aventureuses*, Paris: Gallimard, 69–192

—— (1974), 'Mérimée et le fantastique: en relisant *La Vénus d'Ille*', *Nouvelle revue des deux mondes*, Oct–Dec: 20–27

CARPENTER, S. (1986), 'Metaphor and madness in Mérimée's *La Vénus d'Ille*', *Romance Notes*, 27: 75–81

CASTEX, P.-G. (1951), *Le Conte Fantastique en France de Nodier à Maupassant*, Paris: José Corti

CHAMBERS, R.(1972), 'Gautier et le complexe de Pygmalion', *Revue d'histoire littéraire de la France*, 4: 641–58

—— (1974), *Spirite de Théophile Gautier: une lecture*, Minard, Archives des lettres modernes

—— (1980), 'La lecture comme hantise: *Spirite* et *Le Horla*', *Revue des sciences humaines*, 177: 105–17

—— (1985), *Story and Situation: Narrative Seduction and the Power of Fiction*, Minneapolis: University of Minnesota Press

CHATMAN, S. (1978), *Story and Discourse: Narrative Structure in Fiction and Film*, Ithaca: Cornell University Press

—— (1990), *Coming to Terms: The Rhetoric of Narrative in Fiction and Film*, Ithaca: Cornell University Press

CHIZHEVSKII, D. (1962), 'The Theme of the Double in Dostoevsky', in *Dostoevsky: A Collection of Critical Essays*, ed. by R. Wellek, Englewood Cliffs, NJ: Prentice Hall, 112–29

—— (1979), 'On Gogol's "The Overcoat"', in *Dostoevsky and Gogol*, ed. by P. Meyer & S. Rudy, Ann Arbor: Ardis, 137–60; orig. pub. 1938

COCKRELL, R. (1999), 'Philosophical Tale or Gothic Horror Story? The Strange Case of V.F. Odoevskii's *The Cosmorama*', in *The Gothic-Fantastic in Nineteenth-Century Russian Literature*, ed. by N. Cornwell, Amsterdam: Rodopi, 127–43

COHN, D. (1978), *Transparent Minds: Narrative Modes for Presenting Consciousness in Fiction*, Princeton: Princeton University Press

—— (1990), 'Signposts of Fictionality: A Narratological Perspective', *Poetics Today*, 11/4: 775–804

CORNWELL, N. (1986a), 'Perspectives on the Romanticism of V.F. Odoevskii', in *Problems of Russian Romanticism*, ed. by R. Reid, Brookfield, VT: Gower, 169–208

—— (1986b), *The Life, Times and Milieu of V.F. Odoevskii, 1804–1869*, Ohio: Ohio University Press

—— (1990), *The Literary Fantastic, from Gothic to Postmodernism*, London: Harvester Wheatsheaf

—— (1998), *Vladimir Odoevsky and Romantic Poetics*, Oxford: Berghahn

—— (ed.) (1999), *The Gothic-Fantastic in Nineteenth-Century Russian Literature*, Amsterdam: Rodopi

CRAVENS, C. S. (2000), 'Čapek's *Hordubal* and Dostoevsky's *The Double*: Madness and Free-Indirect Discourse', *Comparative Literature*, 52: 53–71

CROUZET, M. (1992), 'Introduction', in his edition of *Gautier: L'œuvre fantastique: Nouvelles*, Paris: Bordas

CULLER, J. (1974), *Flaubert: The Uses of Uncertainty*, Ithaca: Cornell University Press

—— (1975), *Structuralist Poetics: Structuralism, Linguistics, and the Study of Literature*, London: Routledge and Kegan

DECOTTIGNIES, J. (1962), 'Quelques rapprochements suggérés par *La Vénus d'Ille*', *Revue des Sciences Humaines*, 27: 453–61

DENTAN, M. (1976), '*Le Horla* ou le vertige de l'absence', *Etudes de Lettres*, 9: 45–54

DOHERTY, J. (1992), 'Fictional Paradigms in Pushkin's *Pikovaya Dama*', *Essays in Poetics*, 17/1: 49–66

DOLEŽEL, L. (1980), 'Truth and Authenticity in Narrative', *Poetics Today*, 1: 7–25

—— (1988), 'Mimesis and Possible Worlds', *Poetics Today*, 9: 475–96

EIKHENBAUM, B. (1979), 'How Gogol's Overcoat Was Made', in *Dostoevsky and Gogol*, ed. by P. Meyer & S. Rudy, Ann Arbor: Ardis, 119–36; orig. pub. 1919

FALETTI, H. (1977), 'Remarks on Style as Manifestation of Narrative Technique', *Canadian-American Slavic Studies*, 11/1: 114–33

FANGER, D. (1979), *The Creation of Nikolai Gogol*, Cambridge, Mass.: Harvard University Press

FELMAN, S. (1978), *La Folie et la chose littéraire*, Paris: Seuil

FINNÉ, J. (1980), *La Littérature fantastique*, Brussels: Université de Bruxelles

FISH, S.(1980), 'Literature in the Reader: Affective Stylistics', in *Reader Response Criticism: From Formalism to Post Structuralism*, ed. by J. Tompkins, Baltimore: John Hopkins University Press, 70–100

FITZ, B. E. (1972), 'The Use of Mirrors and Mirror Analogues in Maupassant's *Le Horla*', *French Review*, 45/5: 954–63

FLUDERNIK, M. (1996), *Towards a 'Natural' Narratology*, London and New York: Routledge

FOUCAULT, M. (1972), *Histoire de la folie à l'âge classique*, Paris: Gallimard

FRYE, N. (1957), *Anatomy of Criticism: Four Essays*, Princeton: Princeton University Press

FURST, L. (1984), *Fictions of Romantic Irony*, Cambridge, Mass.: Harvard University Press

GASPERETTI, D. (1989), '*The Double*: Dostoevsky's Self-Effacing Narrative', *Slavic and East European Journal*, 33: 217–33

GEI, N. K. (1983), *Proza Pushkina — poetika povestvovaniia*, Moscow: Nauka

GENETTE, G. (1968), 'Vraisemblance et motivation', *Communications*, 11: 5–21

—— (1972), *Figures III*, Paris: Seuil

—— (1983), *Nouveau discours du récit*, Paris: Seuil

—— (1997), *Paratexts: Thresholds of Interpretation*, trans. by J. Lewin, Cambridge: Cambridge University Press

HAMON, P. (1971), '*Le Horla* de Guy de Maupassant: essai de description structurale', *Littérature*, 4: 31–43

—— (1973), 'Un discours contraint', *Poétique*, 16: 411–45

HARTER, D. (1996), *Bodies in Pieces: Fantastic Narrative and the Poetics of the Fragment*, Stanford: Stanford University Press

HAYMAN, D. & RABKIN, E. (1974), *Form in Fiction: An Introduction to the Analysis of Narrative Prose*, New York: St. Martin's Press

HINGLEY, R. (1962), *The Undiscovered Dostoevsky*, London: Hamish Hamilton

HUME, K. (1984), *Fantasy and Mimesis: Representations of Reality in Western Literature*, New York and London: Methuen

HUTCHEON, L. (1981), 'Ironie, satire, parodie: une approche pragmatique de l'ironie', *Poétique*, 46: 140–55

—— (1988), *A Poetics of Postmodernism: History, Theory, Fiction*, London and New York: Routledge

—— (1994), *Irony's Edge: The Theory and Politics of Irony*, London and New York: Routledge

INGHAM, N. (1974), *E.T.A. Hoffmann's Reception in Russia*, Würzburg: Jag

IRWIN, W. R. (1976), *The Game of the Impossible: A Rhetoric of Fantasy*, Urbana: University of Illinois

ISER, W. (1978), *The Act of Reading: A Theory of Aesthetic Response*, Baltimore and London: John Hopkins University Press

IZMAILOV, N. V. (1973), 'Fantasticheskaia povest'', in *Russkaia povest' XIX veka: istoriia i problematika zhanra*, ed. by B. S. Meilakh, Leningrad: Nauka, 134–69

JACKSON, R. (1981), *Fantasy: Literature of Subversion*, New York and London: Methuen

JAKOBSON, R. (1960), 'Closing Statement: Linguistics and Poetics', in *Style in Language*, ed. by T. A. Sebeok, Cambridge, Mass.: MIT Press

JAUSS, H. R. (1982), *Toward an Aesthetic of Reception*, trans. by T. Bahti, Minneapolis: University of Minnesota Press

JONES, J. (1983), *Dostoevsky*, Oxford: Clarendon Press

JONES, L. (1972), 'The *Conte fantastique* as Poetic Fiction: Critical Definitions Then and Now', *Orbis Litterarum*, 27: 237–53

JONES, M. V. (1987), 'Dostoevsky – Driving the Reader Crazy', *Essays in Poetics*, 12/1: 57–80

—— (1990), *Dostoevsky after Bakhtin: Readings in Dostoevsky's Fantastic Realism*, Cambridge: Cambridge University Press

KARLINSKY, S. (1966), 'A Hollow Shape: The Philosophical Tales of Prince Vladimir Odoevsky', *Studies in Romanticism*, 3: 169–82

—— (1976), *The Sexual Labyrinth of Nikolai Gogol*, Cambridge, Mass.: Harvard University Press

KRISTEVA, J. (1982), *Desire in Language: A Semiotic Approach to Literature and Art*, trans. by T. Gora, A. Jardine and L. Roudiez, Oxford: Blackwell

LANSER, S. (1981), *The Narrative Act*, Princeton: Princeton University Press

LITTLE, T. E. (1982), *The Fantasts*, Amersham: Avebury

LOMAGIN, M. F. (1971), 'K voprosu o positsii avtora v "Dvoinike" Dostoevskogo', *Filologicheskie nauki*, 14: 3–14

LOWRIE, J. O. (1979–80), 'The Question of Mimesis in Gautier's *Contes fantastiques*', *Nineteenth-Century French Studies*, 8: 14–29

MACNAMARA, M. (1986), *Style and Vision in Maupassant's Nouvelles*, Bern: Peter Lang

MAGUIRE, R. (1974), 'The Legacy of Criticism', in his *Gogol from the Twentieth Century: Eleven Essays*, Princeton: Princeton University Press, 3–56

—— (1994), *Exploring Gogol*, Stanford: Stanford University Press

MANN, Iu. (1978), *Poetika Gogolia*, Moscow: Khudozhestvennaia literatura

MOLINO, J. (1980), 'Trois modèles d'analyse du fantastique', *Europe*, 58: 12–26

MONLEÓN, J. (1990), *A Specter is Haunting Europe: A Sociohistorical Approach to the Fantastic*, Princeton: Princeton University Press

MORSON, G. S. (1992), 'Gogol's Parables of Explanation: Nonsense and Prosaics', in *Essays on Gogol: Logos and the Russian Word*, ed. by S. Fusso & P. Meyer, Evanston, Ill.: Northwestern University Press, 200–39

VON MUECKE, D. E. (2003), *The Seduction of the Occult and the Rise of the Fantastic Tale*, Stanford: Stanford University Press

NECHAEVA, V. S. (1979), *Rannii Dostoevskii*, Moscow: Nauka

NEEFS, J. (1980), 'La Représentation fantastique dans *Le Horla* de Maupassant', *Cahiers de l'Association internationale des études françaises*, 32: 231–45

ONEGA, S. & LANDA, J. (1996), *Narratology: An Introduction*, London: Longman

PASCAL, R. (1977), *The Dual Voice: Free Indirect Speech and its Functioning in the Nineteenth-Century European Novel*, Manchester: Manchester University Press

PASSAGE, C. E. (1954), *Dostoevskii the Adapter: A Study in Dostoevskii's Use of the Tales of Hoffmann*, Chapel Hill: University of North Carolina Press

—— (1963), *The Russian Hoffmannists*, The Hague: Mouton

PEACE, R. (1981), *The Enigma of Gogol*, Cambridge: Cambridge University Press

PENZOLDT, P. (1952), *The Supernatural in Fiction*, London: Peter Nevill

PILKINGTON, A. (1975–76), 'Narrator and Supernatural in Mérimée's *La Vénus d'Ille*', *Nineteenth-Century French Studies*, 4: 24–30

PONNAU, G. (1997), *La Folie dans la littérature fantastique*, Paris: Presses universitaires de France

POPKIN, C. (1993), *The Pragmatics of Insignificance: Chekhov, Zoshchenko, Gogol*, Stanford: Stanford University Press

PORTER, L. (1982), 'The Subversion of the Narrator in Mérimée's *La Vénus d'Ille*', *Nineteenth-Century French Studies*, 10: 268–77

PRATT, M.-L. (1977), *Toward a Speech Act Theory of Literature*, Bloomington: Indiana University Press

PRINCE, G. (1982), *Narratology: The Form and Functioning of Narrative*, Berlin: Mouton

PROPP, V. (1958), *The Morphology of the Folk-Tale*, Austin: University of Texas Press

RABKIN, E. (1976), *The Fantastic in Literature*, Princeton: Princeton University Press

RAMSEY, C. C. (1999), 'Gothic Treatment of the Crisis of Engendering in Odoevskii's *The Salamander*', in *The Gothic-Fantastic in Nineteenth-Century Russian Literature*, ed. by N. Cornwell, Amsterdam: Rodopi, 145–69

REID, R. (1986), 'Russian Theories of Romanticism', in R. Reid (ed.), *Problems of Russian Romanticism*, Aldershot: Gower, 1–25

RIMMON[-KENAN], S. (1977), *The Concept of Ambiguity: The Example of James*, Chicago: Chicago University Press

—— (1983), *Narrative Fiction: Contemporary Poetics*, London: Routledge

ROYLE, N. (2003), *The Uncanny*, Manchester: Manchester University Press

RYAN, M.-L. (1991), *Possible Worlds, Artificial Intelligence, and Narrative Theory*, Bloomington: Indiana University Press

—— (1992), 'Possible Worlds in Recent Literary Theory', *Style*, 26/4: 528–53

SCHNEIDER, M. (1964), *Histoire de la littérature fantastique en France*, Paris: Fayard

SCHOLES, R. & KELLOGG, R. (1966), *The Nature of Narrative*, Oxford: Oxford University Press

SHUKMAN, A. (1977), 'The Short Story: Theory, Analysis, Interpretation', *Essays in Poetics*, 2/2: 27–95

—— (1989), 'Gogol's *The Nose* or the Devil in the Works', in *Nikolay Gogol: Text and Context*, ed. by J. Grayson & F. Wigzell, London: Macmillan, 64–82

SICHER, E. (1990), 'Dialogization and Laughter in the Dark, or How Gogol's Nose Was Made: Parody and Literary Evolution in Bachtin's Theory of the Novel', *Russian Literature*, 28: 211–34

SIEBERS, T. (1984), *The Romantic Fantastic*, Ithaca: Cornell University Press

SIMPSON, P. (1993), *Language, Ideology, and Point of View*, London: Routledge

SMITH, A. B. (1969), *Ideal and Reality in the Fictional Narratives of Théophile Gautier*, Gainsville: University of Florida Press

—— (1977), *Théophile Gautier and the Fantastic*, University: University of Mississippi, Romance Monographs, 23

STANZEL, F. (1984), *A Theory of Narrative*, trans. by C. Goedsche, Cambridge: Cambridge University Press

SUCUR, S. (2001), *Poe, Odoyevsky, and Purloined Letters: Questions of Theory and Period Style Analysis*, Frankfurt am Main: Peter Lang

TARGE, A. (1975), 'Trois apparitions du *Horla*', *Poétique*, 24: 446–59

TERRAS, V. (1969), *The Young Dostoevsky (1846–1849): A Critical Study*, The Hague: Mouton

—— (ed.), (1985), *Handbook of Russian Literature*, New Haven and London: Yale University Press

TODOROV, T. (1966), 'Les catégories du récit littéraire', *Communications*, 8: 121–51

—— (1970), *Introduction à la littérature fantastique*, Paris: Seuil

—— (1971), *Poétique de la prose*, Paris: Seuil

TOMASHEVSKII, B. V. (1960), *Pushkin i Frantsiia*, Leningrad: Sovetskii pisatel´

TRAILL, N. H. (1991), 'Fictional Worlds of the Fantastic', *Style*, 25: 196–210

—— (1996), *Possible Worlds of the Fantastic*, Toronto: University of Toronto Press

TURCANU, R. (1998), '*Le Horla* et "l'effet de réel"', *Nineteenth-Century French Studies*, 26/3–4: 387–97

TYNIANOV, IU. (1979), 'Dostoevsky and Gogol: Towards a Theory of Parody', in *Dostoevsky and Gogol*, ed. by P. Meyer & S. Rudy, Ann Arbor: Ardis, 101–18; orig. pub. 1921

VAX, L. (1959), 'L'art de faire peur', *Critique*, 915–42 and 1026–48

—— (1960), *L'Art et la littérature fantastiques*, Paris: Presses universitaires de France

—— (1965), *La Séduction de l'étrange*, Paris: Presses universitaires de France

VON MUCKE, D. E. (2003), *The Seduction of the Occult and the Rise of the Fantastic Tale*, Stanford:

Stanford University Press

WALTON, K. (1978), 'How Remote are Fictional Worlds from the Real World?', *Journal of Aesthetics and Art Criticism*, 37: 11–23

—— (1983), 'Appreciating Fiction: Suspending Disbelief or Pretending Belief?', *Dispositio*, 5: 1–18

—— (1990), *Mimesis as Make-Believe: On the Foundations of the Representational Arts*, Cambridge, Mass.: Harvard University Press

WHYTE, P. J. (1984), 'Du mode narratif dans les récits fantastiques de Gautier', *Bulletin de la Société Théophile Gautier*, 6: 1–19

WILLIAMS, G. (1983), 'The Obsessions and Madness of Germann in *Pikovaya Dama*', *Russian Literature*, 14: 383–96

—— (1989), 'Convention and play in *Pikovaya Dama*', *Russian Literature*, 26, 523–37

WOODWARD, J. (1982), *The Symbolic Art of Gogol: Essays on his Short Fiction*, Columbus, Ohio: Slavica

ZGORZELSKI, A. (1978), 'Is Science Fiction a Genre of Fantastic Literature?', *Science Fiction Studies*, 19: 296–303

ZIOLKOWSKI, T. (1977), *Disenchanted Images: A Literary Iconology*, Princeton: Princeton University Press

INDEX

BRITISH COMPARATIVE
LITERATURE ASSOCIATION

The British Comparative Literature Association, founded in 1975, aims at promoting the scholarly study of literature without confinement to national or linguistic boundaries, and in relation to other disciplines. Through its regular publication *Comparative Critical Studies*, conferences, workshops, the John Dryden Translation Prize competition and other activities, the Association:

- encourages research along comparative, intercultural and interdisciplinary lines, as well as in the fields of general literary studies and literary theory
- fosters the exchange and renewal of critical ideas and concepts
- keeps its members informed about national and international developments in the study of literature
- provides a forum for personal and institutional academic contacts, both within Britain and with Associations and individuals in other countries.

Membership of the BCLA is open to academic members of universities and other institutions of higher learning as well as to graduate students and to other persons with appropriate scholarly interests, both in Britain and abroad. The BCLA is affiliated to the International Comparative Literature Association (ICLA), and membership of the BCLA includes membership of the ICLA.

President Professor Gillian Beer (Cambridge)
Secretary Mrs Penny Brown (Manchester)
Treasurer Dr Karen Seago (London Metropolitan)

www.bcla.org

Enquiries
Mrs Penny Brown
Department of French Studies
University of Manchester
Manchester M13 9PL
E-mail: penny.brown@manchester.ac.uk